New Jersey Day Trips

New Jersey Day Trips

A Guide to Outings in New Jersey
and Nearby Areas of New York,
Pennsylvania, and Delaware

11TH EDITION, REVISED AND UPDATED

Patrick Sarver

RIVERGATE BOOKS
An Imprint of Rutgers University Press
New Brunswick, New Jersey, and London

917.4904
N42d
2007

Based on the original book by Barbara Hudgins.

LIBRARY OF CONGRESS CATALOGING-IN-PUBLICATION DATA

Hudgins, Barbara
  New Jersey day trips : a guide to outings in New Jersey and nearby areas of New
  York, Pennsylvania, and Delaware, 11th edition, revised and updated.
    p.   cm.
  ISBN 978-0-8135-4094-8 (pbk. : alk. paper)
  I. Family recreation—Middle Atlantic States—Guidebooks.   2. Middle Atlantic
  States—Guidebooks.   3. New Jersey—Guidebooks.   4. New York—Guidebooks.
    5. Pennsylvania—Guidebooks.   6. Delaware—Guidebooks.   I. Hudgins, Barbara.
  II. Sarver, Patrick.
  F106.T835   2003

                                                              2002208823

A British Cataloging-in-Publication data record for this book is available
from the British Library

Manufactured in the United States of America

Contents

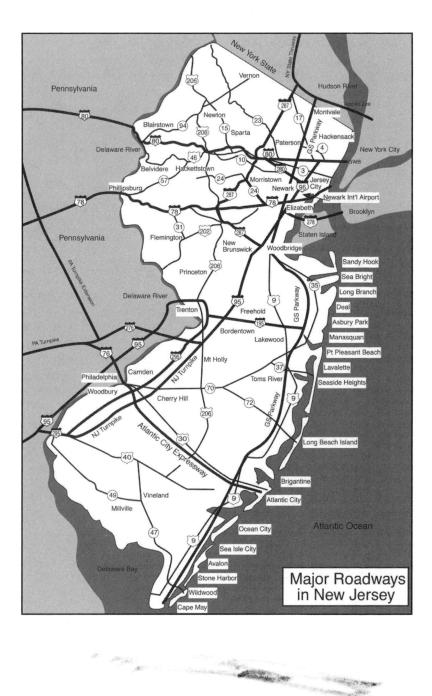

Major Roadways
in New Jersey

Preface

The first nine editions of *New Jersey Day Trips* were published by the Woodmont Press and written solely by Barbara Hudgins. This is the second edition for a new publisher, Rutgers University Press, and a new author, Patrick Sarver, who coauthored the 10th edition with Barbara. This edition follows the format originally established by Barbara, and is still divided into subject categories, such as museums, zoos, gardens, flea markets, and so forth.

Admission fees for many New Jersey attractions have gone up with the same regularity as the state's property taxes. With a publication that comes out every few years, these changes can lead to confusion. Therefore the price points are given in a range with $ signs used as a code.

There is no single way to write a guidebook. You can approach it from the geographical point of view, or from the type of attraction. The advantage of categorizing by type of attraction is that someone who is interested in a particular activity can easily find what is available at a glance. If a teacher has a class in Revolutionary War history, a parent is looking for museums dedicated to children, or a newcomer to the state is looking for outlet shopping and flea markets, each can discover what is available immediately.

Some attractions are only seasonal and are simply not available all the times of the year or are open only on limited days of the week. For example, the governor's mansion in Princeton is open only on Wednesdays. The unofficial summer season at the Shore starts on Memorial Day and ends on Labor Day (although many stretch the season through September). Mountain Creek is a ski area in the winter and a waterpark in the summer; that is why you will find it listed in the chapter on amusement parks as well as the chapter on the outdoors. You will find that some placements are purely arbitrary. When a particular place could belong in more than one category, it is placed where it seems to fit best.

There are a number of new entries in this edition. There are also many nearby out-of-state entries; the length of these has been reduced somewhat to allow for the addition of new places.

Ten Tips for Day Trippers

1. Always telephone first. Places may be closed unexpectedly, or they may change their public hours at any moment.

2. Check Websites when they are available. However, when it comes to hours and prices, they may not be as up to date as the recorded message. Websites are fine for "seeing the place" first and for travel directions.

3. Take along a full-sized map, drinks, snacks, flashlight, extra jacket, and other things you may need.

4. Do not show up during the last half-hour. Places that require guided tours often refuse admittance an hour before closing.

5. Use coupons and "two-fers." Most amusement parks have marketing arrangements with companies for two-for-one admissions with a can, coupon, or other promotion. Also check for discount coupons in brochures, flyers, and newspapers.

6. Go on free days or off-season. State parks, for example, are free off-season.

7. Buy season tickets. This makes sense if you live within close range. Or become a member of a local museum, garden, or zoo.

8. Use your corporate or organizational clout. When companies support institutions, their employees may get a free corporate day or a discount. Members of AAA or AARP often get discounts. Check with your town's recreation department; they may have discount tickets for attractions and events.

9. "Suggested Donation" means just that. If you are visiting for a short time or have a large family with you, you do not have to pay the full suggested donation, but you should pay something.

10. Watch out for extras, such as parking fees and sales tax. Always take along more money than you think you will need.

Prices, Abbreviations, and Hours

For this edition exact prices are not included since they change so quickly from year to year. Instead, a simple range of prices is used with the following code:

$	=	up to $5
$$	=	$5.01 to $10
$$$	=	$10.01 to $15
$$$$	=	$15.01 to $25
$$$$$	=	$25.01 to $35
$$$$$$	=	$35.01 and above

ABBREVIATION: q.v. (which see) refers to a separate entry in the book.

HOURS

Hours of operation can change at any time—and often do. Readers are strongly encouraged to telephone first, especially during off-season and for smaller places. Locally operated historical houses and museums, for example, depend on volunteers, who can be unreliable. Also note that while every effort has been made to include the latest phone numbers and Websites, these can also change at any time. In most cases, for the sake of brevity, we have left out holiday closings. Unless an entry says "Open 365 days" you can assume that most sites, except public parks, are closed on Thanksgiving, Christmas, and New Year's Day. For other holiday closings, check first.

Hours noted within this book pertain to general public admission. There are often special hours and tours for groups and school classes. If you plan a group visit, always call ahead for group reservations, discounted prices, and possible lunchroom privileges.

New Jersey Day Trips

Unique Towns and Tours

Cape May's Victorian hotels and Bed & Breakfasts border the
beachfront at the southern end of the state. *(Photo by Patrick Sarver)*

Princeton

Shades of F. Scott Fitzgerald! Golden lads and lasses walk the well-clipped paths between venerable university halls while russet leaves flutter overhead from rows of sturdy trees. Well, actually, while the setting is still traditional, student styles are very much like those elsewhere—if a bit more upscale. But for a trip to a real university town that blends history, culture, and Gothic college architecture, nothing beats Princeton.

The best way to see the campus is to take the free one-hour tours offered by the Orange Key Guide Service—just go to the welcome desk at the Frist Campus Center. Tours leave at 10 A.M., 11 A.M., 1:30 P.M., and 3:30 P.M., weekdays and Saturdays. Sunday tours are at 1:30 P.M. and 3:30 P.M. (Summer hours vary slightly.) The number for tours is 609-258-1766, and you can also get parking directions. It is not necessary to reserve in advance. Although the Website says these tours are primarily for prospective students, they are for everyone and include history, culture, and a bit of gossip. Here are some of the campus sights on the tour.

1. Nassau Hall: Built in 1756, this Georgian stone structure has survived pillage (by the British, not the students) and major fires in 1802 and 1855. It served as a barracks and hospital for troops of both sides during the Revolution. In 1783 Congress met here for four months while awaiting word that the treaty ending the Revolution had been signed. It now serves as administrative offices for the university. A portrait of Washington by Charles Willson Peale hangs in the Faculty Room along with those of founders, university presidents, and famous alumni.

2. Firestone Library: A beautiful two-million-volume library built in 1948, it is the embodiment of the collegiate Gothic style. Galleries display changing exhibits of rare books and photographs.

3. Woodrow Wilson School of Public and International Affairs: Guides will show you the outside of the striking Robertson Hall, one of the few modern structures on campus. Designed by Minoru Yamasaki, who also designed the World Trade Center, it includes a reflecting pool and the Fountain of Freedom.

4. University Chapel: Built in a Gothic design by Ralph Adams Cram in 1928, it is the third largest university chapel in the country, seating 1,800. A sixteenth-century carved oak pulpit and some of the finest stained glass to be seen this side of the Atlantic makes the chapel an outstanding part of the Princeton trip.

5. Putnam Sculptures: These are a series of massive metal and stone sculptures scattered around the campus as if a giant had decided to distribute his toys among the college buildings. Sir Henry Moore, Jacques Lipchitz, Pablo Picasso, Alexander Calder, and Louise Nevelson are among the twenty sculptors represented.

6. Prospect House: This Tuscan villa built in 1850 was the home of university presidents from 1879 to 1968 but is now used as a Faculty Club and is not open to the public. However, the formally designed garden to the rear is open and very pleasant. The flower garden here was laid out by the wife of Woodrow Wilson.

Not included in the tour, but an important stop, is the Princeton University Art Museum (q.v.). This is a first-rate museum, and—it's free! Paintings include a generous sampling of Americana, Italian Renaissance, and French Baroque. You'll find a good collection of Chinese bronzes, artifacts from Central and South America, a top collection of prints, and a medieval room. Call 609-258-3788 for more information.

If you want to see an Ivy League football game, the Princeton Stadium seats 27,800, and ticket prices are very reasonable. There's also a special parking area for tailgaters a short walk away.

Besides the university, Princeton has pleasant shopping along Nassau Street and Palmer Square, and many good restaurants (among them Lahiere's, the Nassau Inn, and the Alchemist and Barrister). You might also want to look at the Princeton Cemetery at Wiggins and Witherspoon, which holds the remains of Aaron Burr and Grover Cleveland among its many notables. The Princeton Battle Monument, a fifty-foot structure, stands imposingly at Nassau and Stockton Streets, and a walking tour of the area will take you past many lovely old houses. Albert Einstein's former home, at 112 Mercer St., is not open to the public. However, many people take a photograph of it as they pass by. A short drive down from the Einstein house is Princeton Battlefield Park (q.v.), which has lots of greenery and a Revolutionary-era house.

Historic Morven, Drumthwacket (the present governor's residence), and Bainbridge House have separate listings in this book. Self-guided tour maps can be picked up at Bainbridge House, home of the Historical Society of Princeton (158 Nassau St.). Or you can join the walking tours on Sundays at 2 P.M. The McCarter Theatre on University Ave. runs a full program of professional plays, movies, ballets, and concerts. Call 609-258-2787 for details. There are also fairs and community events throughout the year, including a tour of private homes in December.

DIRECTIONS: Rts. 206 or 27 to Princeton (Mercer County). The university is on Nassau Street. **WEBSITES:** (University) www.princeton.edu/main, and (community) www.princetonol.com.

Lambertville, New Hope, and Lahaska

Lambertville

Once a poor relation to New Hope across the river in Pennsylvania, Lambertville has become a top destination for antiques browsers. One reason is the growth of good restaurants, art galleries, funky clothing shops, and quaint townhouses along the banks of the Delaware.

Settled by Emanuel Coryell in 1732, Lambertville started life as a colonial village with a ferry that crossed the Delaware River. In fact, it was called Coryell's Ferry for many years, and a small contingent of the Continental Army crossed here on December 25, 1776, and met the larger group marching on Trenton. The town was also an important stagecoach stop on the New York–Philadelphia run.

In 1834 the Delaware & Raritan Canal opened alongside the Delaware River, and commerce thrived. The workers who dug the canal rented simple rowhouses, much like those in English cities. These were sturdy stone or brick homes, and they dotted the landscape of Lambertville.

The **Marshall House** (60 Bridge St.) is a two-story cream-colored brick townhouse built in 1816. James Wilson Marshall, who was born there, later discovered gold at Sutter's Mill in California. Unfortunately, he staked a claim too late and died broke, but the modest house that bears his name is now the headquarters of the Historical Society.

> **HOURS:** Free tours are held weekends 12–4, Apr.–Oct. The society also holds walking tours of town at 2 on the first Sunday of the month, May–Nov. (**FEE:** $.) There's also an autumn house tour of Lambertville in late Oct. **TELEPHONE:** 609-397-0770. **WEBSITE:** www.lambertvillehistoricalsociety.org.

Although Lambertville remained a sleepy Hunterdon County community for about a century, it was rediscovered in the 1980s. The old workers' houses were spiffed up, and new townhouses were built along the river. The Lambertville railroad station was turned into a two-story restaurant-with-a-view, called, appropriately enough, Lambertville Station. The Coryell Gallery at the Porkyard (8 Coryell St.) features an art gallery up a little alley along with a courtyard with restaurants and cozy bar. The yearly Shad Festival (the last week in April) attracts thousands to town to savor the traditional shad while getting a glimpse of the revived town with lots of crafters and artists on its streets.

The shops and eateries are mostly clustered along Bridge Street (the main thoroughfare) and Union Street, which transects it, but there are plenty of byways to duck into as well. Antiques shops are numerous here, although the prices can be on the steep side. But there are also plenty of reproduction and collectible shops. Some of

Antiques, galleries, restaurants, and a historic atmosphere attract visitors to Lambertville, which overlooks the Delaware River. *(Photo by Patrick Sarver)*

the best restaurants are open for dinner only, but there are several coffee and ice cream shops around town. You'll also find a bevy of Bed & Breakfasts along with two traditional inns, so if you want to sleep over there are plenty of accommodations.

On Wednesday and on weekends, you can also drive south on Rt. 29 for 2 miles for a look at the **Golden Nugget Antique Market** (609-397-0811; www.gnmarket.com), which stands on the left side of the road. There are 250 outdoor tables and 60 inside shops where dealers show collectibles, antiques, art, and doodads. And at the **Rago Arts and Auction Center** at 333 N. Main (609-397-9374; www.ragoarts.com), you'll find year-round auctions of art and furnishings, including estate sales. While there are items in all price ranges, the emphasis here is clearly upscale.

> **DIRECTIONS:** Rt. 202 south to Rt. 179, then right onto Bridge Street.
> **WEBSITE:** www.lambertville.org.

New Hope

Just across the bridge from Lambertville, New Hope, Pennsylvania, has long been the cultural and picturesque capital of Bucks County. On any weekend from spring to fall the narrow sidewalks of this sophisticated oasis are jammed. In the 1920s, landscape painters settled here. By the thirties, Bucks County had become well known as a quiet weekend haven for novelists, poets, and playwrights. And in 1939, the **Bucks County Playhouse** opened in a former gristmill. Now the state theater of Pennsylvania, it offers family musicals and matinee performances as well as midday Children's Theatre on Friday and Saturday from late June to December (215-862-2041; www.buckscountyplayhouse.com).

Another warm-weather attraction is the **New Hope Mule Drawn Canal Boat Ride,** which offers a one-hour ride on the old Delaware Canal. It is a slow and easy way to see the town. It departs from the barge landing at New Street, and several rides are offered daily during the afternoon from May through October and on weekends in April (215-862-0758; www.onthecanal.net). A popular pontoon ride is **Coryell's Ferry,** which offers scenic half-hour rides on the Delaware.

> **ADMISSION:** $$. Discount: Under 12. **LOCATION:** It loads behind Gerensers Exotic Ice Cream Store, 22 S. Main St., during the summer season. **TELEPHONE:** 215-862-2050.
> **WEBSITE:** www.spiritof76.biz/ferry.html.

Railroad enthusiasts will enjoy the **New Hope & Ivyland Railroad,** which departs from a picturesque station at Stockton and W. Bridge Streets and steams through the Bucks County countryside.

HOURS: Daily, late May–Oct.; weekends, Jan.–Mar.; and Fri.–Sun., Apr.–May. There are also special themed and evening rides from spring to Christmas. **ADMISSION:** $$$. Discount: Under 12. **TELEPHONE:** 215-862-2332. **WEBSITE:** www.newhoperailroad.com.

Doylestown-based **James A. Michener Art Museum** now has a branch in Union Square in New Hope, with exhibits on Bucks County art and culture, both past and present (215-862-7633; www.michenerartmuseum.org). Historic house lovers will enjoy the **Parry Mansion** at 45 S. Main St. Guided tours are given May–Oct., weekends, 1–5 (215-862-5652; www.newhopehistoricalsociety.org). And for a more "frightful" time with lots of spooky tales, **Ghost Tours of New Hope** offers lantern walks.

HOURS: 8 P.M. Sat., June–mid-Nov. **LOCATION:** The gathering point is Main and Ferry Streets. **ADMISSION:** $$. **TELEPHONE:** 215-343-5564. **WEBSITE:** www.ghosttoursofnewhope.com.

Even without these extras, there's plenty to see in New Hope. There are numerous shops featuring memorabilia, and if you collect such things as old sheet music, military hats, or miniature dolls, you'll find much to pick from. Sometimes there are also horse-drawn carriage rides that leave from the Logan Inn. Art galleries can be found on Main Street, Mechanic Street, and on Rt. 202. Besides the standard Pennsylvania red barn landscapes, you can find modernistic sculpture and paintings. The kids will be more interested in the toy shops and the knick-knack and candy stores.

One of the charms of visiting a quaint riverside town is eating in a quaint, interesting restaurant, and there are plenty of them in New Hope, most of them along the main drag. Whether you opt for the casual Mother's, riverfront views at the Landing, or one of the many sidewalk cafes, you will be satisfied. The better places fill up on weekends, though, so make reservations as soon as you arrive. There are also a variety of nightspots and clubs that give the town a jazzier tone after 7 P.M.

For more details, stop by the Information Center at 1 W. Mechanic St. (215-862-9990; www.newhopepennsylvania.com).

Lahaska

If you drive west of New Hope onto Rt. 202 west (or just bypass town via the Rt. 202 toll bridge), you will come to Lahaska a few miles up the road. The place to go is **Peddler's Village,** a twentieth-century reconstruction of an eighteenth-century village filled with—what else—shops and restaurants. The landscaping here (by Derek Fell) is outstanding, and a giant waterwheel and floral beds lend the proper tone. The seventy or so shops are mostly the country-store type, but there are several unique boutiques that feature everything from English teapots to Santa Fe windcatchers to special games and toys. Food can be found at seven eateries, including the Golden Plough Inn, the Colonial-style Cock 'n Bull, Earl's, and a few quick-stand places. The atmosphere here is child-friendly. Ten family-oriented festivals throughout the year include Strawberry, Apple, and Scarecrow festivals. There is an indoor "entertainment center" called Giggleberry Fair that includes a restored 1922 carousel, several interactive play areas, and a corner for pizza and hot dogs.

LOCATION: Rts. 202 and 263, Lahaska, PA.
TELEPHONE: 215-794-4000 (Peddler's Village).
WEBSITE: www.peddlersvillage.com.

On the other side of Rt. 202 is an outlet mall called **Penn's Purchase.** It features about three dozen discount and outlet stores designed to attract the bargain-minded crowd. You'll find Hanes, Bass, Bose, and Jones New York among others, and also a fast-food shop (215-794-0300; www.pennspurchase.com).

Atlantic City

Atlantic City keeps reinventing itself with new looks, new styles, and new owners, balancing between being a traditional Jersey Shore resort and a Vegas wannabe. The new Convention Hall and a lighthouse replica create a dramatic entrance into the city, and laser lights highlight the drama at night. There is continuing growth at the Marina, while casino-hotels add new facades and extensions every year on the boardwalk. The emphasis now seems to be shifting to making Atlantic City a well-rounded resort in the Vegas mold, with more upscale shopping and restaurants to complement the casino action.

But there are still amusement arcades, concession stands, and fudge shops. The beach, now bumpy with sand dunes, is not the draw it once was, but the city has added pleasant parks and courtyards to maintain a civilized air.

A tunnel allows cars to proceed directly to the marina's elegant hotels. Harrah's and Trump Marina are long-established there, while the newer Borgata has become the second-largest-grossing casino in the city by appealing to a younger and more upscale crowd with its stylish décor and with its shopping, which is undergoing a major expansion.

Getting There: Bus tours are still a favorite way for people to make a one-day visit. Casinos often give you vouchers for money and other freebies when you arrive, and you must stay 6 hours. Casino-subsidized buses come from all points of New Jersey as well as Philadelphia and New York. Regular buses and trains also service the town. A rail terminal, next to the Convention Center and Shera-ton Hotel, has plenty of taxis available. If you come by car, most casinos have garage parking for a small fee.

Transportation: The best way to get around town is to take the jit-neys that operate along Pacific Avenue behind the hotels. They come frequently, cost $1.50, and travel as far as the inlet and marina. On the boardwalk you can walk on a nice day or take the push-along rolling chairs that cost about $5 for every six blocks (the slow but convenient boardwalk tramcars are now gone). Cabs are plentiful (at hotel entrances) if you want to get away from the boardwalk area. And buses run the length of the island 24 hours a day on Atlantic Avenue.

Hotels: Casino-hotels change their names more often than Holly-wood stars change spouses. On the boardwalk they stretch from the Hilton north to the Showboat. In between, a number of mod-estly priced chain hotels have popped up. Many large hotels now feature a dramatic theme. At Bally's Wild, Wild West you find a domed ceiling that simulates a real sky with sunsets and thunder-storms. Showboat has mechanical cats that play jazz (and live musicians as well). Caesar's Palace is now fitted out with marble atriums, fountains, and statues worthy of Augustus. The Tropicana has a grandiose annex. And the Borgata aims to set the mark for elegance.

Casinos: While a touch of the old glamor of gambling may be left, today the casinos have more of a noisy shopping mall atmosphere. Table games are placed side by side, and slot machines take up more space every year. High rollers are offered special rooms for Baccarat and other exotic games. Minimum bets are posted at each table, with $5 the cheapest and minimums rising as the evening wears on.

Casinos offer lots of variety, including Asian games at the tables and an ever-expanding variety of fruits, bells, pigs, cowboys, and whatnot on the slot machines. Slots now range from a penny to $5. All take paper bills directly, and most now pay out in paper tickets. To cash them in, you still must hike to the cashier or to ATM-like machines. Frequent customers use a "club" card, which gives them back points every time they use the slot machines or tables. Even-tually, one can get enough "comps" to eat in the fancy restaurants, buy in the gift shops, or sleep in the hotel rooms.

Food: There are plenty of first-class restaurants, both in the casinos and the streets beyond. And every casino has a buffet. Some are elegant; some are simply cafeteria food at reasonable prices. They are often crowded, so reserve your time as soon as you arrive. There are also theme restaurants: Planet Hollywood at Caesars, the Hard Rock Café, and the All-Star Cafe at the Taj Mahal are popular with families. Big spenders go to the super-deluxe French, Italian, and Chinese restaurants that every hotel seems to have, but they are usually open only for dinner Wednesday through Sunday. Coffee shops and delis are available almost all the time.

Entertainment: First-class shows, chorus girls, and big-name stars appear at the hotels, but the big names are usually weekend events. There are also piano lounges and comedy rooms. For large concerts, the centrally located Boardwalk Hall now serves as a sports and entertainment center, featuring such events as ice hockey; boxing; pop, rock, and classic concerts; and ballet.

On the boardwalk during summer, the Steel Pier (q.v.) across from the Taj Mahal offers amusement rides, as does the smaller Central Pier. The usual hot dog stands and games of chance bring back the flavor of the "old" Atlantic City. The biggest indoor amusement is **Ripley's Believe It or Not Museum** at New York Avenue. Inside, a hologram-like Robert Ripley at his desk welcomes you to such displays as a Chinese unicorn man, a bottle cap suit, a model of the Sydney Harbor Bridge made out of matchsticks, a section of the Berlin Wall, and many other oddities. Try walking the swaying bridge through the Old Mine Tunnel as the wall spins around you!

ADMISSION: $$. TELEPHONE: 609-347-2001. WEBSITE: www.ripleys.com.

At centrally located Kennedy Plaza there is a deluxe miniature golf course (during season) and a large courtyard for watching random entertainments. Video arcades for youngsters and teenagers are located in most hotels and at several boardwalk concessions.

The new Pier at Caesars, on the site of the old Million Dollar Pier, features high-end retailers like Gucci and Armani, nine restaurants, a wedding chapel, and an indoor light-and-water show. The Quarter, at the Tropicana, is a new shopping and dining area that also features an Imax theater. And Atlantic City Outlets/The Walk (q.v.), a seven-block retail area of upscale outlets, stretches west from Bally's to the Convention Center.

History and Culture: For nostalgia buffs, there's a museum devoted to Atlantic City history plus an art center at the Garden Pier on the boardwalk north of the Showboat. The **Historical Museum** is small but contains a trove of facts and displays everything from Miss America's tiara to a video of historical trends in seaside resorts. The **Art Center** features changing exhibits in three galleries. Both are free. Open daily, 10–4 (609-347-5839 [historical museum] and 609-347-5837 [art center]).

Looking inland and to the right from the Garden Pier, you see Absecon Lighthouse (q.v.), the tallest such structure in New Jersey. There's a cute little lighthouse-keeper's cottage out front with displays. Inside, a passage leads to the lighthouse and 228 steps to a panoramic view of ocean, inlet, and casino hotels.

The **New Jersey Korean War Memorial** in front of the peaceful Brighton Park (next to Bally's Casino) is devoted to veterans of that conflict. Statues of soldiers emerge from a back wall engraved with the names of the 822 New Jerseyans who died in the war. Just a few blocks away, at Pacific Avenue and Dr. Martin Luther King Jr. Blvd., is the imposing **Civil Rights Garden.** It features a brick path through plants, flowers, and ginkgo trees and eleven black granite columns etched with quotations. In the center is a large bronze bell that hovers over a reflecting pool.

On the inlet, close to the large Farley Marina, **Gardeners Basin** is a nautically themed plaza with several points of interest. The Atlantic City Aquarium (q.v.) has helped stir up some interest. The nautical theme is reiterated in the Flying Cloud Cafe, the Back Bay Ale House, a lobster pound, and handful of a seashore-themed shops. You can also catch boat rides at the basin during season for dolphin-watching excursions, deep-sea fishing charters, sightseeing and dance cruises, or even parasailing.

South of Atlantic City is **Lucy the Margate Elephant,** a 65-foot high, tin-plated Victorian architectural "folly" in Margate City. From April to December, you can walk through its wooden interior (which is actually a museum) with a guided tour for a reasonable fee. You can even step outside onto the Howdah on top and view the surroundings. Lucy is at Decatur and Atlantic Avenues (609-823-6473; www.lucytheelephant.org).

DIRECTIONS: (Atlantic City) Garden State Parkway to Exit 38 (Atlantic City Expressway south). **TELEPHONE:** 800-ACVISIT. **WEBSITE:** www.atlanticcitynj.com.

Cape May

While Cape May has been a resort since the mid-1800s, it is only within the last 30 years that it has reached fame as a Bed & Breakfast town, filled with good restaurants, quaint shops, and Victorian charm. The Victorian summer homes of old have been converted into an array of Victorian homes and inns sporting the lively colors of pink, blue, green, and maroon. Gothic cottages, Italianate villas, and mansard and stick-style buildings have become stylishly old-fashioned homes, restaurants, antique stores, and art galleries. All this Victorian revitalization has led Cape May to extend its season almost year-round.

One place to begin a visit is the Visitor Center (Lafayette and Bank Streets), which offers brochures on tours of Victorian inns and whale-watching boats. They can recommend what's best to see if you have limited time. Depending on the season, you can take walking tours, house tours, trolley tours, and tulip tours. A special Victorian Week in October features ten days of antiques, crafts, fashion shows, and tours. Another special event is the Christmas candlelight tours.

Many of these festivities are run by the Mid-Atlantic Center for the Arts (MAC), which operates out of the **Emlen Physick Estate** (1048 Washington St.). The Physick House itself is the scene of a popular, year-round tour. This sprawling 1881 stick-style home is typical of the late Victorian era, both in its multiangled red roof and its charming period furnishings, and is said to have been designed by architect Frank Furness. The interior is very well done, from the ornate fireplaces to the stained glass windows in Dr. Physick's bathroom door. Tours may include costumed docents, and on certain days there is even an actor playing the part of Dr. Physick. There is also a charming Victorian tearoom, a gallery, and a gift shop in the old carriage house. A number of trolley tours travel from the estate to various parts of town and surrounding areas. Along the way, you'll see the colorful historic area, with houses trimmed in carpenter's lace, stores, and fancy restaurants. There are also guided walking tours, and a self-guided audio tour is available.

The Washington Street Mall is a focal point for shoppers, and you can find any number of boutiques and outdoor cafes in this pleasant outdoor mall. (You can also book horse and carriage rides, trolley tours, and inn tours across from the entrance to the mall.) The beachfront has a few modern motels and video game arcades along with the older hostelries. But the major ambience of the town is its restored Victorian past. Inns like the Abbey and the Southern Mansion host afternoon tours of their public rooms at certain hours. Multihouse tours are offered during special events. The MAC also sponsors a Cape May sampler tour and tea with visits to four houses. For a different take on Cape May, the Colonial House (behind Alexander's Inn on Washington Street) allows a look at a simpler

way of life in pre-Revolutionary times. Open daily, 10–2, June 15–
Sept. 15.

There is the beach, of course, which is easily accessible from the
center of town, and you can rent chairs and umbrellas if you want to
stay a few hours (beach badges are required during the summer).
The width of the beach seems to change each season depending on
the winter storms, but the ocean is mild here. A few simple arcades
dot the concrete boardwalk that borders the beach.

Cape May is also known as a restaurant town, and some of the
better-known eateries are the traditional Lobster House at Fisher-
man's Wharf near the entrance to town, the elegant dining room at
Alexander's Inn (653 Washington St.), and the trendy 410 Bank
Street (at that address). Of course there are plenty of less formal eating places, and for some, fried oysters at The Ugly Mug in Washington Mall is seafood heaven.

For information on tours, contact the **Mid-Atlantic Center for the
Arts** (800-275-4278; www.capemaymac.org.) For other information
contact the Chamber of Commerce (609-884-5508; www.capemay
chamber.com).

Another excursion is run by the Cape May Seashore Lines (q.v.),
an old-fashioned train ride that leaves from the depot and stops at
Historic Cold Spring Village during the summer.

> **DIRECTIONS:** Garden State Parkway to Exit 0; continue on Rt. 109
> for 2 miles.

Newark

You don't have to be a foreign visitor to book a tour of Newark. Bus
tours for groups provide a mix of history, sociology, and architecture. There are a variety of tours, including those of the downtown
area, the parks, and the grand old houses of the Forest Hills section.
Did you know that Newark was founded by Puritans? Or that farmers insisted on a broad street so they could bring their cattle to market—the reason such thoroughfares are called Broad and Market?

The downtown tour includes the massive Federal Court Building
and the Essex County Courthouse. The statue of Abraham Lincoln
seated in front of the courthouse was created by famed sculptor Gut-
zon Borglum, who carved Mount Rushmore and also crafted a heroic
statue of soldiers in Military Park. Since Newark was a city of immigrants, each new group raised a church or synagogue as soon as it
arrived. But it was the grandchildren of immigrants who built the
magnificent Sacred Heart Cathedral, a huge Gothic-style cathedral
situated on the edge of Branch Brook Park. The marble interior and
three full rose windows are resplendent. Tours may also encompass

a trip through the park (especially if the cherry blossoms are in bloom) and a glimpse of the little subway that takes riders from the Forest Hills section to downtown in 7 minutes.

Whether you take a group tour or visit Newark on your own, you will probably end up in the Ironbound section, famed for its Spanish and Portuguese restaurants. The narrow streets here are filled with bakeries, groceries, and eateries. The Ironbound is so called because the train tracks and bridges form a triangle of iron that encloses the district. Tourists come for the Portuguese bakeries and the restaurants, such as Iberia, Fornos, and Spain, which are known for their generous portions and reasonable prices. To book a tour, call 973-483-3348; www.newarktours.com.

Greenwich

There are several "forgotten towns" in southwest Jersey—towns that reached their prime back in the eighteenth century when travel by water was more common than going by rough roads. The town of Greenwich on the Cohansey River is such a place. It was started as a colony by John Fenwick, who welcomed Quakers, Baptists, and Presbyterians—groups that were not well tolerated in their previous home in Puritan Massachusetts.

Settlement began in 1683, and the town became an official port of entry from 1695 to 1765. It was a bustling commercial port, and small townhouses in the English style grew up along the central street. In 1774, Greenwich had its own tea party in response to British taxes—the residents burned the English import, which was being kept in a cellar for safekeeping.

Today there is a monument to the Greenwich Tea Party—and many of the eighteenth-century houses along Ye Greate Street still stand. The Cumberland County Historical Society makes its home at one of the oldest, the **Gibbon House** at 960 Ye Greate St. The society conducts tours of the house, a well-furnished 1730 home built as a replica of a London townhouse by the town's leading citizen (open Wed.–Sun., 1–4). The lower floor is furnished as a colonial home, with the second floor more given to a range of historical exhibits. Out back, you'll find a barn museum and an early Swedish log cabin.

Because Greenwich was dependent on maritime trade, a great interest in ships and shipping is apparent there. The **John Dubois Maritime Museum** (open Apr.–Dec., Sun., 1–4) has nautical maps, models of ships, tools, and tons of lore about coastal sailing. Other historical society properties are the Prehistorical Museum (Wed., Sat., Sun., 12–4) and the Lummis Library.

Greenwich is not a tourist town. No arty shops or gourmet lunch spots are tucked into the townhouses. But it is a chance to see a quiet town from the past where the historical district is kept intact. The Cumberland County Historical Society runs all the tours and goes out of its way to accommodate visitors—especially groups. Special yearly events include a juried Craft Faire (856-455-4055; www.cchistsoc.org).

Stockton

Located a few miles north of Lambertville in Hunterdon County, this riverfront town is known for its "small hotel with a wishing well"— the Stockton Inn, in the heart of town. A small but charming business area adds to the town's ambience, as does the handsome Woolverton Inn, a Bed & Breakfast on a hill not far from town.

The area is a popular weekend place for visitors who hike or bike the Delaware & Raritan Canal Path, which is part of the state park bordering the Delaware River. About a mile north of the town you'll find the picturesque **Prallsville Mills** on the left-hand side of Rt. 29. This complex includes a 1790 linseed oil mill, an 1877 gristmill, an 1850 sawmill, a grain silo, and a railroad trestle. Wickecheoke Creek feeds the canal at the mill complex, and there is a canal lock on the grounds. Although the grounds are open daily, the stripped-down interior of the gristmill is open only by appointment and hosts a well-known juried art show in April. The linseed mill houses an art gallery. All the buildings are operated by the Delaware River Mill Society (609-397-3586; http://home2.netcarrier.com/~drms).

Nearby is another picture-taking favorite (especially in the fall): **Green Sergeant's Bridge,** which is the pride and joy of the tiny town of Sergeantsville. This is the last remaining covered bridge in New Jersey, and it's white, not green. (It is named after a man called Green Sergeant.) The bridge crosses Wickecheoke Creek about 1.5 miles west of town.

DIRECTIONS: From Rt. 29, take Rt. 523 to Rt. 604.

Bordentown

Settled in 1682 and one of the oldest towns in New Jersey, Bordentown is no longer quite as thriving a Quaker enclave it once was. Several famous citizens once lived here, among them Clara Barton; Thomas Paine; Francis Hopkinson (a Declaration of Independence signer); and Joseph Bonaparte, king of Spain and brother of Napoleon. Many eighteenth-century buildings are still standing, and the homes of the famous are here as well, although private. Today, the town is primarily working class, but it still possesses an aura of quaintness and history.

Self-guided walking tours begin with a brochure available from the Historical Society, located in the Friends Meetinghouse, which houses a small museum. Unfortunately, it is open only by appointment, but brochures are available at the nearby Old Bookshop on Farnsworth Avenue. None of the forty-five buildings listed are open to the public, but the history and architecture of each are nonetheless interesting. The Gilder House (closed for restoration) includes furnishings from Joseph Bonaparte's estate. Other houses on the self-guided tour are the Shippen House, Francis Hopkinson House, Thomas Paine House, and Joseph Borden House. A Thomas Paine walking tour is held by the Thomas Paine Society at 3:30 P.M. on the second Saturday of the month, Apr.–Dec. (609-424-0301).

The **Clara Barton Schoolhouse** is a prime historical site in town. Miss Barton, who later founded the Red Cross, actually taught here in 1843 for a very short time but made quite an impact. Until then, middle-class children went to private school, and public schools were considered to be for paupers. Barton had to persuade local schoolchildren to attend. There was no fee, but each child was required to bring a stick of wood to keep the stove going. The small red brick building has benches and a raised platform where the teacher sat (in the back of the room, not the front). It is open only for the reserved group-guided tour that the Historical Society offers. However, major sites are open for the Holiday Home Tour on the second Saturday in December.

CONTACT/LOCATION: Bordentown Historical Society, 302 Farnsworth Ave., Bordentown (Burlington County). **TELEPHONE:** 609-298-3779. **WEBSITE:** www.downtownbordentown.com.

Burlington

Another town that saw its heyday years ago when it was the capital of West Jersey and a stronghold of Quakerism is Burlington. Start with guided tours of the **Burlington County Historical Society** complex and a self-guided tour of the adjacent High Street area (hour-long audio tapes are available at society headquarters for a small fee).

The society's museum complex includes three houses from the mid-1700s plus a library/museum. One home was once rented by the family of America's first novelist, **James Fenimore Cooper**, although the writer spent only the first thirteen months of his life here. The **Captain James Lawrence House** right next door is dedicated to pictures and memorabilia of the War of 1812 hero who is best known for his words, "Don't give up the ship!" (During the tour you find out that the Americans actually did give up the ship and the

British won the battle.) Although small, it is well furnished and very interesting. These houses are at 457 and 459 High St. The rest of the complex includes the **Bard-How House** (453 High St.), which is maintained in a simple Colonial style. The society's history and genealogy library and museum gallery, which has permanent and changing historical exhibits, is behind the houses.

   HOURS: Tue.–Sat., 1–5. **ADMISSION:** $. **LOCATION:** 451 High St., Burlington. **TELEPHONE:** 609-386-4773.
   WEBSITE: http://08016.com/bchs.html.

The complex is among more than forty historic sites in Burlington's mile-square historic district, which is covered in a self-guided walking-tour brochure from the county Historical Society. Among the sites on the tour are views of Burlington Island (site of the first New Jersey settlement in 1624) from the riverfront, where you can enjoy an old-fashioned walk with a nice view. Most houses on the walking tour are private, and these include the estate of William Franklin, Benjamin's son and New Jersey's last colonial governor. Other notable buildings are the 1785 Friends Meetinghouse, the 1685 Revell House, the 1856 Ulysses S. Grant House, and the Grubb Estate, a stop on the Underground Railroad, as well as several early day churches. The city also offers guided walking tours for a small fee. For a self-guided tour brochure or guided tour times, visit City Hall at 437 High St. or call 609-386-3993; www.tourburlington.org.

OTHER TOWNS

Ocean Grove: A pleasant Monmouth County seaside town to visit for the beach or for the pretty Victorian buildings that now contain small shops and restaurants, Ocean Grove began as a Methodist Camp Meeting summer colony. It was first filled with tents and then with the colorful stick-style cottages that remain to this day. Although the strict Methodist rules against driving and bicycling no longer apply, it is still a dry town. For those interested in history, there are guided tours that include an inside look at the Great Auditorium (q.v.) as well as an interior of a tent in the town's Tent Colony.

A well-known stop is the 1874 **Centennial Cottage,** which is furnished with Victorian antiques and has a garden with plants and flowers that were popular in the late nineteenth century. Some tours include a stop for tea and sweets at a local B&B. All tours start from the Historical Society's museum at 50 Pitman Ave. (732-774-1869 for hours and schedules; www.oceangrovehistory.org).

Mount Holly: The Burlington County seat was another center of Quaker life in the early days. This quiet little town has several buildings of note on its walking tour. Among the noteworthy buildings are the **Burlington County Prison Museum** (609-265-5476), designed by Robert Mills, architect of the Washington Monument; the Mill Street Hotel; and a restored 1759 schoolhouse where famous Quaker abolitionist John Woolman once taught. The **Woolman Memorial,** three-quarters of a mile away at 99 Branch Street, is a brick Revolutionary-era home that exemplifies late eighteenth-century Quaker life and displays items associated with Woolman (609-267-3226; http://woolmancentral.com; call for hours). Several other stops include the 1796 Old Courthouse Complex, a 1712 log cabin, and a Friends Meeting House used by the British in 1778 and the following year for meetings of the state legislature. Near the center of town, the quaint shops at Mill Race Village feature crafts, gifts, antiques, and dining in a historic setting. A pamphlet for the self-guided town tour is available from the town clerk at Township Hall, 23 Washington St. (609-267-0170; www.mountholly.com). Also, for a small fee pick up a copy of Burlington County Loop Tours, a self-driving guide to the county's Revolutionary War sites, from the Burlington County Cultural & Heritage Department (609-265-5068).

Salem: Salem was an early Quaker settlement in West Jersey. Today, it is the home of a historic district with a large number of Colonial and Victorian houses (856-935-8800). Among important sights around town are the Old Court House, a reproduction of a 1640 Swedish cabin in Johan Prinz Park, and the Goodwin Sisters' House (an 1821 home that was an important stop on the Underground Railroad). Most famous is the historic Salem Oak in the Friends Burial Ground, said to be between 500 and 700 years old. Under its branches a peace treaty was signed with the Lenape Indians in the 1600s. The Salem County Historical Society headquarters is in the **Alexander Grant House,** 79–83 Market St., built in 1721. This nineteen-room museum displays Early American furniture and decorative arts as well as changing exhibits. Living rooms, bedrooms, featherbeds, a 1630s clock, documents signed by Washington and Franklin, and much more are on view. Outside are an 1840s log cabin, the oldest law office in the United States (built in 1735), and a large stone barn with old carriages and tools.

> **HOURS:** Open Tue.–Fri. plus the second Sat. of the month, 12–4.
> **ADMISSION:** Nominal fee. **TELEPHONE:** 856-935-5004.
> **WEBSITE:** www.salemcountyhistoricalsociety.com.

You can also pick up maps here for a walking tour of the local historic area. One Saturday a year, in late April or early May, the Historical Society also hosts an open house for historic homes and gardens in Salem County.

Woodbury: The Gloucester County Historical Society's library at 17 Hunter St. is the place to pick up two tour maps. One is for a walking tour of Old Woodbury, a brochure and map to thirty-five historic, mostly private homes and businesses in town. There's also a driving tour map ($) of forty-eight historic buildings in the county, with a short history of each. Again, most buildings are privately owned. Of particular note is the Historical Society's headquarters, the 1765 **Hunter-Lawrence-Jessup House** at 58 North Broad St. Built in 1785 and altered during Victorian times, it was the home of the Reverend Andrew Hunter, a colonial tea burner, and Captain James Lawrence of "Don't give up the ship!" fame. Today, it serves as a twelve-room historical museum. Displays include Revolutionary and Civil War artifacts, antique toys, samplers, agricultural and architectural displays, and changing exhibits. In the basement display area, there's a fireplace from an old tavern in Gloucester City. Betsy Ross was married next to it.

> **HOURS:** Open Mon., Wed., & Fri., 1–4, and the last weekend
> of the month, 2–5. **ADMISSION:** $. Discounts: for 18 and under.
> **TELEPHONE:** Museum, 856-848-8531; Library, 856-845-4771.
> **WEBSITE:** www.rootsweb.com/~njgchs.

Bridgeton: This town has New Jersey's largest historic district, with more than 2,200 homes and buildings from the Colonial, Federal, and Victorian eras—all in various stages of repair. The strongest ambience is Victorian. The Cohansey River runs through town, and a pleasant riverfront plaza has been built to host concerts, fairs, and walking tours. Across the river is a large park, which includes the small Nail Mill Museum (Apr.–Dec., Tue.–Fri., 10:30–3:30; Sat.–Sun, 11–4; free), the Cohanzick Zoo (q.v.), the New Sweden Farmstead Museum (q.v.), and rhododendron and azalea gardens along the park drive. A walking tour leads to many historic homes and buildings. Stops open to visitors include Potter's Tavern, home of New Jersey's first newspaper (open weekend afternoons; small fee); the Bridgeton Hall of Fame All Sports Museum in the Burt Avenue Recreation Center (Tue.–Sat., 10–12 and 1–3; free); and the George Woodruff Indian Museum in the library on Commerce Street (Mon.–Sat., 1–4, except summer; free.). Some boutiques have opened in the riverfront area, and the city is working to enhance its Victorian ambience. Maps, a film, and arrangements for self-guided audio tours as well as guided bus and walking tours are available at the Bridgeton-Cumberland Tourist Association, 50 E. Broad St., Bridgeton (Cumberland County) (856-451-4802).

Haddonfield: Haddonfield Historic District encompasses almost five hundred Colonial and Victorian houses, buildings, and sites along streets enhanced by trees, brick sidewalks, and gardens. Around 150 of the buildings have historical or architectural significance. Among the most notable are Indian King Tavern and Greenfield Hall (q.v.). Other sites around town include the Fire Company #1 Museum and the discovery site of the first complete dinosaur skeleton. There are also scores of galleries, boutiques, and antiques shops. Stop by the Visitor Center (Mon.–Fri., 11–5; Sat., 10–4) on Kings Court for a self-guided walking tour brochure. The center also has a walking tour map of churches. There are also themed guided tours, including stained glass tours, history and architecture tours, and Haunted Haddonfield tours led by expert guides. Contact the Visitor Center, 114 Kings Hwy. East, Haddonfield (Camden County) (856-216-7253; www.levins.com/haddon.html or www.haddonfieldnj.org).

Millville: The Glasstown Center Arts District along the Maurice River preserves buildings from the 1800s when this Cumberland County town was a major glassmaking center. The district includes Riverwalk, a landscaped walkway along the riverfront; a marina; and the Riverfront Renaissance Center for the Arts, with works from more than a hundred artists. There are also a growing number of galleries in the adjacent business district. Two blocks east on Main Street is the Millville Historical Society and the Baracha Dunn House, built in 1798 (open Wed., Sun., 1–4). Glassmaking is also the theme at Wheaton Arts and Cultural Center (q.v.) north of the town (856-293-0556; www.glasstownartsdistrict.com).

Chester: This Morris County town dates back to pre-Revolutionary War times. The main thoroughfare of town still has a country air to it, even though the surrounding area is suburban. Main Street stores offer a mix of antiques, quilts, jewelry, and cookware—all with a country flavor. Shops that carry lavender and lace are nestled between antiques stores. Lots of special weekend promotions can be found here, including large craft shows in spring and fall at Chubb Park. **LOCATION:** Rts. 124 and 206, Morris County (908-879-4814; www.chesternj.org).

A few miles east of Chester, the upscale community of **Mendham** reminds many of a quiet Connecticut town. A number of interesting antiques shops as well as galleries and specialty shops are centered around the intersection of Rt. 124 and Hilltop Road, where you'll also find the Black Horse Inn, a mainstay of country dining.

Hoboken: Known for its old-fashioned railroad terminal, Stevens Tech, Washington Street nightclubs, and, of course, Frank Sinatra, this Hudson County town is filled with art, music, and food celebrations. There are also many restored brownstones that make you feel like you're in an out-of-the-way corner of Manhattan—except when you can see the real skyline from Hoboken's riverfront walkways and Pier A, just north of the Hoboken Terminal. A nexus for the twenty and thirty-something crowd, Washington Street is the center of the action in Hoboken, where you'll find well-known nightclubs and restaurants, including Maxwell's and the Clam Broth House. **Hoboken Historical Museum,** at 1301 Hudson St. on the waterfront (201-656-2240; www.hobokenmuseum.org), features exhibits, lectures, and tours of homes, gardens, and historic sites (open Tue.–Thu., 2–9; Fri., 1–5; weekends, 12–5). Walking tours include the Historical Museum; Elysian Field, the birthplace of baseball (at 10th and Hudson); Stevens Castle Room at Stevens Tech; the Erie Lackawanna Rail Terminal; and the Hoboken Police Museum. The museum also holds an annual historical house tour in October.

The museum offers self-guided tour maps of the town as well as a Frank Sinatra tour. This includes the site of his boyhood home at 415 Monroe (now only a vacant lot behind a wall) and places where he performed. There's a one-room private museum next door to his home called "From Here to Eternity," which is more like a neighborhood bar with Sinatra memorabilia.

Hoboken also features a number of street festivals throughout the year, including the old-fashioned St. Ann's Feast in the summer (with Italian sausage and peppers) and a jazz/food festival that centers around the Terminal in September (www.hoboken.com).

Flemington: Known for its many Victorian homes, Main Street is the center of a historic district where 60 percent of the buildings are on the national register. These include the Hunterdon County Courthouse, where the Lindbergh baby kidnapping trial took place in 1935, and the historic Union Hotel across the street, where the famous reporters of the age stayed and reported on the trial. The **Fleming Castle Museum** at 5 Bonnell St. was built in 1756. It is open for tours 1–4 P.M. on the second Saturday of the month. Programs include demonstrations by Revolutionary War soldiers as well as music and eighteenth-century life (908-782-4607; www.flemingcastle.com). Other historic buildings of note include the 1846 Doric House, home of the Hunterdon County Historical Society (114 Main St.);

and the Reading-Large House, an impressive home with massive columns built in 1847. There are also a number of Victorian B&Bs in the district. These buildings and houses are open for tours during the Flemington Comes Alive celebration, late Sept.–late Oct. (908-782-2610), which includes a dramatic production of the Lindbergh trial at the courthouse (www.famoustrials.com). Flemington is also a center for outlets (q.v.), as well as specialty shops at Turntable Junction and along Main Street, which has a number of new shops and restaurants.

Hope: Guided walking tours of the Hope Historic District start at 10 A.M. on the first and second Saturdays of the month, June–Oct. The starting point is the Inn at Millrace Pond, a restored gristmill on Rt. 519 that is also a Bed & Breakfast and upscale restaurant. The 1½ hour tour ($$; under 12 free) of this historic Warren County village, which was founded in 1769 by Moravians, includes a community church (Gemeinhaus) and Moravian cemetery as well as the 1769 gristmill and other historic stops. Along the way, you pass gift and antiques shops and many historic private homes. Stop by the Help Our Preservation Effort (H.O.P.E) historical library and exhibit center on Walnut Street. The historical society museum, which houses a small collection of local historic photos and artifacts, is around the corner on High Street (open Sun. afternoons, June–Oct.). For H.O.P.E. tours, call 908-459-9177.

Cranbury: This historic Middlesex County town settled in 1697 offers a pleasant place to stroll along tree-shaded streets lined by early American homes. The highlight of its national historic district is the **Cranbury Museum** on Park Place, which is open Sunday afternoons. This 1834 structure combines half a dozen nicely done period rooms with interesting historical exhibits. You can also pick up a self-guided walking tour brochure here. This is a quiet town, not given much to tourism, but you'll find a handful of antiques shops and cafes with sidewalk tables as well as a used-book store. The Cranbury History Center (open Mon. and Thu., 10–1), the Historical Society's library, is across the street from a pleasant park and scenic mill pond. There's also an annual house tour on Cranbury Day in early October (609-655-2611; www.cranburyhistory. org/museum/index.html).

ANTIQUES TOWNS

There are also a number of smaller towns scattered throughout the state that offer both old-fashioned charm and antiques shops. Here are some of the more notable ones.

Mullica Hill: The Gloucester County village of Mullica Hill has long attracted buyers to its country-style antiques stores. Antique dolls, books and ephemera, toys, furniture, together with collectibles and arts-and-crafts items can be found in a passel of stores. Antiques collectives include King's Row Antique Center, 46 N. Main St.; Old Mill Antique Mall, 1 S. Main St.; and the Warehouse, 2 S. Main St. There are also numerous individual shops that include crafts, furniture, and dolls as well as antiques. LOCATION: Junction of Rts. 322 and 45 (856-881-6800; www.mullicahill.com).

Hopewell: A colonial town known for its antiques and pleasant atmosphere lies a few miles northwest of Princeton in Mercer County. A number of antiques shops along W. Broad Street plus the Tomato Factory (a group enterprise) makes this a nice destination for a country outing. The Hopewell Museum (q.v.), the Off-Broad-Street Theatre, and the Hopewell Valley Bistro & Inn and Failte Coffee House add character to this historic town.

Boonton: Boonton Historical Society Museum, 210 Main St. (Sat., 1–4), offers walking tours of Main Street, Ironworks Hollow, and Ironworks Residential Historic District on five Saturdays, Apr.–Sep. (973-402-8840; www.boonton.org/historical). A self-guided tour map is also available at the museum. This Morris County town is also the site of the New Jersey Firemen's Museum (q.v.). But it's probably best known as a browser's town, with more than twenty antiques shops in operation.

Lafayette: A small country enclave on Rt. 15 in Sussex County is the home of the Lafayette Mill Antiques Center, where a group of fifty-five dealers runs an antiques cooperative in a picturesque converted 1842 mill (973-383-0065; www.millantiques.com). The mill, open Thu.–Mon., is next to the Millside Café, which has an upstairs art gallery. There are half a dozen or more other interesting antiques shops around town. A few miles south, the town of **Andover** has about a dozen antiques shops, including the Scranberry Coop (Rt. 206 south of town), which has 150 dealers under one roof and quite a variety of merchandise (open Wed.–Sun.).

Clinton: The Red Mill Museum Village (q.v.) and Hunterdon Museum of Art (q.v.) on opposite banks of the South Branch of the Raritan River are the main draws in town, but the historic Main Street area offers a number of art galleries, antiques stores, restaurants, and gift shops. Across the bridge is Clinton House, an inn dating back to 1743. The surrounding town has some interesting nineteenth-century homes. Take Rt. 78, Exit 15.

Red Bank: The Antiques Center at Red Bank, which hosts about 150 dealers in three large buildings (195, 195A, and 226 W. Front St.), has been around for a long time. Usually open daily but call 732-741-5331 for hours. In recent years, this Monmouth County town has become more upscale, and the Broad and Front Streets area has evolved into an interesting collection of shops, coffeehouses, hip restaurants, and galleries—a nice place for walking and window shopping. The riverfront area is the scene for several music and family festivals (www.redbankartsantique.com and www.redbankrivercenter.org).

Frenchtown: With four blocks of antiques shops, galleries, and boutiques on Race and Bridge Streets leading to the old-fashioned Delaware River bridge, this small town on the banks of the Delaware provides an interesting stop in Hunterdon County. The Frenchtown Inn, Race St. Cafe, and Bridge Street Cafe also give this quaint small town more than its share of restaurants of note (www.frenchtown.com).

Allentown: Located on the far western edge of Monmouth County (just 10 miles east of Trenton) is a historic town that offers an old-fashioned historic district. The Shops at the Old Mill as well as antiques and specialty shops along S. Main Street are popular draws. There's also an interesting nature trail along Doctors Creek in Heritage Park, next to the mill.

Mauricetown: A small nineteenth-century town south of Millville on the Maurice River features many charming Victorian homes built by oystering and whaling captains. Stop by the Historical Society in the Edward Compton House on Front Street (open Sun., 1–3; call 856-785-1137). There are also a few antiques shops around the Cumberland County town, and there are Christmas house tours the second Sunday in December.

Where Washington Slept, Ate, and Fought

One of the largest land battles of the Revolution is reenacted every June at Monmouth Battlefield State Park near Freehold. *(Photo courtesy of Monmouth Battlefield State Park, 2003. Photographer: Michael F. Smith)*

Jockey Hollow

The winter of 1779–1780 was the coldest in a century. On December 1, 1779, General George Washington entered Morristown and took up residence at the house of Mrs. Jacob Ford, Jr. Meanwhile, 4 miles away at Jockey Hollow, 10,000 men chopped down 600 acres of oak, walnut, and chestnut trees to build more than 1,000 log huts along the slopes of the "hollow." Severe snowstorms hindered their work and delayed the supply of meat and bread they needed to survive.

Starvation confronted the army, which also suffered from inadequate clothing, disease, and low morale. So terrible was the winter of the Morristown encampment that many troops finally mutinied. But the history books only seem to tell you about Valley Forge. Why? Because New Jersey didn't have very good public relations—not until recently, anyway.

Today there are several reconstructed huts on the site, which is administered by the National Park Service. But first, go to the Visitor Center, which gives full information about the encampment. There's a mini-theater where an 11-minute film begins at the touch of a button. The story is told by typical foot soldiers huddled in a simple hut waiting for rations and money that take forever in coming. After the film, you can move on to a mock-up of a soldiers' hut and see the straw beds, muskets, and clothing used at the time.

From the Information Center, proceed out the back door to the **Wick Farm.** The farmhouse was occupied by both the Wick family (owners of a farm that included Jockey Hollow) and General Arthur St. Clair and his aide. A vegetable/herb garden, a well, and a horse barn surround the wooden cottage. Inside, there is often a guide dressed in colonial garb cooking, melting down candles, or just answering questions. A tour shows the little bedroom of Tempe Wick, the family bedroom, the general's office/bedroom, and the kitchen.

From there, drive to the open slopes of the winter encampment and visit the simple soldiers' huts on the hill or the various brigade lines. Altogether there are 27 miles of hiking trails within the park, so there's plenty of walking space. On special weekends there are often demonstrations, musters, or other doings both at the Wick Farm and near the reconstructed huts.

> **HOURS:** Daily, 9–5. Closed major holidays. **ADMISSION:** Adults, $ (includes all of MNHP). Under 16 free. **LOCATION:** Take Rt. 287 to Rt. 202 to Tempe Wick Rd. (south of Morristown). Follow signs. **TELEPHONE:** 973-543-4030. **WEBSITE:** www.nps.gov/morr.

Washington's Headquarters

For another look at the Morristown encampment go to Washington's Headquarters (the Ford Mansion), which is part of the overall site called Morristown National Historic Park. It's only a short drive away. You enter at a separate museum (scheduled to reopen later in 2007 after remodeling), where displays emphasize the role of the citizens of Morristown and how they reacted to the soldiers in their town. Other exhibits include military paraphernalia, such as surgeon's tools, mess kits, muskets, and uniforms. Two movies are shown periodically in the auditorium. The films were shot on location both here and in Jockey Hollow, and contrast the warmth and food available to officers at the mansion with the hungry, freezing men camped only 4 miles away. A lively ball scene was filmed in the central hall of the Ford Mansion.

A park ranger, usually in period dress, will then take you on a tour of the Ford Mansion across the lawn. It's a solid frame Colonial-style house—by no means a mansion in the modern sense. As you enter the long central hallway, you notice how well such halls were suited for line dances such as the Virginia reel. The house was offered as headquarters to Washington by Mrs. Ford, a widow with four children. The Ford family lived in two rooms while the general and his staff occupied the rest of the house. The furnishings are authentic to the period and many are true Ford family pieces. Beds include the canopied master bed used by Washington. Highboys, chest-on-chests, wall maps, and lots of straw mattresses are all on display.

Despite the rigors of the Morristown encampment, the Ford Mansion was a comparatively elegant abode for the chief of staff. From here, Alexander Hamilton (who was Washington's aide-de-camp) courted Betsey Schuyler, who was staying at the nearby Schuyler-Hamilton house (q.v.). The historic park also includes other sites, such as Fort Nonsense.

HOURS: Museum: Daily, 9–5; mansion tours, daily, 10–4.
Closed major holidays. **ADMISSION:** Adults, $ (includes all sites in MNHP). Under 16 free. **LOCATION:** Rt. 287 to Exit 36 or 36A to Morris Ave. East, Morristown (Morris County). Follow signs to Washington's Headquarters. **TELEPHONE:** 908-766-8215. **WEBSITE:** www.nps.gov/morr.

Dey Mansion

A solid Dutch farmhouse built in the early Georgian style in the 1740s, the Dey Mansion was Washington's headquarters for three months during the summer and fall of 1780. Here Washington was able to keep an eye on the British in New York, while staying close to food and forage for his army. Furnishings reflect the status of the Dey family, who were quite well-to-do (Theunis Dey was a colonel in the militia). An interesting feature of this house is its separate kitchen (connected to the main house for use during the colder months.) A separate kitchen was practical, for if it caught fire, it would not take the rest of the house with it. The house is filled with well-kept furnishings and many family portraits from the period. You can also see Washington's bedroom and the office where he tended to his correspondence.

Outside there are picnic facilities, a replica blacksmith shop, and other outbuildings. The house is part of Preakness Valley Park, and a golf course is quite close to the mansion. The Bergen County Militia offers special reenactments on the front lawn on special occasions.

HOURS: Wed.–Fri., 1–4:30; Sat. & Sun., 10–12 & 1–4:30.
ADMISSION: $. **LOCATION:** 199 Totowa Rd., Wayne (Passaic County).
TELEPHONE: 973-696-1776.
WEBSITE: www.passaiccountynj.org/historicalattractions.htm.

Wallace House

During the winter of 1778, the well-provisioned British army stayed in New York City, while the American army camped out in the Watchung Mountains in Middlebrook. The winter of 1778–1779 was rather mild, much more pleasant than those at Valley Forge or Morristown. The soldiers lived in tents and later built log cabins, but General Washington stayed 4 miles away at the best house in the area. It was owned by John Wallace, a wealthy Philadelphian who had built the twelve-room Georgian in the then-rural area as a retirement home. Washington rented out only four rooms for himself and his staff at a price of $1,000, while the Wallace family used the rest of the home.

The Wallace House is a solidly built wood structure with wide plank floors and painted walls. A guide takes you through the parlors, dining room, and bedrooms, which have been refurnished to reflect the Wallace family lifestyle of the 1780s, including family portraits on the walls. The room where Washington slept has a canopied four-poster bed, typical toiletry articles on the dresser, and a Chinese porcelain bathtub. The formal parlor does not look large, but it is said up to thirty people ate there when General and Mrs. Washington entertained. Tours start at the nearby interpretive center, with video tours of both the Wallace House and Old Dutch Parsonage.

HOURS: Wed.–Sat., 10–12 & 1–4. Sun., 1–4. Closed federal and state holidays. **ADMISSION:** Free. **LOCATION:** 71 Somerset St., Somerville (Somerset County). **TELEPHONE:** 908-725-1015.

Old Dutch Parsonage

From the Wallace House you can cross the street diagonally to the red brick house known as the Old Dutch Parsonage (there is usually one guide for both places.) This was the dwelling place of Reverend John Frelinghuysen, minister of the Dutch Reformed Church. Later it became the home of the Reverend Jacob Hardenbergh, who married Frelinghuysen's widow. Hardenbergh was one of the "Fighting Pastors" of the Revolutionary War who condemned the British from the pulpit. However, he is best known as the founder of Queens College, which later grew into Rutgers University. Hardenbergh was a frequent host to General and Mrs. Washington when they stayed close by in the Wallace House. (The parsonage was moved to its present location in 1913.)

The displays at the parsonage are meant to reflect the life and times of this Dutch pastor. The building is experiencing ongoing restoration to Hardenbergh's time at the end of the Revolution. Tours could best be described as "restoration tours," with explanations of the historic clues that restorers look for when they determine how a house was originally constructed. One large front room is kept as a social hall for open houses and music programs throughout the year. Featured are music, singing, and even colonial dances. Upstairs, there are changing exhibits on social history related to the house.

HOURS, LOCATION: Same as Wallace House. **ADMISSION:** Free.

The Old Barracks

Set in the midst of bustling downtown Trenton, the Old Barracks, with its red-painted porches, is an authentic reminder of the past. This is the only standing barracks of the type used by the British to house troops in colonial America. It is also the place where Washington and his troops surprised Hessian soldiers after crossing the Delaware on Christmas night in 1776 and turning the tide of the Revolution.

This U-shaped fieldstone building was originally built in 1758 during the French and Indian War because American colonists objected to the billeting of British troops in private homes. A year later an officers' house was added. In 1776 the British and Hessian mercenaries used it until the Americans gained control, after which it became a hospital for the wounded. After the war, the building went through a series of ups and downs until the Old Barracks Association saved it in 1899.

A guided tour starts in the Officers' House, where you can see the relative comfort of the upper ranks. A full restoration has opened up plenty of space in the main barracks. A long barracks room, complete with bunk beds, as well as storage areas are on view. Interpretative history with costumed guides is emphasized. In different rooms, costumed docents adopt various "characters." They will show such things as how to load a musket or care for the wounded.

On Thursdays and Saturdays, you can usually see demonstrations of colonial bread baking.

An annual reenactment of the Battle of Trenton and the "Ten Crucial Days" takes place on the weekend after Christmas during Patriot Week, with lots of cannons and reenactors in the streets. Washington also stops by for a visit on his birthday.

HOURS: Tue.–Sat., 11–5; Sun., 1–5. Closed major holidays.
ADMISSION: $$. Discounts: Seniors, students. Under 6 free.
LOCATION: Barracks St. at West Front St., Trenton (Mercer County). Take Willow St. exit from Rt. 29 south. **TELEPHONE:** 609-396-1776.
WEBSITE: www.barracks.org.

Washington Crossing State Park (New Jersey)

This popular park covers 991 acres stretching east from the banks of the Delaware in Titusville and commemorates the crossing that led to the most important victory of the war's early years. On Christmas Night 1776, General Washington crossed the icy Delaware from Pennsylvania with 2,400 men, plus artillery and supplies. The crossing took 9 hours, and the men and officers converged on this spot on the Jersey side. The ensuing surprise attack on Trenton gave a sweet taste of victory to the discouraged American troops.

The Visitor Center is filled with information on this and other early battles of the Revolutionary War, plus displays on the uniforms and muskets of the time. There are a variety of exhibits and two videos on the crossing and events over the following 10 days. New Jersey's role in the Revolution is presented by the extensive Swan collection of eighteenth-century armaments and other artifacts.

Elsewhere in the park are open fields for Frisbee throwing, an excellent nature center, an open-air amphitheater featuring summer shows, hiking trails, and many picturesque picnic groves. Near the Delaware River sits a monument marking the spot where the troops disembarked, as well as two historic houses. One of these, the **Johnson Ferry House,** is a refurbished 1740 farmhouse and inn furnished with period furniture, with a colonial herb garden outside. The house also hosts special events and demonstrations of Revolutionary-era cooking, crafts, and home life. The small Nelson House across Rt. 29 stands even closer to the river. A separate group administers tours there.

HOURS: Visitor Center, Wed.–Sun., 9–4:30; shorter winter hours. Johnson Ferry House: guided tours, Wed.–Sat., 10–12 and 1–4; Sun., 1–4. Park open dawn to dusk. **ADMISSION:** Free, but there is a parking fee ($) on summer weekends. **LOCATION:** Rts. 29 & 546, Titusville (Mercer County). **TELEPHONE:** Park, 609-737-0623;

Visitor Center, 609-737-9303; Ferry House, 609-737-2515.
WEBSITE: www.state.nj.us/dep/parksandforests/parks/washcros.html.

Washington Crossing Historic Park (Pennsylvania)

Across the river, the site of the embarkation is the focus of a large park that stretches up the Delaware River in two sections. In the McConkey's Ferry section, a modern Visitor Center offers brochures, a theater for a film about the crossing, and tickets for the historical buildings in the park. Some of these buildings are within easy walking distance. The first is the **McConkey Ferry Inn,** where Washington and his staff ate just before the crossing. It is fixed up as a travelers' inn with tables set with pewter and a bar and grill. Nearby are three other historic houses built in 1817–1830, a general store, and a boathouse with replicas of the Durham longboats used for the crossing. Traveling 3.5 miles north, you come to the Thompson's Mill section of the park, which includes a wildflower preserve, a 110-foot-high observation tower on Bowman's Hill, an 1830s gristmill, and the **Thompson-Neely House,** which is built of Delaware River ledgestone and dates back to 1702.

Tickets for guided tours of all the historic houses are reasonably priced. The Visitor Center, movie, and self-guided walking tour are free. An annual re-creation of the crossing takes place every Christmas Day, when the general and his contingent row over to the other side, weather permitting.

> **HOURS:** Tue.–Sat., 9–5; Sun., 12–5. **ADMISSION:** Guided tour, $.
> Discounts: Seniors, children. Under 6 free.
> **LOCATION:** Across Delaware River bridge from Titusville. North on
> PA Rt. 32 to the Thompson's Mill section. **TELEPHONE:** 215-493-4076.
> **WEBSITE:** www.ushistory.org/washingtoncrossing.

Fort Lee Historic Park

Set in scenic Palisades Interstate Park with a view of the Hudson, the George Washington Bridge, and Manhattan, Fort Lee commemorates a defeat, not a victory. The park is only 33 acres but contains a modern Visitor Center, meandering paved paths, a picnic area, reconstructed gun batteries and earthworks, and an authentic eighteenth-century soldiers' hut. The park is actually a quarter mile east of the original Fort Lee, named after General Charles Lee, who helped defend New York City.

Washington planned Fort Lee as a bulwark against the British navy's control of the Hudson River. With forts on both sides of the river and sunken ships in the river channel, Washington felt he could keep British ships at bay. However, General Howe forced the

Americans out of Long Island and then New York City. In November 1776, when General Cornwallis ferried 6,000 men across the Hudson north of the fort, Washington ordered an immediate retreat. Weapons and other military supplies had to be left behind. It was a devastating blow that led to the darkest days of the Revolution, inspiring Thomas Paine's "The American Crisis" and his famous line, "These are the times that try men's souls."

Today, you can see replicas of the abandoned cannon in the park and view the story on Plexiglas panels in the Visitor Center. A short film and displays of muskets are also on view. Down at the soldiers' hut, costumed guides interpret colonial life on summer weekends and for school groups. As part of the larger interstate park, good hiking trails and scenic overlooks are found nearby.

> **HOURS:** Visitor Center, Mar.–Dec., Wed.–Sun., 10–5. **ADMISSION:** $ parking fee, Apr.–Oct. **LOCATION:** Hudson Terrace, Fort Lee (Bergen County). Take last exit before George Washington Bridge. Turn left off Hudson Terrace. **TELEPHONE:** 201-461-1776. **WEBSITE:** www.njpalisades.org/flhp.htm.

Farther north, the **Kearney House,** along the Hudson at the Alpine Boat Basin, was long thought to have served as Cornwallis's overnight headquarters. Later research cast doubt on this notion and placed the British general's landing a mile or so to the south. But the belief did lead to the preservation of the four-room house as the nation's only historic site dedicated to a wartime enemy. Three rooms are furnished in nineteenth-century style and one contains exhibits of the Palisades Interstate Park in the 1920s.

> **HOURS:** Open weekends and holidays, May–Oct., 12–5. **LOCATION:** Alpine Approach Rd., Alpine. **TELEPHONE:** 201-768-1360, ext. 208. **WEBSITE:** www.njpalisades.org/kearney.htm.

Monmouth Battlefield State Park

Although not a complete victory, the Battle of Monmouth on June 28, 1778, proved that American troops, honed by Von Steuben's training at Valley Forge, could win against British regulars in open field fighting. Today's park covers the scene of that hot day's artillery battle in which General Charles Lee ordered a retreat (later reprimanded by Washington), and a legendary lady named "Molly Pitcher" (whose real name was Mary Hays) became a heroine.

The rolling fields, woodlands, and orchards at Monmouth Battlefield are now peaceful, with several miles of nature trails. A large Visitor Center provides information and displays, including relief maps of the battle and videos of a reenactment of the fight as well as battle artifacts recovered from the area. Here you can pick up a map of the battlefield and nearby historic sites and visit the small gift shop. Picnic facilities are nearby. In the park you will find the **Craig House** (off Rt. 9 south at Schibanoff Rd.; open Wed., Sun., 12:30–4, late Apr.–early Nov.), which was occupied by the British and where the wounded were tended during the fight. It has now been restored to its colonial appearance with period furnishings. The site of Molly Pitcher's well was near the Continental Army's artillery line on Perrine Ridge. On the last weekend in June, you can see an annual reenactment of the battle.

> **HOURS:** Park, open daily, 8–4:30; spring & fall, 8–6; Memorial–Labor Day, 8 a.m.–8:30P.M.. Visitor Center, daily, 9–4.
> **ADMISSION:** Free. **LOCATION:** Rt. 9 or Rt. 33 to Bus. Rt. 33 (Freehold Rd.), Manalapan (Monmouth County). One mile west of Rt. 9. **TELEPHONE:** 732-462-9616.
> **WEBSITE:** www.state.nj.us/dep/parksandforests/parks/monbat.html.

Red Bank Battlefield

A small but decisive battle to defend Fort Mercer took place here on October 22, 1777. The Hessian army was soundly beaten even though they greatly outnumbered the Continentals. The fort, along with Fort Mifflin on the Pennsylvania side, guarded the Delaware River and prevented British ships from reaching occupied Philadelphia, so the defense of Fort Mercer was quite important. Although British ships got through after Fort Mifflin was lost, the victory at Red Bank, along with one at Saratoga, New York, three days earlier, convinced France to aid America's fight against the British. The picturesque park contains old cannons and monuments and some earthworks of Fort Mercer. Admission to the 1748 **Whitall House,** where the wounded were cared for, is free. Inside, there is a parlor, a room used as a field hospital, a working colonial kitchen (demonstrations on the third Sunday of the month, Apr.–Oct.), an exhibit room on the battle, and an archeology room with a video on the park and historic artifacts that have been recovered there. There is also an herb garden just outside. The annual 18th Century Field Day, with a battle reenactment and other events, is held the third Sunday in October, and Colonial Christmas tours are held the second Friday and Saturday in December. Visitors can also enjoy Delaware River-front pathways and a pier as well as an adjacent picnic area.

> **HOURS:** Grounds, daily, dawn to dusk; house: Apr.–Sept., Wed.–Sun., 1–4; Oct.–May, Wed.–Fri., 9–12 & 1–4. **ADMISSION:** Free.
> **LOCATION:** 100 Hessian Ave., National Park (Gloucester County).

TELEPHONE: 856-853-5120. WEBSITE: www.co.gloucester.nj.us/ Government/Departments/ParksnRec/redbank.htm.

Indian King Tavern

Set in the town of Haddonfield, which looks as if it stepped out of the past, this public house, or tavern, was the site where the legislative council and general assembly of the New Jersey legislature officially declared New Jersey a state in 1777. Among the many military figures who passed through Haddonfield and are likely to have visited the tavern were General Anthony Wayne, Count Kasimir Pulaski, and the Marquis de Lafayette. The rooms shown by the guide include the keeping room (where food was brought in from a separate outside kitchen), bar, dining room, Assembly room, the legislative council/public bedroom, and the innkeeper's family bedroom.

> **HOURS:** Wed.–Sat., 10–12 & 1–4; Sun., 1–4. Closed major holidays and Wed. after holidays. **ADMISSION:** Free. Groups by appointment only. Children under 12 must be accompanied by an adult. Guided tours are ongoing; just ring the doorbell for the next tour.
> **LOCATION:** 233 Kings Highway, Haddonfield (Camden County).
> **TELEPHONE:** 856-429-6792. **WEBSITE:** www.levins.com/tavern.html or www.state.nj.us/dep/parksandforests/historic/indianking.

Historic New Bridge Landing

Historic New Bridge Landing, known for the wooden bridge that allowed the Continental Army from Fort Lee to escape Cornwallis in 1776, is an 18-acre park that includes a number of historic buildings.

The **Steuben House**, built in 1752, with a further addition built in 1765, is an example of early Dutch Colonial architecture. The house was confiscated during the Revolutionary War because the owners, the Zabriskie family, were loyal to the British. Its position on the Hackensack River made it a strategic prize for both sides, and it was the site of several skirmishes during the Revolution. Washington headquartered here in September 1780. The house was presented to Baron von Steuben in 1781 for his service in training the troops during the war. (Seven years later, after renovating the house, he sold it to the son of the Loyalist from whom it was seized.) Noticeable in the furnishings here is the emphasis on local craftsmen and on the Dutch influence in Bergen County. Some fine specimens of the local colonial crafts include a New Brunswick kas (Dutch armoire) and an old settle (a table that converts into seating).

The **Campbell-Christie House** was built in 1774 by Jacob Campbell in New Milford, and it served as a tavern in the late 1700s after it was bought by John Christie. The inventor J. Walter Christie, born in the house in 1865, worked on pioneer submarines, developed front-wheel drive for cars and trucks, and is the father of the modern tank. The house, moved here in 1977, serves as the headquarters of the Bergen County Historical Society and houses the society's collection of furniture and historic objects. It is open and staffed for special events and on the second Sunday of the month.

The Demarest House Museum (J. Paulison Homestead), a Bergen Dutch sandstone cottage with two rooms built in the 1790s, was moved behind the Steuben House from nearby River Road in 1956. At the time, it was believed to be a home of the family of early pioneer Samuel Demarest. It is open and staffed only during special events (201-261-0012).

HOURS: Steuben House, Wed.–Sat., 10–12 & 1–5; Sun., 2–5.
ADMISSION: Free. **LOCATION:** 1209 Main St., River Edge
(Bergen County). Take River Edge exit from Rt. 4.
TELEPHONE: 201-487-1739. **WEBSITE:** www.bergencountyhistory.org.

Covenhoven House

One of four historic houses administered by the Monmouth County Historical Association, it is significant for its role in the Battle of Monmouth. Henry Clinton, commander of the British troops at the battle, stayed at the home from Friday, June 26, until Sunday, June 28, 1778. After the battle, he and his troops left Freehold for New York. The main section of the home is in Georgian style and furnished according to a 1790 inventory of William A. Covenhoven, the well-to-do farmer who owned the property. A mural depicting a sea battle and walls decorated in a blue-and white Delft pattern were discovered in a bedroom during restoration.

HOURS: May–Sept., Thu.–Sat., 1–4. **ADMISSION:** $. Discounts: Seniors, children. Under 6 free. **LOCATION:** 150 West Main St., Freehold
(Monmouth County). **TELEPHONE:** 732-462-1466.
WEBSITE: www.monmouth.com/~mcha/historichouses.html.

Proprietary House

This mansion is a true Palladian villa, known as High Georgian in America. It was built in 1763 for the last royal governor of New Jersey (who was Benjamin Franklin's "natural" son, William). However, Franklin did not move in until 1774. When the Revolutionary War began, he was arrested—for, unlike his famous father, he chose the Tory side. Benjamin Franklin made two visits in 1775 but could not talk his son into switching allegiance.

The house suffered much damage during the war and was gutted by fire in 1792. After that it had as many ups and downs as a soap opera heroine. It was a popular seaside hotel and then was sold at a sheriff's auction. There were "rich" years as a merchant's abode, then a downward slide. Restoration began some years ago. Special exhibits are on view throughout the year.

Although the house is sparsely furnished and the restoration work incomplete, during a tour you can get a feel for its dimensions. The true Palladian windows, the high ceilings, and the Adamesque fireplace are evident. The governor's drawing room, also called the "Great Parlour," is dramatic and includes an unusual 1780 painting of King George III on glass. The most charming room in the building is the downstairs vaulted wine cellar constructed of red brick, where teas are held (extra fee) on Wednesday afternoons. A display room shows relics and photos of the restoration. There is also a gift shop in the housekeeper's room on the first floor.

HOURS: Wed., 10–4; Sun. by appt. **ADMISSION:** $. Under 12 free.
LOCATION: 149 Kearny Ave., Perth Amboy (Middlesex County).
TELEPHONE: 732-826-5527. **WEBSITE:** www.proprietaryhouse.org.

Boxwood Hall

Also known as the Boudinot Mansion, this very nicely furnished Colonial house is not far from the main drag in Elizabeth. Built in 1750, it was the home of Elias Boudinot, president of the Continental Congress, during the Revolution. George Washington had lunch here on the way to New York and his inauguration as president. Alexander Hamilton lived here for 3 years, and Lafayette stayed at the house in 1820 on his return to America. House furnishings include both the Colonial and later Empire style. The master bedroom also contains displays on local history.

HOURS: Mon.–Sat., 9–12 & 1–5. **ADMISSION:** Free.
LOCATION: 1073 East Jersey St., Elizabeth (Union County).
Off Rts. 1 and 9. **TELEPHONE:** 908-282-7617. Call first.

Buccleuch Mansion

Currently closed for renovation, this handsome Georgian mansion is set in Buccleuch Park with nicely landscaped surrounding gardens. Originally built in 1763, White House Farm, as it was then known, was sold to an English army officer in 1774. The house was confiscated by the Americans in 1776, but British troops reoccupied New Brunswick by December. The banister still retains the marks of the soldiers' musket barrels from the occupation, which lasted until 1777. After the war, Colonel Charles Stewart, Commissary General of the Revolutionary Army, became the owner. At this time, White House Farm was visited by George Washington, John Hancock, and Alexander Hamilton, all of whom loved the setting. Much of Buccleuch Mansion's furnishings today are of nineteenth-century origin. Rooms include a Victorian parlor and a drawing room with Queen Anne pieces.

LOCATION: Easton Ave. to Buccleuch Park, New Brunswick (Middlesex County). **TELEPHONE:** 732-745-5094.

Rockingham

Washington lived in this house when it was in Rocky Hill in 1783 while Congress met in nearby Princeton, awaiting the signing of the Treaty of Paris to end the Revolution. Actually, both George and Martha stayed here and entertained extensively for about 3 months. Guests included Thomas Jefferson, James Madison, and Thomas Paine. It is best known as the house where the "Farewell Address to the Armies" was composed.

A handsome, medium-sized two-story colonial with front porch, the house was once part of an estate of 350 acres with barns, coach house, and granary. It has been moved three times, the latest in 2001 to a Kingston Township location very close to its previous site.

Tours by costumed docents lead through two floors of Rockingham's furnishings, which include such period pieces as Chippendale sets, burnished bureaus, canopied beds, and an antique tea service. The study where the Farewell Address was composed is shown with the ink stand and green cloth on the table. There's even a life-sized replica of Washington. Outside, there's a sizable kitchen garden displaying colonial herbs and vegetables in front of the house. Open hearth cooking is also demonstrated during special events. Plus, there's a children's museum in an adjacent former eighteenth-century wash house.

HOURS: Mon.–Sat., 10–12 & 1–4; Sun., 1–4. **ADMISSION:** free.
LOCATION: Laurel Rd., Kingston (Somerset County).
TELEPHONE: 609-683-7132. **WEBSITE:** www.rockingham.net.

OTHER REVOLUTIONARY WAR SITES

Princeton Battlefield State Park: A short decisive battle was fought here on January 3, 1777, just a week after the famous crossing of the Delaware. General Hugh Mercer was mortally bayoneted during this battle. Within the park, you can visit the Thomas Clarke House, a refurbished 1772 home used as a hospital following the battle. The two-story house is furnished with period pieces as it was during the Revolution, including the room where Mercer died. There are also two rooms with displays on the Revolution, including weapons and artifacts from the park's grounds. Across the road, a colonnade and gravesite mark where twenty-one British and American soldiers died. **HOURS:** Park, 9 A.M. to dusk; house, Wed.–Sat., 10–12 & 1–4, Sun., 1–4. **ADMISSION:** Free. **LOCATION:** 500 Mercer Rd., Princeton (Mercer County). **TELEPHONE:** 609-921-0074. **WEBSITE:** www.state.nj. us/dep/parksandforests/parks/princeton.html.

Washington Rock Park: This huge outcropping on Rock Road atop Watchung Mountain offers a 30-mile panorama that includes New York City. Washington used it in 1777 during the Middlebrook encampment to track the movements of the British army. The park has limited parking space, but there are a few picnic tables. Green Brook (Somerset County). **ADMISSION:** Free. **TELEPHONE:** 201-915-3401. **WEBSITE:** www.state.nj.us/dep/parksandforests/parks/washrock.html.

Drake House: During the battle of the Watchung Mountains, Washington used this house as his command headquarters. Although there is a Colonial bedroom where he is supposed to have rested, the house was later remodeled. There is a Colonial kitchen, bedroom, and dining room, while the parlor and library reflect the Empire and Victorian styles. Upstairs rooms are devoted to changing exhibits on local history. **HOURS:** Sun., 2–4. **ADMISSION:** $. Discount: Children. **LOCATION:** 602 W. Front St., Plainfield (Union County). **TELEPHONE:** 908-755-5831. **WEBSITE:** http://drakehousemuseum.tripod.com.

Schuyler-Hamilton House: This nice little Colonial home is squeezed into a dead-end street off Morris Avenue a few blocks east of the Morristown Green. This is where Alexander Hamilton courted Betsey Schuyler when he was aide-de-camp to Washington at the nearby Ford Mansion. **HOURS:** Sun., 2–4. **ADMISSION:** $. **LOCATION:** 5 Olyphant Place, Morristown (Morris County). **TELEPHONE:** 973-267-4039.

Allen House: Since this 1740 house was operated as the Blue Ball Tavern during the Revolutionary War, two major rooms here have been furnished in that manner. Tables are set with pewter, there is a bar and grill with whiskey jugs, and so forth. It was a meeting place for local revolutionaries, who fought a skirmish with Loyalists here (a Continental soldier died on the stairway). The upstairs is currently undergoing restoration and historic reinterpretation. **HOURS:** May–Sept., Thu.–Sat., 1–4. **ADMISSION:** $. Under 6 free. **LOCATION:** Rt. 35 & Sycamore Ave., Shrewsbury (Monmouth County). **TELEPHONE:** 732-462-1466. **WEBSITE:** www.monmouth.com/~mcha/historichouses.html.

Marlpit Hall: Built in the mid-1700s, this home of a prominent Tory remained in the family until the 1930s. During the Revolution, Edward Taylor was arrested and lost his wealth and status because of his ties to the Loyalist Party and for passing information to his son, George, who was a colonel in a local Loyalist unit. Today, the home's furnishings reflect the Dutch and English colonial period of the eighteenth century into the early nineteenth. **HOURS:** May–Sept., Thu.–Sat., 1–4. **ADMISSION:** $. Discounts: Seniors, children. Under 6 free. **LOCATION:** 137 Kings Highway, Middletown (Monmouth County). **TELEPHONE:** 732-462-1466. **WEBSITE:** www.monmouth.com/~mcha/historichouses.html.

John Abbott II House: As the British advanced on Trenton in 1776, state funds were hidden in this house, which was built in 1730. The Redcoats found some of it, but most—hidden in a tub of broken crockery—was overlooked. Today, costumed docents guide you through this two-story Colonial with an 1840s addition, where you see the contrast between the early Quaker lifestyle and the more elaborate Victorian parlor. **HOURS:** Weekends, 12–5. **ADMISSION:** Free. **LOCATION:** 2200 Kuser Rd., Hamilton Township (Mercer County). **TELEPHONE:** 609-585-1686.

Behind the Abbott House is the **Civil War and Native American Museum,** which contains three rooms of memorabilia, including weapons, surgical equipment, and other displays on a local Civil War training camp. A Civil War reenactment is also held nearby in late July. **HOURS:** Apr.–Nov., weekends, 1–5. **ADMISSION:** Free. **TELEPHONE:** 609-585-8900. **WEBSITE:** www.campolden.org.

Hancock House: In a raid on March 21, 1778, nine Continental soldiers and Judge William Hancock were killed here and twenty others were wounded. This 1734 house has five rooms filled with period furnishings. There's also a Swedish Colonial cabin on the site, salvaged from another area home, where it was discovered encased in later construction. **HOURS:** Wed.–Sat., 10–2 & 1–4, Sun., 1–4. **ADMISSION:** Free. **LOCATION:** Rt. 49 at Hancock's Bridge, 5 miles south of Salem (Salem County). **TELEPHONE:** 856-935-4373. **WEBSITE:** www.fohh.20fr.com.

Solitude House: Built in 1720 and enlarged over the years, this was the manager's home for the nearby Union Forge Ironworks. John Penn, last royal governor of Pennsylvania, was held as a prisoner here in 1777–1778, and a copy of a letter from Penn is on display. Aaron Burr visited often, and George Washington stayed briefly because the forge supplied his army with cannonballs. Only recently opened to the public and in the process of restoration, this house has two period rooms as well as exhibits on local history and archeological artifacts from the grounds. A path leads to a scenic nineteenth-century stone dam and to a small remaining wall of the early forge. **HOURS:** May–Nov., Sun., 2–4. **ADMISSION:** Free. **LOCATION:** 7 River Rd., High Bridge (Hunterdon County). **TELEPHONE:** 908-638-3200. **WEBSITE:** www.highbridge.org/heritage.html.

Burrowes Mansion: Built in 1723, this Georgian house belonged to Major John Burrowes, known locally as the "corn king," who mustered the First New Jersey Company in his backyard during the Revolution. A month before the Battle of Monmouth, loyalists raided the house looking for Burrowes's son. Believing he was hiding in the attic, they fired their muskets through the floorboards—to no avail, as their target had already fled. The bullet holes are still there, however, and are among the highlights of the guided tour. The house today contains a mixture of period furnishings and history exhibits, with Colonial as well as Victorian rooms. Later this was the home of late nineteenth century New Jersey governor Joseph Bedle, whose crib is still here along with his portrait, which hangs in the music room. **HOURS:** First and third Sun. of each month, 2–4. **ADMISSION:** Free. **LOCATION:** 94 Main St., Matawan (Middlesex County). **TELEPHONE:** 732-566-5605.

Cannon Ball House: Built in 1740, this house was used as a hospital during the Battle of Springfield in 1780. During the battle, the house was struck by a cannonball, which is now on display. One of only four structures standing after the British burned the town, today the house has been renovated to its original appearance and is the Springfield Historical Society's headquarters. It has five Revolutionary-era rooms, some Civil War items, early tools, a battle diorama, and a colonial garden. Open for four special events during the year and by appointment. **LOCATION:** 126 Morris Ave., Springfield (Union County). **TELEPHONE:** 973-912-4464.

Osborn Cannonball House Museum: This colonial saltbox farmhouse run by the Scotch Plains–Fanwood Historical Society was built around 1760. It features a restored kitchen and three rooms decorated to reflect its original Colonial style plus a Victorian parlor. Outside, you can enjoy a colonial herb and flower garden noted for its historical accuracy. The house received its name from a cannonball fired at the British in 1777 that hit the house instead—while Mary Osborn was providing soldiers with food and clothing. **HOURS:** Costumed docents lead tours 2–4 P.M., the first Sun. of each month and on special holidays, except Jan.–Feb. **LOCATION:** 1840 Front St., Scotch Plains (Union County). **TELEPHONE:** 908-322-6700.

NEARBY OUT-OF-STATE SITE

Valley Forge National Historic Park

It is known as "The Crucible of Victory" because the 10,000 men who emerged from the harsh winter had coalesced into a well-trained fighting force. The encampment, which lasted from December 19, 1777, to June 19, 1778, is now commemorated in a 3,466-acre park. It is so big you must start with a map or a bus tour. The modern Welcome Center offers an 18-minute film and a small exhibit of Revolutionary military equipment. From here you board buses, which operate in warm weather, for a tour that stops at key sites and features a taped narration. Or you can rent or buy a tape to use if you drive the tour route yourself. Among the important sites are the National Memorial Arch, earthen fortifications, the parade ground where Von Steuben trained and reviewed the troops, soldiers' huts, Artillery Park, and headquarters of several of Washington's generals. Costumed soldiers welcome you to Washington's Headquarters. There is a small additional fee here in season. Costumed personnel are also often at the soldiers' huts. The park has picnic grounds, bicycle trails, snack bar, souvenir shop, and lots of beautiful scenery. There is a small entrance fee April through November, and a fee for bus tours, tapes, and entry to some historic houses.

HOURS: Open daily except Christmas, grounds open sunrise to sunset, Washington's Headquarters, 9–5. For buses, warm weather only.
LOCATION: Visitor Center, Junction of PA 23 and N. Gulph Rd., Valley Forge, PA. Take Exit 326 from Pennsylvania Turnpike.
TELEPHONE: 610-783-1077. **WEBSITE:** www.nps.gov/vafo.

Historic Homes
of the Rich and Famous

The dining room at Morven Museum and Garden in Princeton
is filled with furniture owned by Elias Boudinot, president of
the Continental Congress. *(Photo by Patrick Sarver)*

Lambert Castle

Situated on a hillside below the cliffs of the Garret Mountain Reservation on the border of Paterson and Clifton, Lambert Castle is impressive inside and out. Designed and built by silk manufacturer Catholina Lambert in nineteenth-century opulence, it was inspired by castles he saw during his childhood in England. This 1892 sandstone and granite mansion stands like a medieval castle with rounded towers and turrets, recalling images of long-bow archers repelling invaders.

It wasn't invading hordes that undid Lambert, however, but the silk strike of 1913 and a decline in the American silk trade. Many of Lambert's prized European paintings and fine furnishings had to be sold to pay his debts (five of his Renoirs are now at the Metropolitan Museum). He retained the house, though, until his death in 1923. Soon after, it became part of the Passaic County park system, along with Garret Mountain Reservation, which encompasses hundreds of acres of woods, picnic grounds, and an impressive overlook atop the cliffs behind the castle. Lambert's hilltop observation tower still stands there and is currently undergoing restoration. The view from the castle also remains impressive, encompassing the city of Paterson and the New York skyline to the east.

The castle today is the home of the Passaic County Historical Society, and its first-floor rooms (dining room, music room, breakfast room, front hall, Lambert's office, and private art court) contain a number of Lambert's possessions, including some of his artwork and a 13½-foot-high marble and onyx clock made for the 1867 Paris Exhibition. On the second floor you'll find numerous paintings and artifacts related to local history. The third floor contains changing exhibits. Also of note is a stained-glass window above the stairway memorializing Lambert's daughter Florence, who died in her early twenties. Volunteers provide ongoing tours, and the castle also has a small gift shop. *Note:* From mid-October to mid-December, furnishings are removed to accommodate a Holiday House Boutique fundraiser.

HOURS: Wed.–Sun., 1–4 (Jul.–Aug., 1–5). **ADMISSION:** $.
Discounts: Seniors, children. Under 5 free. **LOCATION:** 3 Valley Rd.,
Paterson (Passaic County). Exit 57 off Rts. 80 and 19.
TELEPHONE: 973-881-2761. **WEBSITE:** www.lambertcastle.org.

Walt Whitman House

A narrow row house in Camden contains the rooms where the poet who sang of America lived out the last eight years of his life. This national historic landmark offers a glimpse into his life. Whitman's original letters, personal belongings, the bed in which he died, and the death notice that was nailed to the front door in 1892 have all been preserved. There is also a collection of rare nineteenth-century photos, including the earliest known image of Whitman taken in 1848. (Whitman was the most photographed person in America in his time.)

Accumulations of furniture (much of it the housekeeper's, which she brought with her when she took over the job), books, pipes, and other memorabilia are here. Whitman had a paralytic stroke, and some of the house's contents were given to him by friends during his disabled period. A bathtub kept in the bedroom is typical of the many gifts his friends collected for him. A settee there was for his visitors.

Surprisingly, this house has only a few rooms on each floor. Whitman spent the money collected by friends on an elaborate mausoleum in Harleigh Cemetery, 2 miles away. The house has been returned to its original look, with mustard-colored walls, wallpaper, and fading furniture. A guide will show you displays of books, manuscripts, and photographs. The house is close to the Camden waterfront area and the Benjamin Franklin Bridge.

HOURS: Wed.–Sat., 10–12 & 1–4; Sun., 1–4. Call first. **ADMISSION:** Free. **LOCATION:** 328 Mickle Blvd., Camden (Camden County). Two blocks from waterfront attractions. **TELEPHONE:** 856-964-5383. **WEBSITE:** www.state.nj.us/dep/parksandforests/historic/whitman.

Edison National Historic Site

This National Park site consists of the Edison Laboratory Complex in downtown West Orange, and Glenmont, Thomas Edison's home, a mile away in the private enclave of Lewellyn Park. The laboratory section includes a Visitor Center with exhibits of Edison's inventions, a separate chemistry lab, a huge storage section of elephant ears and other unusual resources, and a replica of the "invention factory." Also on the grounds is a replica of the original "Black Maria," where early films were shot.

Ongoing renovation keeps the labs closed. There will be structural changes, but one thing that will remain the same is Edison's golden oak library, where his cot, desk, and 10,000 volumes of books still stand. The huge clock on the wall is stopped at 3:27—the time on October 18, 1931, when Edison died.

As for Glenmont, the rambling Queen Anne–style house where Edison lived with his second wife, Minna, is a warm family home filled with carved oak woodwork, oriental rugs, and mementos from world visitors. The house has recently been renovated and cleaned, and surrounding gardens (including the gravesite) reflect Edison's time here. There's also a new garden shop at the house.

HOURS: House: Wed.–Sun. Tours start on the hour, 10–4.
(Check Website for scheduled lab reopening.)
LOCATION: Main St. & Lakeside Ave., West Orange (Essex County).
TELEPHONE: 973-736-0551. **WEBSITE:** www.nps.gov/edis.

Morven Museum and Garden

This gracious Georgian Colonial mansion has been the home of five governors, two senators, and at least one millionaire. Richard Stockton, a leading colonial attorney and signer of the Declaration of Independence, built this historic Princeton residence in 1758. His wife, poet Annis Boudinot Stockton, named it "Morven" after the mythical kingdom in a popular epic poem. The house was occupied by British troops for a time during the Revolutionary War when Richard was taken prisoner. After he died in 1781, Annis remained there. She hosted members of the Continental Congress during their Princeton stay in 1783, when they convened in Nassau Hall. (The president of the Congress, Elias Boudinot, was her brother.) Descendants of the Stockton family (for whom both Stockton, New Jersey, and Stockton, California, are named) kept ownership of the house for many years. Later, Robert Wood Johnson of the Johnson & Johnson pharmaceutical firm purchased the house and added a pool and modern conveniences.

In 1945, Governor Walter Edge bought the house and later deeded it to the state to be used either as an official residence for governors or a museum. After years as a governors' abode, the mansion and surrounding 5 acres of gardens and lawns became too small for official functions. The official residence was moved in the 1980s, and Morven returned to museum status. Today the gardens have been replanted to their original colonial look, and the house has been renovated as a history museum, a museum for decorative arts, and a restored eighteenth-century mansion. One gallery offers exhibits on Morven's residents. Elsewhere, the Boudinot Collection (on loan from the Princeton Art Museum) features colonial and federal art owned by the Boudinot family. And the dining room has been furnished with Elias Boudinot's possessions, as it would have been around the time of the Revolution. There's also a special Tour & Tea on Wednesdays in the Garden Room.

HOURS: Wed.–Fri., 11–3; Sat.–Sun., 12–4. Tours start at 15 min. past the hour. **ADMISSION:** $. Discounts: Seniors, students.
LOCATION: 55 Stockton St. (Rt. 206), Princeton (Mercer County).
TELEPHONE: 609-924-8144. **WEBSITE:** www.historicmorven.org.

Grover Cleveland Birthplace

Grover Cleveland, the only U.S. president born in New Jersey, spent his early childhood in this pleasant manse. The clapboard house was built in 1832 for the pastor of the First Presbyterian Society. Two years later, the Reverend Richard F. Cleveland obtained that position. Grover was born here in 1837, but four years later the pastor moved his family to Buffalo.

The home is set on a busy street in Caldwell. Although not large, it does have a nice garden and ample parking space. This state historic site is a house museum that also includes exhibits on Cleveland's life and presidency. The open-hearth kitchen looks more like one from colonial times, but these were still common in many households in the 1830s. Other items of note include Cleveland's cradle and original family portraits. A number of later pieces from Cleveland's presidency in the exhibit gallery reflect the richer, more ornate world of the 1880s. A large chair from his executive office in the White House as well as several other pieces show both Cleveland's girth and his station in life.

A picture of Mrs. Frances Cleveland, a beautiful young woman whom he married when she was 21 and he was 49, adorns the house, along with memorabilia from their marriage. Frances was the daughter of Cleveland's business partner, and she turned down his marriage proposal several times before she finally said yes. She was the youngest First Lady ever, and their marriage was the first to take place in the White House. Their first baby, Ruth, was a media icon and later became the namesake of the popular candy bar. Much memorabilia and photographs of Cleveland and his administration can be found here. Cleveland was the only president to be elected to two nonconsecutive terms and is best remembered for that distinction.

After his second term, Cleveland retired to Princeton, where he served as lecturer and trustee. He became friends with Woodrow Wilson, who was president of the university at that time. Cleveland is buried in the Princeton Cemetery.

HOURS: Wed.–Sat., 9–12 & 1–5; Sun., 1–6. Call first. **ADMISSION:** Free.
LOCATION: 207 Bloomfield Ave., Caldwell (Essex County).
TELEPHONE: 973-226-0001.
WEBSITE: www.state.nj.us/dep/parksandforests/historic/
grover_cleveland/gc_home.htm.

Ballantine House

One of the pleasures of visiting the Newark Museum is touring the Ballantine House next door. You enter this opulent late Victorian townhouse from an interior passageway in the museum proper. This corridor is filled with Belleek and other decorative china. Inside, a foyer depicts the history of the Victorian home as a haven from the outside world. In fact, you get a short course in cultural history before you enter the actual house. The Ballantines were a Scottish family who rose from poor immigrants to wealthy beer barons within the span of two generations. They built this house in fashionable Washington Park when they had "arrived." But this three-story Renaissance Revival townhouse is shown not only as a family home but also as an emblem of the Victorian upper class of the 1880s, with their manners and aspirations.

A hallway leads you to the public rooms on the first floor—the library, dining room, reception room, and parlor. While you cannot go completely into the rooms, you can see everything perfectly from behind the room barriers. It is a marvelous job of restoration, with the colors brighter and the furniture cleaner than it probably ever was in its heyday. In the high Victorian period the term "interior decoration" was taken literally and every inch of space was covered, plastered, paneled, draped, or otherwise prettified. The dining room, for instance, features oak and cherry parquet floors, mahogany woodwork, a ceiling of molded papier-mâché panels between painted plaster beams, and walls of leather-looking paper. Add to that a brick and wood fireplace, small stained glass windows, tapestried chairs, and a table sparkling with white linen, and you get a scene of solid bourgeois luxury that was meant to impress the guests. Other rooms include the delicate French-style parlor and the somber reception room where visitors would wait while their calling cards were brought to the family. A magnificent stained glass window with its rising sun presides over the stairwell. On the second floor the family bedrooms and exhibits of china and silver are on view. The silver includes some niceties of formal dining, such as pickle forks and place-card holders. The Ballantine House provides not only insights into Victorian living, but its legacy of manners and mores as well.

HOURS: Wed.–Sun., 12–5; Oct.–June., weekends 10–5.
ADMISSION: Included with museum. **LOCATION:** 49 Washington St., Newark. Enter through Newark Museum. **TELEPHONE:** 973-596-6550.
WEBSITE: www.newarkmuseum.org.

Bainbridge House

This small brick building, wedged between businesses on Princeton's busy Nassau Street, stands opposite Princeton University. Built in 1766 by Job Stockton, cousin of Declaration of Independence signer Richard Stockton, the house was also the birthplace of Captain William Bainbridge, a hero of the War of 1812 and commander of the U.S.S. *Constitution.* It may have provided housing for Congress when it met in Princeton in 1783. Today it serves as headquarters for the Historical Society of Princeton. A typical small home of a well-to-do family of the late eighteenth century, it features a long-term exhibit on Princeton history as well as short-term displays on social history, notable people and events, and architecture. There's also a small museum shop, and the society conducts tours of Princeton from here. Anyone can join the 2 P.M. Sunday walking tour. Self-guided maps are also available.

> **HOURS:** Tue.–Sun., 12–4. Weekends only, Jan.–Feb. **ADMISSION:** $$.
> Discount: Children. **LOCATION:** 158 Nassau St., Princeton
> (Mercer County). **TELEPHONE:** 609-921-6748.
> **WEBSITE:** www.princetonhistory.org.

Ringwood Manor

If they ever film a Chekhov play in New Jersey, Ringwood Manor would make a perfect setting. This rambling manor house set on a rise overlooking a small lake is a prime example of a Victorian country estate.

The house goes back to 1807, when it was built by ironmaster Martin Ryerson, replacing an earlier colonial structure. One side of the house has been furnished to reflect that original house, with the

Ringwood Manor is a Victorian mansion that presides over a classic estate setting in Ringwood State Park. *(Photo by Patrick Sarver)*

gracious colonial dining room and parlor part of the tour. Relics of the old-iron forge days dot the landscape. A cannon from the USS *Constitution* and a section of iron chain that stretched across the Hudson during the Revolution are placed on the terrace as a salute to the early iron products forged in this area.

But it is the 51-room expanded manor with a porte cochere designed by Stanford White that gives Ringwood its high Victorian look. In 1853, it became the country home of Peter Cooper, the industrialist and philanthropist who founded Cooper Union and ran for president as the candidate of the short-lived Greenback Party. Later his son-in-law, Abram S. Hewitt, took over. Hewitt, who served as a congressman from New York and was New York City mayor, enlarged and modernized the house to later nineteenth-century taste. It became a pleasant haven filled with antiques and cottage furniture. The Victorian rooms include bedrooms with lace curtains, parlors filled with paintings, a heavy oak stairway, and bronze chandeliers.

The manor presides over one corner of a huge state park in the Ramapo Mountains. Each section of the park has its own tollgate and parking fee (during the summer season). Shepherd's Lake has a lovely swimming, canoeing, and picnic area and therefore is by far the most popular area of the park, filling up early on weekends. During warm weather, there are also art exhibitions in the Barn Gallery on the grounds (Wed., Sat., Sun. & holidays, 1–4).

HOURS: Park, daily, dawn to dusk. Manor House, Memorial Day to Labor Day, Wed.–Sun., 10–3. **ADMISSION:** Summer parking fees, $. **LOCATION:** 1304 Sloatsburg Rd., Ringwood (Passaic County). Rt. 287 to Exit 57, then follow signs. **TELEPHONE:** 973-962-7031. **WEBSITES:** www.ringwoodmanor.com, or www.state.nj.us/dep/parksandforests/parks/ringwood.html.

Skylands Manor

In another section of Ringwood State Park you can find Skylands, a 44-room Tudor-style mansion that looks like an English castle. Skylands is best known for the state botanical gardens (q.v.), but the first-floor rooms of the mansion are open for limited Sunday afternoon tours and a long weekend in early December, when it is decked out for Christmas.

The house and gardens as they appear now were built in 1922 by architect John Russell Pope (who also designed the Jefferson Memorial) for investment banker and garden connoisseur Clarence Mackenzie Lewis. Many of the rooms are paneled in oak, often carved with such oddities as sea monsters, cupids, and dragons' heads as well as more classical designs. The formal dining room has Elizabethan panels from an English manor house. The Great Hall features European stained glass medallions in leaded windows dating to the sixteenth and seventeenth centuries as well as a huge marble mantelpiece. The stone terrace with its view of flowering trees and statuary is quite romantic. At one time the holdings covered almost 2,000 acres, but the house and gardens now encompass around 96 acres. While the gardens and trails are part of the state park and open all the time, tours of the mansion are handled by the Skylands Association. A private catering company also handles weddings and corporate functions inside the mansion.

> **HOURS:** First Sun. of month except Jan. & Feb., 12–4. **ADMISSION:** $.
> Discounts: Seniors, children. Under 6 free. Summer parking fee, $.
> **LOCATION:** Morris Rd., Ringwood (Passaic County). Rt. 287 to Exit 57,
> then follow signs. **TELEPHONE:** 973-962-9534. **WEBSITES:** www.njbg.org,
> or www.state.nj.us/dep/parksandforests/parks/ringwood.html.

Liberty Hall Museum

Liberty Hall, an estate on the Essex/Union county border, was the enclave of two illustrious families—the Livingstons and the Keans. It has been converted into a "living history" museum tucked behind corporate buildings across from Kean University.

William Livingston built the original colonial homestead in 1772. A member of the Constitutional Convention, Livingston was the first elected governor of New Jersey. When one of his daughters married John Kean, the two families became entwined. The house is full of history. John Jay, the first chief justice of the Supreme Court, married Livingston's daughter Sarah in the front hall. When he was a teenager, Alexander Hamilton lived in one of the upstairs bedrooms for a year. And in 1780, during the Revolutionary War, British soldiers invaded the home—the hatch marks of their sabers are still evident on the banisters. They fled when they thought they saw the ghost of Hannah Caldwell, a minister's wife who had been killed in the nearby Battle of Springfield, on the staircase.

Since the Kean family lived in Liberty Hall until the 1970s, the furnishings are original to the house and represent all the eras it encompasses: Colonial, Victorian, Edwardian, art deco, and modern. Many people still remember the elegant lifestyle of the last of the family, Mary Alice Kean, to inhabit the house. Reminiscent of that lifestyle is the Afternoon Tea, available on Wednesdays, 2–4, on the glass porch overlooking the formal gardens. (Reservations required/separate fee.) Regular tours include the Visitor Center (where there's a ten-minute video on the house narrated by former governor Tom Kean), outbuildings, and the surrounding gardens (a formal English parterre, a rose garden, fruit trees, and a large horse chestnut planted in 1772). A separate gardens and grounds tour is also available. Special events, such as an 1890s baseball game and reenacted Revolutionary War battles, are also featured on particular weekends, as are workshops like pumpkin carving, apple picking, and garden photography.

> **HOURS:** Wed.–Sat., 10–4; Sun., 12–4. Closed Jan.–Mar.
> **ADMISSION:** $$$. Under 6 free. **LOCATION:** 1003 Morris Ave., Union.
> **TELEPHONE:** 908-527-0400. **WEBSITE:** www.libertyhallnj.org.

Macculloch Hall

This 1810 Federal-style structure has furnishings that are quite handsome. These include oriental rugs, huge crystal chandeliers brought over from the Twombly estate in Madison (now a Fairleigh Dickinson University campus), and an original portrait of Washington by Charles Willson Peale. There are ten period rooms, with quality furnishings from the eighteenth and nineteenth centuries throughout. Macculloch Hall is a museum of the decorative arts, with half the house dedicated to changing galleries. Temporary exhibits vary, so anything from a cache of English teapots to quilts to vases might be shown in the museum rooms.

A permanent gallery is also dedicated to Thomas Nast, the famous cartoonist whose vitriolic drawings helped topple the corrupt Boss Tweed in New York. (Nast's house, a private residence, is diagonally across the street). His depictions of Santa Claus created the classic image we now know. Nast also created the donkey and elephant as symbols of the political parties. The Republican Party of New Jersey was also founded in this house. In addition there is a very pleasant English garden behind Macculloch Hall one can wander through. The mansion is tastefully decorated for Christmas tours and offers special exhibits at other times of the year.

> **HOURS:** Wed., Thu., & Sun., 1–4. **ADMISSION:** $. Under 12 free.
> **LOCATION:** 45 Macculloch Ave., Morristown (Morris County).
> Two blocks south of South St. (Rt. 124). **TELEPHONE:** 973-538-2404.
> **WEBSITE:** www.macullochhall.org.

Drumthwacket

On any Wednesday you can visit Drumthwacket, the governor's mansion in Princeton, for a tour of the gracious Greek Revival building that has been refurbished to the hilt. The governor will not be in, of course. For two hours, this white-columned house belongs to those who pay for its maintenance, namely New Jersey residents.

With its two-story Ionic columns and wide veranda, Drumthwacket will remind many of the plantation houses of the Deep South. Indeed, Charles Olden, who built it in 1835, had spent nine years in New Orleans and was impressed by southern architecture. Olden later became governor of New Jersey in 1860.

A docent explains the history of the building as you move from room to room. Moses Taylor Pyne bought the estate from Olden's widow in 1893. Pyne named the house Drumthwacket, which is Scottish-Gaelic for "wooded hill." He added two wings, one of which includes a striking Gothic-and-Tudor library with wood paneling from an English church, a Caen stone fireplace, and canvas panels on the ceiling that look like medieval bookplates. You can also visit the Governor's Study, which features an unusual two-sided desk.

The dining room is most impressive. The nineteenth-century Sheraton mahogany table is often set with Tiffany sterling silver candelabra and an ornate punchbowl—part of a 57-piece service originally commissioned for the first USS *New Jersey* in 1906—and gold-trimmed Lenox china with the seal of New Jersey. The hand-painted chinoiserie wallpaper is also impressive. Across the hall, in a comfortably furnished living room, a special exhibit of New Jersey porcelains from the studios of Cybis and Boehm are displayed. There are historic paintings and furnishings throughout the house, including a Charles Willson Peale portrait of Washington, an 1879 landscape by Asher B. Durand, a 1765 Chippendale secretary, and a 1797 tall case clock. Outside, you can wander through the lovely formal terraced gardens behind the house and visit the Olden House, the original farmhouse that now houses the gift shop. From late November to mid-December, the house is decorated for Christmas.

HOURS: Wed., 12–2. Tours start at noon. Reservations needed. Closed in August and late December. **ADMISSION:** Free.
LOCATION: 354 Stockton St. (Rt. 206), Princeton (Mercer County).
TELEPHONE: 609-683-0057, ext. 3. **WEBSITE:** www.drumthwacket.org.

William Trent House

The founder of Trenton—so to speak, because his house and property were known as Trent's Town—William Trent built his stately home in 1719. It was later the residence of four governors. "A genteel brick dwelling house, three stories high, with a large, handsome staircase and entry," wrote one early observer. It was built in the Georgian style and is furnished with eighteenth-century English and colonial pieces according to a 1724 inventory done just after Trent died.

Guided tours are run by knowledgeable volunteers who give out many tidbits of information. They will point out teacups without handles, which were early imports from China, and the front parlor chandelier with removable "arms" (candleholders that were used to light the way to bed). In the master bedroom is a trundle bed for the children that pulled out from the main, canopied bed. Although this was a wealthy colonial household, it was not unusual for children to sleep in the same room as their parents. A Visitor Center in an adjacent carriage house includes a gift shop.

HOURS: Daily, 12:30–4. **ADMISSION:** $. Discounts: Students, children. **LOCATION:** 15 Market St., Trenton. **TELEPHONE:** 609-989-3027. **WEBSITE:** www.williamtrenthouse.org.

Kuser Farm Mansion

The country home of Fred Kuser was built in 1892 as both a vacation home and a working farm. The family had financial interests in hotels, beer, cars, and more but is best known for its connection with 20th Century Fox movie studio. Fred's brother Anthony helped William Fox start his motion picture company with a $200,000 loan. (Anthony later donated High Point State Park to New Jersey, including the tall monument he had built there.) The connection continued for years, with the Kuser family showing movies using a specially constructed screen in their dining room well into the

The Kuser Farm Mansion in Hamilton was built as a Queen Anne-style summer "cottage" in 1892. *(Photo by Patrick Sarver)*

1960s. While the house is not a place of super luxury (it was meant for casual summer entertaining and family get-togethers), it displays meticulous workmanship. Specially trained German craftsmen worked on the ornately carved mantelpieces throughout the 22-room house. Double floors, heavy woodwork, stained glass windows, and a bedroom featuring a Delft tile fireplace are among the notable details. The 45-foot dining room features a heavily ornate table and chairs that were the hallmark of the Victorian age.

The Kuser Mansion and surrounding farm were sold to Hamilton Township in the mid-1970s to be used as a public park. The outdoor area includes a gazebo and many picnic tables and has a pleasant, quiet atmosphere. There are also summer concerts on the grounds. Last tour begins half an hour before closing.

HOURS: House, May–Nov., Thu.–Sun., 11–3. Weekends only Feb.–Apr. Call first. **ADMISSION:** Free. Christmas open house and other special events. **LOCATION:** 390 Newkirk Ave., Hamilton Twp. (Mercer County). Rt. 295 to Kuser Rd. exit, north to Ferrante Ln. **TELEPHONE:** 609-890-3630.

Stickley Museum at Craftsman Farms

This was the home of Gustav Stickley, a well-known furniture designer of the early twentieth century, who was also the foremost American spokesman for the Arts and Crafts movement. His large, wooden, somewhat chunky furniture is often referred to as "Mission" style. Stickley also published a journal called *The Craftsman* (hence the name of the farm), which printed his house designs. Although he was not a trained architect, his plans appealed to those who disliked the overly ornate houses of the Victorian age. Since local builders used these plans, there are many Craftsman-style houses in New Jersey. They are typically two-story, with large overhanging eaves, a porch supported by round, wooden columns, and windows that are grouped together. When styles changed and his furniture and house plans were no longer popular, Stickley went bankrupt. Nowadays, Stickley furniture is back in vogue.

Craftsman Farms was saved from developers a few years ago. There are 26 acres left of the original 650-acre tract. The main house—a large log cabin with a stone chimney—was originally intended as a clubhouse for a boys' farm. This explains the huge kitchen and the 50-foot-long living room and dining room. The home features rounded ceiling beams and hammered copper fireplace hoods and, of course, Stickley furniture—most of it original to the house. Tours take about 45 minutes and include a short walk around the sloping acreage. An interesting museum shop sells books on the Arts and Crafts movement, pottery, textiles, and other art items. Many special events, plus brown-bag Wednesday lectures, are featured here.

HOURS: Apr.–mid-Nov., Wed.–Fri., 12–3; Sat., 10–4; Sun., 11–4.
ADMISSION: $$. Discounts: Seniors, children. Under 6 free.
LOCATION: 2352 Rt. 10 West #5, Parsipanny (Morris County). Rt. 287 to Rt. 10 west to Powder Mill Estates. Follow signs.
TELEPHONE: 973-540-1165. **WEBSITE:** www.stickleymuseum.org.

NEARBY OUT-OF-STATE HOMES
Nemours
None of the fabulous homes of the super-rich in America are more palatial than Nemours, the former residence of Alfred I. DuPont outside Wilmington in the Brandywine Valley. The mansion, built in 1909, is a modified Louis XVI French chateau. The landscaped gardens are in the French formal style and include marble statues, cascading fountains, and a series of terraces. The hand of Louis XVI seems to be everywhere, a tribute to the Gallic origins of the DuPonts.

Inside, the home displays vast elegance. The gold and white dining room has ornate moldings on walls and ceilings, Rococo-style paintings, and a chandelier worthy of the Phantom of the Opera. The reception room, living room, and other public rooms are equally fabulous with inlaid ceilings, marble tiled floors, rich oriental rugs, and carved walls. Furniture includes both genuine antiques, such as George Washington's chair, as well as fine copies of Louis XVI furnishings.

There's a downstairs tour of a restaurant-sized cooking area as well as a bowling alley, a billiard room, and a furnace room. After the house tour you board a minibus for a garden tour. Fountains and pools, colonnades and balustrades, marble Cupids and Dianas, and a reflecting pool and fountain create a mini-Versailles. Tours are limited and reservations highly suggested. No children under 16.

HOURS: May–Nov.; tours, Tue.–Sat. at 9, 11, 1, & 3; Sun. tours: 11, 1, & 3.
ADMISSION: $$$. **LOCATION:** Rockland Rd., Wilmington, DE.
Inside Alfred I. DuPont Institute. **TELEPHONE:** 302-651-6912.
WEBSITE: www.nemours.org/internet?url=no/mansion/index.html.

Winterthur
Henri DuPont, grandson of the founder of the DuPont empire, was a great collector of American decorative arts. Winterthur is his crowning achievement. Although he actually lived in this mansion, he turned it into a veritable museum. Whole rooms were transported

into the house. The main mansion contains 175 rooms, many of them decorated in a pre-1860 style. You will find dining rooms, kitchens (including walls, ceilings, and fireplaces) placed panel by panel inside the mansion. Several style periods are shown: seventeenth century, William and Mary, Queen Anne, Chippendale, Federal, Empire, and Victorian. Each piece is documented. The Duncan Phyfe room, for instance, had its architectural elements removed from a house in New York. There's a striking plantation dining room removed in its entirety from a South Carolina home, a New England kitchen, a Shaker bedroom, a New York parlor, and a flying staircase copied from an estate in North Carolina.

The museum galleries are on the other side of the main building. These include displays of furniture, china, and silver and explanations of their social significance, plus a Touch-It Room for children. The separate Dorrance Gallery houses a wonderful collection of eighteenth-century tureens from the Campbell Soup Collection.

There are also extensive gardens where azaleas and dogwoods bloom in spring. A tram takes you through the gardens from the main Visitor Center, where you can also buy tickets, pick up maps, or check out the book and gift shop. Rugs, chairs, and china are for sale at the Gallery and Plant Shop. General admission includes galleries, shops, and gardens but not the mansion tour.

HOURS: Tue.–Sun., 10–5. **ADMISSION:** Prices vary for different house tours, general and garden tours. **LOCATION:** N.J. Turnpike or Rt. 295 to Delaware Memorial Bridge, then north on I-95 to Rt. 52 (Exit 7), then left to Winterthur. **TELEPHONE:** 800-448-3883.
WEBSITE: www.winterthur.org.

Franklin D. Roosevelt Home

As president during the Great Depression and World War II, Roosevelt was both blamed and praised for cataclysmic changes in American life. Roosevelt's charming boyhood home has always been identified with the man. Now a National Historic Site, the Hyde Park complex consists of the family home, beautiful grounds overlooking the Hudson River, and the Roosevelt Library and Museum. The white, classically proportioned country house called "Rosewood" is not overly large and can accommodate tours of only a limited number of people.

In the main hall, you see the heavy furnishings that characterized a country home of the 1890s. Further on, the pretty Dresden Room is brightened by the colorful floral drapes and upholstery picked out by Sara Roosevelt in 1939 shortly before the king and queen of England visited. The whole house, in fact, shows much more the influence of Franklin's mother, Sara, than of his wife, Eleanor. Upstairs is FDR's boyhood bedroom and other family and guest rooms.

At the FDR Library, a museum section contains gifts from foreign rulers, cartoons, photographs, and a passing glimpse of both the Depression and World War II. There are also re-creations of rooms from the White House and sections of the Rosewood home. Outside, next to the rose garden, are the graves of both FDR and Eleanor. In another section of the estate, Val-Kill, the Eleanor Roosevelt Historic Site, is open to viewers from a separate road.

HOURS: Daily, 9–5. **ADMISSION:** Adults, $$$. Under 16 free.
LOCATION: Hyde Park, NY. Take Garden State Parkway to N.Y. Thruway to Exit 18. Cross Mid-Hudson Bridge, then Rt. 9 north for 7 miles. Follow signs. **TELEPHONE:** 854-229-9115. **WEBSITE:** www.nps.gov/hofr.

Vanderbilt Mansion

If the Roosevelt home radiates quiet wealth, the Vanderbilt Mansion exudes conspicuous consumption. A marble palace in the style of the Italian Renaissance, it is set on large grounds overlooking the Hudson. The mansion's furnishings are closer to French Rococo than Italian Renaissance. The huge marble reception hall opens to both the dining room and drawing room. The dining room, which seated thirty, and the beautifully furnished drawing room were the scene of gala balls. A small side room called the Gold Room attracts tourists to its ceiling painting, which depicts scantily clad maidens floating in an azure sky.

The upstairs bedrooms of Mr. and Mrs. Vanderbilt were certainly fit for a king and queen. Walls of embroidered silk and a bed with a marble gate around it were copied from a French queen's bedroom for the one Mrs. Vanderbilt used. Mr. Vanderbilt merely had a canopy with a crown above his bed and true Flemish tapestries on the walls.

Tours begin at the Visitor Center, where a film about the estate is shown. The mansion is open only by guided tour. You can walk around the grounds yourself, and check out the formal gardens. Advance registration during foliage season is recommended.

HOURS: Daily, 9–5. Closed major holidays. **ADMISSION:** Adults, $$. Under 16 free. **LOCATION:** Use Hyde Park directions.
TELEPHONE: 854-229-9115, 800-967-2283 (advance registration).
WEBSITE: www.nps.gov/vama.

Kykuit

You may never be as rich as Rockefeller, but you can visit the family estate near Tarrytown, NY. The mansion was the country home of four generations of Rockefellers: John D., John D. Jr., Nelson, and Nelson's children. The furnishings and the magnificent terraced grounds show the influence of the first three generations. John D., who started the fortune, did not believe in conspicuous consumption. The original stone house, called "Kykuit" (Dutch for "lookout"), was not particularly ornate. It was later remodeled in the Renaissance Revival style. You'll find rooms decorated in various ways, including a beautiful Adamesque side room. The most spectacular is the two-floor music room, with graceful balconies rimming the oculus, an oval ceiling opening. Eighteenth- and nineteenth-century furniture along with Chinese vases from various dynasties are found in the first-floor rooms.

What makes Kykuit unique is the incorporation of modern paintings and sculptures into classic and Victorian surroundings. Both Nelson and his mother, Abby Aldrich Rockefeller, were major art collectors. Most of the modern paintings, rugs and lithographs are downstairs in a separate gallery. Kandinsky, Picasso, Motherwell, and "Op Art" from the 1960s are on display.

The gardens, originally landscaped by William Bosworth in the Italian Villa style, are built in a series of terraces down the hill. The view of the hills, the Hudson, and the Palisades beyond is spectacular. The terraces include a stone teahouse, a rose garden, and a nine-hole golf course.

The tour, run by Historic Hudson Valley, begins at the Visitor Center at Philipsburg Manor. You watch an introductory film, then board a bus to the mansion.

HOURS: Mid-May.–early Nov., weekdays exc. Tue., 10–3; weekends, 10–4. **ADMISSION:** Adults, $$$$. Discounts: Seniors, students. **LOCATION:** Upper Mills, North Tarrytown, NY. Take Tappan Zee Bridge, then Rt. 9 north for 2 miles. **TELEPHONE:** 914-631-3992. **WEBSITE:** www.hudsonvalley.org.

Lyndhurst

A few minutes south of the Tappan Zee Bridge, this Gothic Revival "castle" was first built in 1838 by New York City mayor William Paulding. In 1880 it became the summer home of railroad tycoon Jay Gould. The crystal greenhouses were once the foremost indoor gardens in America. The house, with its turreted towers and manicured lawn, is often used in commercials as an example of the good life.

Today the estate is owned by the National Trust for Historic Preservation. Visitors are led through the home by tour guides (although you are also allowed to take a self-guided audio or brochure tour instead). Among the stops are an ornate dining room with enough carved woodwork to fill a Gothic church, the butler's pantry, an elegant parlor, and the art gallery—a huge drawing room filled with paintings, stained glass windows, and a view of the Hudson.

Upstairs, the tour includes living quarters, highlighted by the Duchess's guest bedroom. Much of the interior is wood or plaster painted to look like stone to enhance the medieval look. A short walk away, the renovated carriage house offers a lunch cafe. The gift shop and a museum gallery can be found in a separate carriage house. You can also walk around the sweeping lawns, as well as the rose garden, perennial beds, and conservatory.

> **HOURS:** Mid-Apr.–Oct., Tue.–Sun. and Mon. holidays, 10–5;
> Nov.–Apr., weekends, 10–4. **ADMISSION:** Adults, $$.
> Discounts: Seniors, students. Under 12 free.
> **LOCATION:** 635 S. Broadway (Rt. 9), Tarrytown, NY, one-half
> mile south of Tappan Zee Bridge. **TELEPHONE:** 914-631-4481.
> **WEBSITE:** www.lyndhurst.org.

Sunnyside

Home of Washington Irving, America's first internationally famous author, Sunnyside was built in a whimsical manner to suit Irving's taste. The reconstructed house is a mélange of the Dutch, the Spanish, and the quaint, with wisteria growing up its walls. It was built on the banks of the Hudson with several acres of lovely grounds, including an icehouse and swan ponds. At the Visitor Center a charming film about the Legend of Sleepy Hollow is shown.

The house is shown by guided tour only, and because the rooms and hallways are small, the tour can be a little cramped. Docents costumed in top hats or hoop skirts take you through the canopied bedchamber, the parlor, and up and down the stairs to the other household rooms. It is modestly furnished in early nineteenth-century style, but hosted many a famous visitor. Irving's brother and his children lived in the house and maintained the household for him. Since Irving lived abroad for seventeen years, he acquired a taste for the English romantic garden, which he translated to the acreage at Sunnyside. Picnicking is allowed on the grounds, and there is a cafe on weekends. The Sleepy Hollow Church and graveyard are nearby.

> **HOURS:** Apr.–Oct., 10–5; Nov., Dec. 10–4. Daily except Tue.
> Weekends only in March. **ADMISSION:** Adults, $$. Discounts: Seniors,
> children. Under 5 free. **LOCATION:** Tappan Zee Bridge to Tarrytown,
> NY, then Rt. 9 south to Sunnyside Lane. **TELEPHONE:** 914-591-8763.
> **WEBSITE:** www.hudsonvalley.org.

Boscobel

A stately Federal mansion set on the banks of the Hudson River (it was moved 15 miles from its original location), Boscobel was begun by Morris Dyckman in 1804. Dyckman, who made his money as an arms dealer, was able to afford the best furnishings. Although he died before the house was finished, his wife moved in and furnished it elegantly. A large central hall, sweeping stairway, patterned wallpaper, Duncan Phyfe furniture, china, glass, silver, and a bevy of whale-oil lamps reflect an era of early and gracious wealth. The wide lawns, the elegant rose garden, and the view of West Point across the river add to the air of quiet gentility. Guides take you through the home, but you may peruse the outdoor vistas on your own. A small gift shop is in a separate building.

> **HOURS:** Apr.–Oct., daily except Tue.; tours, 9:30–5; Nov. & Dec., 9:30–4. Closed Jan.–Mar. **ADMISSION:** Adults, $$. Discounts: Seniors, children. **LOCATION:** 1601 Rt. 9D, Garrison, NY, 8 miles north of Bear Mountain Bridge. **TELEPHONE:** 845-265-3638.
> **WEBSITE:** www.boscobel.org.

Pennsbury Manor

Here is a complete re-creation, on the original site, of the beautiful manor house built by William Penn on the banks of the Delaware. Located 25 miles above Philadelphia in what was then a wilderness, the estate includes many outbuildings, such as a bake and brew house, a smoke house, icehouse, and stable. Although everything was built from scratch in the 1930s, great care was taken to follow the letters and journals of Penn regarding this self-sufficient estate.

There are two striking things about Pennsbury Manor. One is the earliness of the period. The house was built in the late seventeenth century (Penn lived there only from 1699 to 1701), so the furnishings reflect the heavy Jacobean hand. The other is its surprising elegance. Although nothing is lavish, the furnishings are richer than one would expect of a Quaker leader. As the guide points out, while Penn was a great believer in equality, he was still the proprietor, entitled to receive an annual fee for each parcel of land sold.

After a tour of the bedrooms, parlors, and counting rooms, a walk through the grounds is in order: first to the barge landing, then the herb garden, the barnyard, and the orchards. A brew/bake house where great vats of ale were mixed and where huge ovens baked loaves of bread is close by. There are regularly scheduled tours (usually four a day). And you can tour the grounds yourself.

HOURS: Apr.–Nov., Tue.–Sat., 9–5; Sun., 12–5. Call for winter hours and special Christmas hours. **ADMISSION:** Adults, $$. Under 6 free. **LOCATION:** 400 Pennsbury Memorial Rd., Morrisville, PA. **TELEPHONE:** 215-946-0400. **WEBSITE:** www.pennsburymanor.org.

Andalusia

Nicholas Biddle was one of America's first millionaires, and the Biddle name still connotes a sense of grace, polish, and old money in the Philadelphia area. Andalusia came to him through marriage. He transformed it in 1834 into one of the outstanding examples of Greek Revival architecture in the Northeast. Its white pillars and architrave will remind you of many antebellum Southern mansions. The house faces the Delaware River, and its large sloping green lawn runs down to the water. On this lawn you will find both a billiard room and a Gothic "ruin" that was built that way. This was not uncommon in the 1830s, when the romantic novels of Sir Walter Scott and excavations in the Middle East had Americans crazy over anything medieval, Greek, Turkish, or Egyptian. Inside the mansion, furniture varies from polished Regency buffets to odd-shaped Greek-style chairs and other American Empire designs. The music room, with its delicate pianoforte and whale-oil lamps, brings visions of genteel ladies offering an evening musicale to local gentry. There are extensive grounds, which include a hedge walk, a grape arbor, and another huge house not open to visitors. Tours are for groups only, but one can go through with a minimum of seven people for a set price.

HOURS: By reserved tour only. **LOCATION:** Bensalem Twp., Bucks County, PA. **TELEPHONE:** 215-245-5479. **WEBSITE:** www.andalusiahousemuseum.org.

Pearl S. Buck Home

Bucks County, Pennsylvania, was a haven for writers in the 1930s. Most of the literary celebrities of that time moved on to other pastures. But Pearl S. Buck, who reached the zenith of her fame during the pre–World War II period (she won the Nobel Prize in 1938), remained here in her lovely country home until her death in 1963. The stone and wood house seems to typify the Hollywood picture of a writer's country retreat: a huge floor-to-ceiling brick fireplace, great expanses of polished wood flooring, overstuffed sofas, and walls lined with books. Add to this a collection of Asian lamps and tables, screens, and sculptures, and you get a picture of Pearl S. Buck, author and admirer of Chinese culture. There's even a tapestry given to her by the Dalai Lama that has images of one thousand

Buddhas. At one point there were also nine adopted Amerasian children in the house, which explains the generous dimensions and open spaces of the home.

Visits to the home are by guided tour only. The tour includes a look at the room where Ms. Buck's awards and prizes are displayed and the study where she wrote her works. Outside is a lovely old-fashioned patio, lots of green rolling hills, and a separate shop where you can purchase Asian pieces and other souvenirs. The Pearl S. Buck Foundation, dedicated to helping Amerasian children who were abandoned by their fathers, is located in a big red barn not far from the house. A film about the foundation often precedes the tour.

HOURS: Tours, Tue.–Sat., 11, 1, & 2; Sun., 1 & 2, Mar.–Dec. Closed Jan. & Feb. **ADMISSION:** Adults, $$. Discount: Seniors. Under 6 free. **LOCATION:** 520 Dublin Rd., Perkasie, PA. Rt. 202 south to Rt. 313 west to Dublin, PA. Turn left on Maple Ave., which becomes Dublin, then go one mile. **TELEPHONE:** 215-249-0100. **WEBSITE:** www.psbi.org.

Restored
and Reconstructed
Historic Villages,
Farms, Mills, and Homes

The Stagecoach Inn, built in the 1700s, is one of thirty historic structures at Waterloo Village, the largest restored historic village in the state. *(Photo by Patrick Sarver)*

Waterloo Village

With thirty historic structures, this is the largest restoration in New Jersey, offering homes and mills scattered along a scenic wooded terrain beside the Musconetcong River. The village complex covers over 5,000 acres and includes buildings ranging from a 1760s inn to an 1870 Victorian mansion. Since Waterloo prospered during the

Revolutionary War as an iron works and also during the nineteenth-century period of the Morris Canal and Sussex Railroad, the buildings reflect Colonial, Federal, and Victorian styles.

There are three areas: the main Canal Village plus the smaller Lenape Village and Rutan Farm. Guides are dressed according to the period. A blacksmith and a potter are usually on hand at their workplaces and will answer questions. Docents are in each house. The hostess in the Canal House, for instance, demonstrates a clockwork weasel that was used to draw the wool yarn into a skein. At the gristmill, you can watch the guide upstairs pour corn kernels between two huge grinding stones. Then you head downstairs where the waterwheel is turning and discover cornmeal pouring out the spout, while another guide explains the process. At the Homestead, where three generations of the Smith family lived when they owned Waterloo, there are some nicely furnished period rooms.

There's a lot of walking to do here, with several homes and inns, a general store, a sawmill, blacksmith shop, and the Canal Museum to visit. The 1859 Methodist church looks as if it came straight out of Vermont. The Stagecoach Inn was a popular stop for travelers in the 1700s and 1800s. Behind Canal Village is the Rutan Farm, moved here from elsewhere in Sussex County, which includes an 1835 cabin plus pens of animals. A long walk along the lake takes you to the separate Lenape Indian village, which looks as it would have in the 1600s. A longhouse, animal skins drying on a pole, and the accoutrements of tribal life are here, together with a guide who explains the customs—including the fact that the women owned everything in the village.

Food is available at the Pavilion Cafe or Towpath Tavern, or you can bring your own for a picnic. There's also a museum store. Horse-drawn carriages are available weekdays in summer and nonfestival weekends all season. Canal Town walking tours are held from late morning to midafternoon. There's also a tented amphitheater for classical and folk music events. The larger pop and rock concerts take place in a field a mile outside the village proper.

HOURS: Late May–early Sept., Wed., 12–4; Thu., Fri., 11–4; weekends, 11–5. **ADMISSION:** $$. Discounts: Seniors, children. Under 6 free. **LOCATION:** Byram Twp. (Sussex County). I-80 to Exit 25 to Rt. 206 north. Follow signs. **TELEPHONE:** 973-347-0900. **WEBSITE:** www.waterloovillage.org.

Red Mill Museum Village

An old red mill with a churning waterwheel sits by a 200-foot-wide waterfall to create the picturesque environment for this museum village. In fact, the red mill is one of the most photographed structures in New Jersey. It is the hub of a village that includes smaller buildings scattered along the banks of the South Branch of the Raritan River. In the small complex you'll find a log cabin, little red schoolhouse, general store/post office, blacksmith shop, tenant house, carriage shed, quarry with stone crusher, and an information center.

The 1810 mill offers several floors of exhibits. The agricultural development of the region is followed with a series of displays of tools and country life. Everything from barrels to baskets is shown, with the sound of the water from the wheel always within earshot. The small gift shop has a pleasant country ambience. The museum also runs a series of specials to attract the crowds. These include Revolutionary and Civil War encampments, spring and fall antiques shows, summer concerts, and the Haunted Mill for Halloween weekend. (Extra fee for events.)

HOURS: April to mid-Oct., Tue.–Sat., 10–4; Sun., 12–5. **ADMISSION:** $$. Discounts: Seniors, children. Under 6 free. **LOCATION:** 56 Main St., Clinton (Hunterdon County). Exit 15 off Rt. 78. **TELEPHONE:** 908-735-4101. **WEBSITE:** www.theredmill.org.

Batsto Village

Once a self-contained community in the heart of the Pinelands, this village is now part of Wharton State Forest, the largest parkland in the state. Pine, oak, and cedar woods, open lowlands, and a sparkling lake provide a scenic backdrop for a place that preserves the lifestyle of bygone days in the South Jersey pines. Founded in 1766, Batsto was once the center of the bog iron industry in New Jersey, and its iron provided armaments for the Revolution. Later, in the 1800s, glass was manufactured here, then lumbering and cranberry farming were tried. As you approach, you find a handsome farm surrounded by split-rail fences with horses and ducks in view.

William Richards bought the ironworks in 1784, and it remained in his family's hands for ninety-two years. The Richards Mansion has an eight-story mansard-roofed tower rising from its center. The rooms inside are filled with the furniture of the well-to-do families who lived there, and the wall-to-wall library of Joseph Wharton, the financier who bought the complex in 1876, is most impressive. So is the dining room, with a table that could seat thirty-six. And from the third floor, there's a narrow, twisting stairway up to the tower, which offers a 360-degree panorama of the village and surrounding Pinelands.

The Richards Mansion stands at the heart of Batsto, a restored iron and glassmaking village in the Pinelands. *(Photo by Patrick Sarver)*

The first stop at Batsto is the Visitor Center. If you want the mansion tour, buy your tickets immediately, for only fifteen people are admitted at a time. The tour takes 45 minutes and is very comprehensive. A walk-through museum at the Visitor Center features local history, with tools and other artifacts accompanied by colorful display panels. There is also a nice-size gift shop.

Except for the mansion tour, you can stroll the village on your own. Among the structures are the General Store, a post office (where you can have your postcard hand-stamped), a barn with farm animals, and a few workers' houses. During the summer, the houses usually have some craftsmen inside—a weaver or a potter at work. The working sawmill is usually open only Sunday afternoons in summer.

The farm with its unusual main house, surrounding barns, and wide-swept fields all in the middle of the Pine Barrens has the true look of a place from another time. A nature center, a nature trail, a picnic area, and a large lake where fishing is allowed are all part of the grounds.

HOURS: Grounds, daily, dawn to dusk. Village, daily, 9–4:30.
ADMISSION: Mansion, $. Discount: Children. Under 6 free.
Parking fee summer weekends. **LOCATION:** Rt. 542, Wharton State Forest (Burlington County). Rt. 9 to Rt. 542 west. Garden State Parkway to New Gretna exit to Rt. 9 south to Rt. 542.
TELEPHONE: 609-561-0024. **WEBSITE:** www.batstovillage.org.

Historic Allaire Village

Set in Allaire State Park, this complex was an active workers' community during the nineteenth century. The huge brick blast furnace is left over from the bog-iron days when James P. Allaire bought the ironworks in 1822 to supply iron to his marine steam engine works in New York City, the largest in the country. He then sought to establish a self-contained community because of its isolation. But after 25 years, competition from high-grade iron ore brought economic ruin to the region. In 1850 Allaire moved to the village and retired. A well-documented display on the ironworks can be found in the Visitor Center.

During warm-weather weekends (including Fridays) you will find docents dressed in 1830s costumes in the various buildings. They talk about village life, and perhaps a blacksmith or pattern maker will be about. You can also view the church, which has a unique feature—its steeple was erected on the wrong end. There's a pond, a bakery with fresh bread, and a gift shop (open Wed.–Sun.), plus several other houses. During the week, when the docents may not be around, you can walk around the grounds and take pictures. Groups can reserve tours. On warm-weather weekends there are always lots of activities, including crafts and antiques fairs, with hayrides in October and lantern tours in late November and December.

While at Allaire, be sure to ride the **Pine Creek Railroad**, a narrow-gauge rail line that runs a short trip on both diesel and steam locomotives. It is close to the parking lot. For information call 732-938-5524. The park also offers nature trails, bicycle trails, and picnic areas. During the summer, a hot dog and ice cream concession may be open next to the Visitor Center.

> **HOURS:** Park, dawn to dusk. Buildings, summer, Wed.–Sun., 11–5; May, Sept.–Oct., weekends, 10–4. Visitor Center, Mar.–mid-Dec., Wed.–Sun., 10–4; daily in summer, 10–5. **ADMISSION:** $ for parking on summer weekends. **LOCATION:** Allaire State Park, Rt. 524, Wall Twp. (Monmouth County). Garden State Parkway to Exit 98; go 2 miles west. **TELEPHONE:** 732-938-2371 (park); 732-919-3500 (village). **WEBSITE:** www.state.nj.us/dep/parksandforests/parks/allaire.html.

Millbrook Village

One of New Jersey's best-kept secrets is this nineteenth-century village set in the Kittatinny Mountains. It is run by the National Park Service as part of the Delaware Water Gap National Recreation Area (q.v.). On Saturdays from May to October, guides dressed in period costumes of the 1860–1880 era lead tours and demonstrate various crafts at some of the buildings. During Millbrook Days, the first full weekend in October, more than one hundred volunteers demonstrate crafts from the last century. At other times, you may walk around the village yourself, although the houses may not be open.

The original Millbrook Village was a small enclave of houses and stores clustered around a gristmill that opened in 1832 beside Van Campens Brook. Since the mill served grain farmers in the surrounding countryside, the town became the social and commercial center of the community. A hotel with taproom, a smithy, a general store, and a simple white-steepled church are among the buildings that surrounded the original mill.

Millbrook reached its zenith around 1875. The village declined after 1900 and by mid-century only a blacksmith remained. What you see here now is a re-creation of Millbrook at its height. Today, the village has two dozen well-kept homes, a school, blacksmith and woodworking shops, barns, a general store, and a church.

> **HOURS:** Grounds, daily, dawn to dusk. Buildings, Saturdays, Memorial Day to early Oct., 9–5. **ADMISSION:** Free. **LOCATION:** Warren County. Rt. 80 west to last exit in N.J. (Millbrook exit). Turn right, follow Old Mine Road 12 miles north. **TELEPHONE:** 908-841-9531. **WEBSITES:** www.nps.gov/dewa/indepth/sites/mv.html and www.millbrooknj.com.

Tuckerton Seaport

Do you know what a sneakbox is? If you don't, you can find out about the duck hunters, clammers, and fishermen who worked the bays and tidal creeks along the Jersey shore at this seaport village. Hunting for waterfowl, dredging for oysters, building boats, and carving decoys was a way of life that has just about disappeared. Tuckerton Seaport is a memorial to these baymen and a tourist destination at the same time.

The cornerstone of the village is the replicated Tucker's Island Lighthouse (the original washed away along with its island in the 1920s). Inside is a museum, with exhibits on lighthouses, pirates (Captain Kidd and others), and buried treasure along with examples of duck decoys and lifesaving and other local lore. Outside, about fifteen wooden buildings (some no larger than shacks) line the edge of Tuckerton Creek. Wooden walkways take you from one structure to the next. These include a decoy carving shop, the Perrine Boat Works, a sawmill, an instructional clam house, and the Hotel de Crab. At the boat works a docent describes sneakboxes and the role of these small hunting craft in the local economy. In another house, a decoy maker explains how he hollows out the inside and places the head in various positions.

Although decoys are considered icons of folk art, they began as simple utilitarian objects for duck hunters. Duck hunting was once a viable occupation for Tuckerton residents, but so many regulations curtailed both waterfowl hunting and bay fishing that this way of life has practically come to an end.

The Yacht Club building emphasizes marine ecology and offers several interactive exhibits for the kids, along with a gift shop and a Lenni-Lenape Indian exhibit. Upstairs are exhibits on local environments, maritime history, and research done at the nearby Jacques Cousteau National Estuarine Research Reserve. And since you can't have a seaport without seafood, Skeeters, a replica of a local summer cottage, serves fried clams, fried oysters, fries, and hamburgers. Lots of special events here, including a boat parade and a big gun and decoy show in September. There are also day-long classes on boat building, decoy carving, and other maritime-related skills on many Saturdays (extra fee).

HOURS: Apr.–Dec., daily, 10–5. Jan.–Mar., weekends, 10–4.
ADMISSION: $$. Discounts: Seniors, children. Under 5 free.
LOCATION: 120 W. Main St. (Rt 9), Tuckerton. Garden State Parkway to Exit 58. Take Rt. 539 south to Rt. 9 traffic. Turn right, go 1,500 feet. The seaport is across from Lake Pohatcong.
TELEPHONE: 609-296-8868. **WEBSITE:** www.tuckertonseaport.org.

Historic Cold Spring Village

A delightful little restored village can be found among the pine trees on a quiet stretch of road not far from Wildwood and Cape May. Historic Cold Spring Village has much charm. The twenty-five historic buildings are set along two country lanes that have a mid-nineteenth-century look. Almost all of them have been moved here from elsewhere. They range from the Colonial to the large Grange Hall, which dates back to 1897. Inside the various structures, you'll find a printer at his shop, an 1820s schoolhouse complete with resident schoolmistress, a tinsmith punching holes in tin, and a blacksmith working at his forge. These are docents and craftspeople who explain what they are doing while they work. There's also a barn where you can see rag rugs being woven.

There are bits of country nostalgia here, such as an old-fashioned water pump, a farm enclosure with sheep and other animals, and walkways made of crushed clamshells. A horse-drawn carriage is a big hit with children.

The Welcome Center offers displays on local history and an orientation video. For those who get hungry, the village has an ice cream store and bakery. Full meals are available at the Old Grange

Restaurant. Weekends there often have special events, such as musical groups on Saturdays at 6:30 P.M. at the gazebo, contests, and so forth. A special excursion train, the Cape May Seashore Lines (q.v.) stops at the Cold Spring Village Station en route to and from Cape May in summer.

> **HOURS:** Father's Day to Labor Day, Tue.–Sun., 10–4:30; Memorial Day, early June & Sept., weekends. **ADMISSION:** $$. Discounts: Seniors, children. Under 5 free. **LOCATION:** 720 Rt. 9, Cold Spring (Cape May County). Garden State Parkway to Exit 0, Rt. 109 N, and follow the signs. **TELEPHONE:** 609-898-2300. **WEBSITE:** www.hcsv.org.

Wheaton Arts and Cultural Center

Set around a green, with buildings styled in 1888 gingerbread, this village is a nice, clean spot on the outskirts of Millville that is dedicated to the glass industry that still flourishes in this corner of New Jersey. One of its main attractions is the Museum of American Glass, which has the most comprehensive collection of American historical glass in the country. It's housed in an elegant Victorian building and includes glass items that go back to colonial times. Collectors will enjoy the world's largest bottle plus paperweights, medicine bottles, and contemporary glass. There are exhibits on colonial glassmaking, Victorian glass, the local glass industry, and art glass. One large hall hosts changing exhibits on such subjects as the development of glassmaking to Tiffany glass. You'll learn everything you ever wanted to know about bottles, Sandwich glass, and cut and pressed glass.

Another attraction is the glassworks, where visitors can watch from a gallery above while gaffers plunge their rods into the blazing furnaces and then shape the glass into bowls, wine glasses, bottles, and paperweights. At these "shows" an announcer with a mike explains just what the gaffer is doing. This is hot work, and even from the gallery you can feel the intensity of the furnace. Visitors can also make their own paperweights, bowls, or vases here. For a fee, you'll get instruction on how to make your individual creation. Call to reserve. The village has also become a center for glass "sculptors" who specialize in glass art.

Other buildings include a craft studio where you can see woodcarvers, potters, and others going about their work. The craftspeople's handiwork plus the art glasswork can be purchased in the museum shops on the village green. The Down Jersey Folklife Center offers changing exhibits on the diverse ethnic crafts of the region such as Japanese origami, Puerto Rican music, or Ukrainian embroidery. For kids there's a small play area, an 1876 schoolhouse to peek at, and an 1897 train station with a 10-minute miniature train ride (extra fee).

The General Store sells penny candy from an old-fashioned glass jar. For food, take a short walk to the restaurants just outside the gates. Special-event weekends feature everything from marbles and fire engine musters to fine craft festivals, antiques shows, and Civil War reenactments.

HOURS: Tue.–Sun., 10–5; Fri.–Sun. only, Jan.–Mar. **ADMISSION:** $$.
Discounts: Seniors, students. Under 6 free. Reduced winter rates.
LOCATION: 1501 Glasstown Rd., Millville (Cumberland County).
Exit 26 off Rt. 55. **TELEPHONE:** 800-998-4552.
WEBSITE: www.wheatonvillage.org.

East Jersey Olde Towne

This is a collection of colonial houses set around a pretty village green on 12 acres in Johnson Park, Piscataway. The buildings were moved here from other localities in central Jersey or are reconstructions of local historical buildings. Started years ago by a professor interested in preserving the heritage of the Raritan Valley, the village today has several buildings open for guided tours.

One is the Smalleytown Schoolhouse, where students learned their lessons in the 1800s or faced wearing a dunce cap or, even worse, punishment with a paddle. Another is the FitzRandolph House, built in the mid-1700s, which represents a typical farmhouse of the Raritan Valley. The Vanderveer House, built along the North Branch of the Raritan River in Bedminster in 1745, had more elegant furnishings, reflecting its wealthy mill owner, Jacobus Vanderveer. (This house was willed to his younger son, while a similar one given to his older son still stands along Rt. 206 and is being restored there as a museum.)

The Church of the Three Mile Run is a typical Dutch structure with a pyramid roof and an interesting history—it is an exact reproduction of an early 1700s church. (It can also be used for weddings.) A brick tavern and a barracks building are partially open or are used for administration. The whole village has white picket fences, brick pathways, and an authentic kitchen garden behind one of the houses.

The village is administered by the Middlesex County Cultural and Heritage Commission, and while you can walk around the green and take pictures, you can only enter the buildings (except for the Visitor Center) during the limited guided-tour hours.

HOURS: Tue.–Fri. & Sun., 8:30–4:30. Tours at 1:30. **ADMISSION:** Free.
LOCATION: 1050 River Rd. (Rt. 18) at Hoes Lane, Piscataway (Middlesex

County). Rt. 287, Exit 9, to River Rd. **TELEPHONE:** 732-745-3030;
Middlesex County C&H Commission, 732-745-4489.
WEBSITE: www.co.middlesex.nj.us/culturalheritage/village.asp.

Longstreet Farm

For those who want to recapture the sights and smells of farm life a
century ago, a visit to Longstreet Farm fills the bill. Although the
farm is kept to the 1890s era, the machinery here was used well into

The fields at Longstreet Farm in Monmouth County are plowed
just as they were in the 1890s to prepare them for spring planting.
(Photo by Patrick Sarver)

the 1920s and may bring back memories to those born on a farm. Old-fashioned combines and tractors, an apple corer, and other antique farm machines are kept in a series of barns and sheds. Animals are present, although not in profusion. There are pigs lying in the mud as well as horses, cows, sheep, and chickens. Open-slatted corncribs that allow the air to circulate are on view. The milking shed is fitted out in the old way, with slots for the cow's head and buckets for hand milking. The carriage house contains a variety of buckboards.

Since Longstreet is a living historical farm, the workers dress in casual 1890s clothes as they go about their farm chores. During summer there is a historical camp for children in which the kids help out. Other hands-on programs are held for all ages, as well as festivals, demonstrations, and classes. The main farmhouse, which dates to the late 1700s, offers tours on weekends and holidays. It contains a number of well-done rooms in late Victorian style, with a majority of the furnishings belonging to the family that lived here for generations.

Longstreet is part of Holmdel Park, which is filled with attractive landscapes. A sheltered picnic area offers tables and a snack bar. In a pond below the shelter, ducks swim gracefully by. And beyond, a cultivated arboretum presents a colorful view of flowering crabapples, rhododendrons, and hundreds of shade trees.

HOURS: 10–4 daily, summer 9–5; farmhouse, Mar.–Dec., weekends and holidays, 12–3:30. **ADMISSION:** Free. **LOCATION:** 44 Longstreet Road, Holmdel (Monmouth County). Garden State Parkway to Garden State Arts Center exit, follow Keyport Rd., look for signs. Off Holmdel Rd. **TELEPHONE:** 732-946-3758. **WEBSITE:** www.monmouthcountyparks. com/parks/longstreet_revised.asp.

Howell Living History Farm

This active farm in Mercer County is set in the turn-of-the-century style. Various stages of mechanization are shown: the reaper reaps and binds mechanically, but it does not thresh. The wheat is bound by machine, but the machine is pulled by a plodding draft horse. The wagon that picks up the bound sheaves is also available for hayrides.

There's plenty of acreage, and you feel the farm's bucolic atmosphere from the moment you walk down the dirt road to the farmhouse. You pass sheep, pigs, and goats—all safely behind fences. A renovated barn serves as the Visitor Center. The early 1800s farmhouse itself is a simple one, with a furnished parlor, antique kitchen, and gift shop. School groups are welcome here to take part in seasonal activities. On Saturdays, a professional farmer is on hand to guide the draft horse in plowing, sowing, and reaping. Several Saturdays are devoted to such things as hayrides, tree planting, and a Fall Festival. Special events, such as a 4-acre maze in a cornfield, are held in season. Visitors are invited to help plant, cultivate, and harvest crops, care for animals, or make soap, butter, and ice cream. There are also week-long farm camps for kids.

HOURS: Apr.–Nov., Tue.–Sat., 10–4, Sun., 12–4. Dec.–Jan., Sat., 10–4. Feb.–Mar., Tue.–Sat., 10–4. Programs, Sat., 11–3. **ADMISSION:** Free. Fee for children's crafts and maze. **LOCATION:** Valley Rd., Howell Twp. (Mercer County). Two miles south of Lambertville on Rt. 29, then 2 miles east on Valley Rd. **TELEPHONE:** 609-737-3299. **WEBSITE:** www.howellfarm.org.

The Hermitage

Known primarily as an outstanding example of nineteenth-century Gothic Revival architecture, the original Hermitage was a two-story brownstone erected in 1750. During the late eighteenth century it was owned by Lt. Colonel Prevost and his charming wife, Theodosia. At that time, the house was host to George Washington, James Monroe, Alexander Hamilton, Marquis de Lafayette, and Aaron Burr, among others. When Colonel Prevost died, Burr wooed his widow. In 1782, Burr and Theodosia married in the parlor of the Hermitage.

Twenty-five years later, Dr. Elijah Rosencrantz bought the house (which his family retained for 163 years). In 1847 the structure was remodeled into a picturesque Gothic Revival home. Steep gabled roofs trimmed with carpenter's lace and diamond-paned windows give it the Victorian look we often associate with Charles Dickens. In fact, one of the several programs given at the house is a performance of *A Christmas Carol.* The Hermitage portrays the upper middle-class life of the late Victorian period, including furnishings, personal items, and papers of the Rosencrantz family. There are also changing exhibits based on the museum's large collection of antique clothing (448 women's gowns alone), which includes fans, handbags, and handmade lace. Special events include a costume exhibition and two craft boutiques that last four weeks during fall and spring. Special prices for these.

HOURS: Wed.–Sun., 1–4; last tour, 3:15. **ADMISSION:** $. Discount: Children 6–12. Under 6 free. **LOCATION:** 335 N. Franklin Tpk., Ho-Ho-Kus (Bergen County). Rt. 17 to Hollywood Ave. exit, then west to Franklin Tpk. **TELEPHONE:** 201-445-8311. **WEBSITE:** www.thehermitage.org.

Whitesbog Village

Unlike strawberries, blueberries were cultivated rather recently—1916 to be exact. That's when Elizabeth White, together with a researcher, found the best blueberry bushes in Pemberton Township and cultivated them on the family farm. She also figured out how to package them. Elizabeth was the daughter of J. J. White, who owned the largest cranberry bogs in the state (hence the name Whitesbog). Like most cranberry growers he used hundreds of migrant workers to harvest the dry crop and had about forty full-time workers on site. The workers (and the management) lived in a company town with small homes, a general store, post office, school, pay office, barrel factory, and cranberry-processing buildings. The blueberries were a means to raise a crop in June and July, since cranberries aren't harvested until September.

This old company town deep in the Pinelands is slowly being restored by the Whitesbog Preservation Trust. The General Store is the Visitor Center, and a few other buildings display agricultural tools and antique engines. Pictures of immigrant workers from Philadelphia handpicking the berries in the early 1900s are part of the museum. There are picnic tables here and a kiosk with maps for walking and driving tours, so even if the village isn't open you can explore the surrounding fields and forest. There are also numerous cranberry bogs at this 3,000-acre site. Events include a Blueberry Festival in late June, and a Pinelands Month Celebration in early October, with Piney music, exhibitors, and tours. There are also Cranberry Harvest Tours and Sunset Hayrides in October plus special guided walks on selected weekends.

HOURS: Grounds, dawn to dusk. Visitor Center, Feb.–Dec., Sat. & Sun., 10–4. **ADMISSION:** Free. **LOCATION:** Brendan T. Byrne State Forest, Pemberton Twp. (Burlington County). Rt. 70 to Rt. 530; 4 miles east of Browns Mills. **TELEPHONE:** 609-893-4646.
WEBSITE: www.whitesbog.org.

Historic Speedwell

Historic Speedwell in Morristown was the scene of one of the most important American achievements. Here, Samuel Morse and Alfred Vail spent years perfecting the electromagnetic telegraph, which later gave rise to radio and television. One thing you learn from a visit to this green and pleasant village compound: you don't have to be a scientist to be an inventor. Morse was a portrait painter by profession. At the Vail House (the main building of the complex), you can see the portraits Morse painted of the senior Mr. and Mrs. Vail. Other rooms in the house show an early middle-class Victorian lifestyle, with period furniture that includes an 1860s Steinway pianoforte, four-post canopy beds, and a "French hat" circular bathtub.

The original Vail money came from their ironworks. The carriage house is devoted to an exhibit concerning the making and molding of iron machinery and to the ironworkers themselves. The foundry was best known for its early steam engines. In fact, the first transatlantic steamship engine was built here in 1819.

The factory building, originally built as a gristmill (there's a covered water wheel) and then used for cotton weaving, now features an exhibit about the telegraph. Vail and Morse held the first public demonstration of this new wonder here in 1838. An exhibit of documents, models, and instruments illustrates the invention and development of the telegraph. A new, updated exhibit is in the works. Other historic buildings on the site include several Colonial and Early American buildings, such as the L'Hommedieu House, which is now the renovated Visitor Center and includes a large gift shop, changing historical exhibits, and a classroom.

Historic Speedwell is on the old homestead of the Vail family across from a picturesque dam where the Vail ironworks once stood. Lots of special events and classes are held on weekends, and a summer history camp is available.

HOURS: Apr.–Oct., Wed.–Sat., 10–4; Sun., 12–4; last tour at 4.
ADMISSION: $. Discounts: Seniors, children. Under 4 free.
LOCATION: 333 Speedwell Ave. (Rt. 202) at Cory Rd., 1 mile north of Morristown. **TELEPHONE:** 973-540-0211.
WEBSITE: www.parks.morris.nj.us/speedwell/home.html.

Fosterfields

An old-fashioned farm that dates from the turn of the century, Fosterfields is run by the Morris County Park Commission. The large farm has many agricultural implements on display and a variety of farm animals, including horses, pigs, and cows. There is also a large plowing field and many outbuildings as you walk along the road from the Visitor Center toward the house on the hill.

The main house, the Willows, has been faithfully restored. It is a handsome Gothic Revival farmhouse built in the 1850s (for a grandson of Paul Revere) with many original furnishings intact. The farm was later owned by the Fosters, and tours of the house reflect the life of the young Caroline Foster, growing up in the early twentieth century. Of notable interest are the marble fireplaces and the trompe l'oeil walls painted to look like wood paneling. These tours are given only on specific days and cost a bit extra.

On weekends from spring to fall there are demonstrations of such farm tasks as plowing, sowing seed, or threshing. Perhaps the women at the farmhouse will be washing clothes and setting them out to dry, or someone will milk a cow. Often, visitors are allowed to get involved in butter-churning and other farm chores. There are several barns to walk through, as well as the farm superintendent's home and an antique sleigh and carriage house.

The Visitor Center has farm displays and also offers a short film on the history of Fosterfields. Here is where you can pick up brochures, buy tickets to the Willows, and get information on special activities and events—whether it's story time, hay raking, or a Civil War encampment.

HOURS: Apr.–Oct., Wed.–Sat., 10–5; Sun., 12–5; house: Thu.–Sun., 1–3:30. **ADMISSION:** $. Discounts: Seniors, children. Under 4 free. **LOCATION:** 73 Kahdena Rd., Morris Twp. (Morris County). Just off Rt. 510/124. **TELEPHONE:** 973-326-7645. **WEBSITE:** http://parks.morris.nj.us/aspparks/ffmain.htm.

Barclay Farmstead

A few blocks behind a typical Cherry Hill strip mall, you'll find this peaceful 32-acre parcel of greenery that features a Federal-style, three-story red-brick farmhouse. The house, with its central hall and staircase, connecting parlors, seven fireplaces, and period furnishings reflects the life of the early nineteenth century. It also reflects the Quaker heritage of this part of southern New Jersey, with period furnishings reflecting their simple lifestyle. The one-time farm also includes a working blacksmith shop, a corn crib, and a spring house. The sizable herb garden behind the house has also been restored. Docents interpret life here circa 1816, when the Thorn family inhabited the farmstead, and are in costume for specific events and school programs. On the second floor there's a small gift shop, and a historical library on the third.

The farmstead is also kept as a recreational and open-space area for the town, so there are "plant-a-patch" gardens, a picnic area, and a small playground on site. Several nature trails lead from the house through woodlands to the north branch of the Cooper River.

HOURS: Tue.–Fri., 12–4; first Sun., 1–4. **ADMISSION:** Free for Cherry Hill residents; others, $. **LOCATION:** 209 Barclay Lane, Cherry Hill (Camden County). Off Rt. 70. **TELEPHONE:** 856-795-6225. **WEBSITE:** www.barclayfarmstead.org.

Acorn Hall

A fine example of a mid-Victorian Italianate style, this house has been featured in *Victorian Homes* magazine. With 90 percent of its furnishings original to the house, the downstairs is set off by two parlors with Carrara marble fireplaces and a dining room with an elegantly set table and marble-topped étagère that matches the fireplace. Upstairs, the original master bedroom has a rosewood bed and chest, while the later master bedroom offers changing exhibits on local historical themes. There are a number of other interesting rooms as well. Outside, the old oak for which the house was named is now gone, but you'll still find a well-kept lawn with a pleasant Victorian garden and gazebo. Tours by docent only.

> **HOURS:** Mon. & Thu., 10–4; Sun., 1–4. **ADMISSION:** $$.
> Discounts: Seniors, students. **LOCATION:** 68 Morris Ave.,
> Morristown (Morris County). **TELEPHONE:** 973-267-3465.
> **WEBSITE:** www.acornhall.org.

Merchants and Drovers Tavern

Built around 1795, this four-story Federal-style structure served as an early public meeting place for merchants, politicians, and farmers as well as a stagecoach stop for travelers. Owned by the same family from 1798 to 1971 and operated continuously as an inn until the 1930s, this hotel has remained largely unchanged over the years. Two parlors, a taproom, kitchen, twelve bedrooms, and servant quarters have recently been carefully restored to an 1820s appearance and furnished with period antiques and reproductions. There are also interpretive exhibits on early tavern life and stagecoach transportation in the long room on the second floor. The tavern also hosts special events, including evening candlelight tours. Also on the property is the 1735 Terrill Tavern, which houses a museum shop.

> **HOURS:** Thu., Fri., and first & third Sat., 10–4. Second and fourth Sun.,
> 1–4. Tue. by appointment. **ADMISSION:** $. Discounts: Seniors, students.
> **LOCATION:** Rt. 27 and Westfield Ave., Rahway (Union County).
> **TELEPHONE:** 732-381-0441. **WEBSITE:** www.merchantsanddrovers.org.

Israel Crane House

A handsome house built in the Federal period and then remodeled in the Greek Revival style, the Crane House was moved from its original site to the present location by the Montclair Historical Society. The tour starts in the basement exhibit room with a video on the history of the house. Costumed docents give guided tours throughout the three-story building with Federal and Empire-style furnishings. Behind the main house is a two-story kitchen building reconstructed to resemble the 1840 kitchen that once existed. Open-hearth cooking demonstrations are held most Sundays, Oct.–May.

Beyond the kitchen building is a pleasant backyard planted with flowers and herbs in eighteenth-century fashion. And beyond that is the Museum Shop/Visitor Center (Sun., 2–5). The first floor exhibits an 1800s general store. A few books and gifts based on historic themes are available for purchase. Upstairs you'll find an old-time schoolroom.

The society also owns Evergreens: The Schultz House Museum, at 30 North Mountain Ave. This large stick-style Victorian house is open for 3 P.M. tours by reservation only on the first and third Sundays of the month, Apr. to Oct. (**ADMISSION: $$.**)

HOURS: Sun., 2–5. **ADMISSION:** $. Discount: Children. Under 11 free. **LOCATION:** 110 Orange Rd., Montclair (Essex County). Off Bloomfield Ave. **TELEPHONE:** 973-744-1796. **WEBSITE:** www.montclairhistorical.org.

Miller-Cory House

Every Sunday during the school season, volunteers cook, spin, or perform seasonal tasks in and around this 1740 farmhouse. The everyday, humdrum tasks of colonial life—from soap making to herb drying—are emphasized here. The house, the adjacent Visitor Center, and a separate kitchen and kitchen garden comprise this small enclave of colonial life. In pleasant weather, wool spinners and other workers may be found outside. The separate kitchen is the scene of soup and bread making by volunteers who use an open-hearth and beehive oven.

Guided tours of the house proper take about half an hour. The tour is thorough and includes everything from how to tighten the rope on a colonial bed to how to make utensils from a cow's horn. Schoolchildren and adults will find the house tour highly educational, while preschoolers may be content to simply mosey around the grounds. They can tour the herb garden, visit the museum shop, or watch the outdoor volunteers at work. There is a special Sheep-to-Shawl festival in the spring.

HOURS: Mid-Sept.–mid-June, Sun., 2–4. **ADMISSION:** $. Discount: Students. Under 6 free. **LOCATION:** 614 Mountain Ave., Westfield (Union County). Rt. 22 to Mountain Ave. **TELEPHONE:** 908-232-1776. **WEBSITE:** http://westfieldnj.com/mc/index.htm.

OTHER NEW JERSEY HISTORIC SITES

Long Pond Ironworks: Founded in 1766 by a German ironmaster who brought five hundred ironworkers and their families to build an ironworks along the upper Wanaque River, the area originally contained a blast furnace and a large forge. Operations expanded during the Civil War but ceased in 1882 when the industry converted to anthracite furnaces. What is left consists of a few buildings and the remnants of such iron-making structures as furnaces, casting house ruins, ice houses, and large waterwheels. At this time, the only building open to the public is the old Country Store, which houses a museum full of displays, artifacts, and relics of life here. **HOURS:** Tours of the furnace area and village at 10, 12, and 2 on the second weekend of the month (times vary), Apr.–Nov. Special events are also held from time to time. The museum is open weekends, 1–4, Apr.–Nov. **ADMISSION:** Donation requested. **LOCATION:** The village is adjacent to Monksville Reservoir, a popular fishing area. W. Milford Twp. (Passaic County), Rt. 511, 2 miles east of Greenwood Lake. **TELEPHONE:** 973-657-1688 (Friends of Long Pond Ironworks). **WEBSITE:** www.longpondironworks.org.

Historic Walnford: This 36-acre historic district in Crosswick Creek Park is a former country estate and mill village. The Georgian-style Waln House, built in 1773, is the largest pre-Revolutionary residence in Monmouth County. It has been restored to an early twentieth-century appearance, preserving the various changes made by five generations of the Waln family and their descendants. The picturesque nineteenth-century gristmill on Crosswicks Creek was powered by turbine rather than a waterwheel—the peak of stone gristmill design when it was rebuilt in 1872. Today it also includes exhibits on gristmill operations and operates most weekends, April through November. An 1879 carriage house, along with a caretaker's cottage, barn, wagon house, and other outbuildings and farm structures preserve this atmosphere of this historic farm village. **HOURS:** Daily, 8–4:30. **ADMISSION:** Free. **LOCATION:** Walnford Rd., Upper Freehold Twp. (Monmouth County). Off Rt. 539, south of Allentown. **TELEPHONE:** 609-259-6275. **WEBSITE:** www.monmouthcountyparks.com/parks/walnford.asp.

Peter Mott House: The Underground Railroad was a pre–Civil War phenomenon: a series of "safe houses" where runaway slaves escaping from the South could find food, shelter, and guidance to the next stop. Many of these railroad "stations" were run by white Quaker farmers. But there were free black men in the north who also took on this task. Such a man was Peter Mott, whose home stands in Lawnside, the only historically African American incorporated community in the northern states. This two-story, white clapboard house, built in 1845, has been restored, with two rooms shown as a typical "house museum." Occasionally there are temporary exhibits on the importation of slaves from Africa, the Underground Railroad, and the Jim Crow era. **HOURS:** Sat., 12–3. **ADMISSION:** $. **LOCATION:** 26 Kings Ct., Lawnside (Camden County), Rt. 295, Exit 30, south on Warwick, right on Gloucester Ave., then left on Moore to Kings Ct. **TELEPHONE:** 856-546-8850. **WEBSITE:** www.petermotthouse.org.

Belcher-Ogden Mansion: This house originally belonged to John Ogden Jr., one of the first settlers in Elizabeth, and was built between 1680 and 1722. Later, from 1751 to 1757, Royal Governor Jonathan Belcher lived in this historic Georgian residence. **HOURS:** Tours by appointment only. **LOCATION:** 1046 E. Jersey Ave., Elizabeth (Union County). **TELEPHONE:** 908-581-7555. **WEBSITE:** www.visit historicalelizabethnj.org/belchermansion.html.

Greenfield Hall: This well-furnished, handsome Georgian building, built in 1841, includes Early American furniture, including tallcase clocks from the 1700s, tools, a toy and doll collection, and Victorian dresses displayed in period rooms. The hall, which is the headquarters of the Historical Society of Haddonfield, also has changing exhibits on local history as well as a museum shop. **HOURS:** Wed.–Fri. and first Sun. of the month, 1–4. Special events are also held throughout the year. **LOCATION:** 343 King Highway East, Haddonfield (Camden County).

Samuel Mickle House: Next door to Greenfield Hall and built in the 1730s, it houses the Historical Society's library, including photos, maps, old books, and genealogical records. **HOURS:** Tue. & Thu., 9:30–11:30, and 1–3 the first Sun. of each month. **TELEPHONE:** 856-429-7375. **WEBSITE:** www.historicalsocietyofhaddonfield.org.

Township of Lebanon Museum: The museum is in a white 1825 schoolhouse restored with all its desks, textbooks, and inkwells in place. Reserved school tours are booked and classes taught. The second floor offers exhibits displaying a permanent Lenape Indian collection plus special exhibits. **HOURS:** Tue., Thu., 9:30–5; Sat., 1–5. **ADMISSION:** Free. **LOCATION:** 57 Musconetcong River Rd., Hampton (Hunterdon County). **TELEPHONE:** 908-537-6464. **WEBSITE:** www. lebanontownship.net/museum.shtml.

Holcombe-Jimison Farmstead: The farmstead features the oldest remaining stone house in Hunterdon County, built in 1711 and being restored for tours, as well as several other buildings and an herb garden. The bank barn is used as a museum of rural life and displays early plows and other farming tools, sleighs, meat grinders, bottles, and assorted implements. Visitors can also find a complete dentist/

doctor's office on the second floor. Beyond the main barn, the wagon shed shelters a printing press and a blacksmith shop, where there are demonstrations during special events, such as a celebration of farming on the second weekend in September. Across the yard you'll find an old-time barbershop, general store, and a shed filled with old farm vehicles. **HOURS:** May–Oct., Sun., 1–4, and Wed., 9–12. **ADMISSION:** $. Discounts: Seniors, students. Under 6 free. **LOCATION:** Rt. 29 just north of Lambertville. **TELEPHONE:** 609-397-2752. **WEBSITE:** www.holcombe-jimison.org.

New Sweden Farmstead Museum: Seven log structures commemorate the 350th anniversary of the first Swedish settlement in America in the Delaware Valley in 1638. This small settlement includes a blacksmith shop, storehouse, threshing barn, residence, barn, and smokehouse. Tours present the lifestyle and contributions of early Swedish settlers, who introduced the log cabin to America. **HOURS:** Sat., 11–5; Sun., 12–5, mid-May through Sept. **ADMISSION:** $. Discounts: Seniors, children, students. Under 6 free. **LOCATION:** City Park, Bridgeton (Cumberland County). **TELEPHONE:** 856-451-9785. Call first. **WEBSITE:** www.co.cumberland.nj.us/tourism/new_sweden_farmstead_museum.

Fort Mott State Park: Fort Mott was part of a coastal defense system designed for the Delaware River in the late 1800s that included Fort Delaware on Pea Patch Island and Fort DuPont across the river. The fortifications seen today at Fort Mott were erected in 1896 in anticipation of the Spanish-American War. Today, you can see maritime history exhibits at the Welcome Center and wander through the old batteries following interpretive signs. **HOURS:** Daily, 8–8 in summer and Sept. weekends; 8–6 in spring and fall; 8–4 in winter. **LOCATION:** 454 Fort Mott Rd., Pennsville (Salem County). Off Rt. 49. **TELEPHONE:** 856-935-3218. **WEBSITE:** www.state.nj.us/dep/parksandforests/parks/fortmott.html.

From Fort Mott, Three Forts Ferry carries visitors to the other two forts (seasonal operation; for ferry information, call 302-832-7708). **Fort Delaware** on Pea Patch Island is the most impressive of the three forts and was built in 1847. During the Civil War, it served as a major Union military prison. The pentagon-shaped fort is surrounded by a moat and resembles a castle. Tours, exhibits, and demonstrations on military weaponry and domestic skills of the time are presented by costumed docents acting in historical character to bring the era to life (302-834-7941; www.visitthefort.com).

Just outside Fort Mott at Supawna Meadows National Wildlife Refuge is a 115-foot lighthouse, built with an unusual metal exoskeleton. Open for visitors 12–4 the third Sun. of the month, Apr.–Oct. (856-935-1487). Also nearby is Finn's Point National Cemetery, where most of the 2,700 soldiers who died on Pea Patch Island during the Civil War are buried.

Church Landing Farm: This three-story Gothic Revival farmhouse museum on the Delaware features rooms furnished as they were around 1860. Guided tours through this well-furnished period home relate the area's history, including the days when a ferry carried worshippers to church across the river to Wilmington and New Castle. The grounds include flower and herb gardens, as well as outbuildings containing a one-room maritime museum, Riverview Beach Park memorabilia, and an 1880 wash house. The riverfront at the farm includes a scenic view of the Delaware Memorial Bridge. "A Day at the Farm" is held every spring, featuring early farm crafts as well as a Civil War encampment. **HOURS:** Wed. & Sun., 1–3. **ADMISSION:** \$. Discounts: Seniors, students. Under 6 free. **LOCATION:** 86 Church Landing Rd., Pennsville (Salem County). Off Rt. 49, half a mile south of Rt. 295. **TELEPHONE:** 856-678-4453. **WEBSITE:** www.pv historical.njcool.net/museum.html.

D.A.R. Van Bunschooten Museum: This 1787 Dutch Colonial house was the home of the Reverend Elias Van Bunschooten, who served the Dutch Reformed Church in northwestern New Jersey for forty years. Operated by the Daughters of the American Revolution, the house is furnished with an impressive collection of Early American and Victorian antiques, all original furnishings. Some rooms have Early American furnishings while others reflect Victorian times or later. You'll find such treasures as a 1740 Hepplewhite sideboard, a French musket shipped to America by Lafayette, a Stickley/Mission-style desk, and a bed that belonged to Revolutionary War heroine Molly Stark. Outside there is a huge barn, ice house, and privy. The guided tour by a costumed decent also includes the Wagon House, where carriage and farm implements await. The big event here is Christmas in July, with crafters and demonstrations. **HOURS:** May 15 to Oct. 15, Thu. & Sat., 1–4. **ADMISSION:** \$. Discount: Children. **LOCATION:** 1097 Rt. 23, 4 miles north of Sussex (Sussex County). **TELEPHONE:** 973-875-5335. **WEBSITE:** www.rootsweb.com/~njdar/Chinkchewunska/ museum.html.

Old Millstone Forge Museum: The longest-operating blacksmith shop in America, it was used from the mid-1700s until 1959. Today the blacksmiths make iron wares for area historical museums when they aren't giving demonstrations or explaining the history of blacksmithing. The best thing here is that you can put on a safety apron and glasses and be a blacksmith for a day as you receive lessons while you make something for yourself—usually a simple hook. You can always return another time and make something more advanced. Wear cotton clothes and closed shoes. Also of note is a small metal marker at 6 feet high at the door, denoting the high-water mark during Hurricane Floyd in 1999. No amenities. **HOURS:** Sun., 1–4, Apr.–June, mid-Sept.–Nov. **ADMISSION:** Donation. **LOCA-TION:** N. River St., Millstone Borough (Somerset County). **TELEPHONE:** 908-448-6624. **WEBSITE:** www.oldmillstoneforge.org.

Barnegat Heritage Village and Museum: Here you can get guided tours of several small historic structures with period furnishings from other locations. These include the Lippincott-Faulkinburgh House, built in the 1700s; Edwards House, built by a Revolutionary War soldier; a 1900 barber shop; and a butcher shop, built with lumber from the storm-wrecked Barnegat lightkeeper's house. **HOURS:** Sat., 1–4, Memorial to Labor Day. **LOCATION:** Barnegat Historical Society, 575 E. Bay Ave., Barnegat (Ocean County). Garden State Parkway, Exit 67. Follow Bay Ave. east through town. **TELEPHONE:** 609-698-5284. **WEBSITE:** www.barnegathistoricalsoc.com.

Cooper Mill: At this 1826 gristmill you can see corn and wheat ground into meal before your eyes. Costumed staff give guided tours (which last as long as you want) upon request during open hours. Last tour starts at 3:30. For tickets to the mill and displays on local history, start at the Visitor Center, a restored nineteenth-century home across the parking lot. The mill also hosts seasonal events, such as blacksmithing and cider pressing. **HOURS:** July & Aug., Fri.–Tue., 10–5. May, June, Sept., & Oct., weekends only. **ADMISSION:** $. **LOCATION:** Rt. 513/124, Chester (Morris County). One mile west of Rt. 206. **TELEPHONE:** 908-879-5463. **WEBSITE:** http://parks.morris.nj.us/aspparks/coopermillmain.asp.

Kearny Cottage: This picturesque 1781 four-room cottage near Raritan Bay was once the home of poet Elizabeth Lawrence Kearny (half-sister of James Lawrence, the War of 1812 hero). It is now used as a house museum. **HOURS:** Tue. & Thu. afternoons (but call first). **LOCA-TION:** 63 Catalpa St., Perth Amboy. **TELEPHONE:** 732-826-1826.

Shippen Manor: Part of the Oxford Furnace Historic District, this Georgian mansion is constructed of stone walls 2 feet thick and features three immense chimneys. Built by the well-known Philadelphia Shippen family in 1754, the house was a center for an iron manufacturing area. Original iron firebacks in chimneys, period furniture, and a cellar kitchen are featured. Each room reflects a different time period, from colonial through Victorian. Tours are given by costumed docents. There are occasional cooking demonstrations, and often a musician or vocalist performs at the house. The lawn is used for Sunday evening concerts in summer and for other special events. **HOURS:** First and second Sun., 1–4. **ADMISSION:** $. Discount: Seniors. Under 12 free. **LOCATION:** 8 Belvidere Ave., Oxford (Warren County). **TELEPHONE:** 908-453-4381. **WEBSITE:** www.wcchc.org.

Somers Mansion: The oldest house in Atlantic County, it has an unusual roof shaped like an upside-down ship's hull and contains nice furniture and local memorabilia. Tours at this state historic site are given by docents. **HOURS:** Wed.–Sat., 10–12 & 1–4; Sun., 1–4. Call first. **LOCATION:** Entrance on Rt. 52 just north of the Somers Point Circle, Somers Point (Atlantic County). **TELEPHONE:** 609-927-2212.

Smithville Mansion: The home of industrialist and inventor Hezakiah B. Smith near Mount Holly was built in the 1840s and lies at the heart of what remains of his industrial village. The tour starts at the Visitor Center, which has displays and photos on Smith and his business, then winds through his Victorian mansion. There is a formal double parlor and dining room with elegant antiques, upstairs bedrooms that include a bed that belonged to President Polk, a billiard room, and a large annex that included a bowling alley. A surrounding park includes industrial ruins, a scenic lake, and trails. **HOURS:** May–Oct., Wed., Sun. tours at 1, 2 & 3. **ADMISSION:** $. Discounts: Seniors, students. Under 6 free. **LOCATION:** Smithville Rd., Eastampton (Burlington County). North off Rt. 38. **TELEPHONE:** 609-265-5068.

Strauss Mansion: The 21-room, Queen Anne-style 1893 "summer cottage" of Adolph Strauss sits high atop a hill overlooking Atlantic Highlands. The foyer, parlor, and Victorian bedroom are filled with fine antiques, oak paneling, and stained glass while the dining room and several upstairs rooms offer exhibits on local history. **HOURS:** Sun., 1–4. **ADMISSION:** Free. **LOCATION:** 27 Prospect Circle, Atlantic Highlands (Monmouth County). **TELEPHONE:** 732-291-7603. **WEBSITE:** www.atlantichighlandshistory.org.

Hamilton-Van Wagoner House: The tour of this 1817 Dutch Colonial-style home by costumed docents begins in the basement with a short video on the area and the people who lived in the house. Upstairs, there are two Victorian rooms—a parlor and library—plus a Federal-period bedroom and parlor and a colonial dining room and kitchen. The second floor offers changing exhibits on area history. There's also a small gift shop in the basement. **HOURS:** Mar.–Dec., Sun., 2–4. **ADMISSION:** $. **LOCATION:** 971 Valley Rd., Clifton (Passaic County). Off Rts. 46 and 3. **TELEPHONE:** 973-744-5707. **WEBSITE:** www.passaiccountynj.org/historicalhousemuseums.htm.

Ledgewood Historic Park: There are three buildings here. The 1815 King Store, which ceased business in 1927, still has a lot of its original merchandise on the shelves. The 1883 Homestead has a restored parlor, two exhibit rooms, and a dining room with a large wall mural of the English countryside. The 1770s Silas Riggs Saltbox has been restored and furnished in its original Colonial style. **HOURS:** Second Sun. of month, 1–4. **ADMISSION:** Free. **LOCATION:** 209 Main St., Ledgewood (Morris County). Off Rt. 10 East. **TELEPHONE:** 973-927-7603. **WEBSITE:** www.roxburynewjersey.com/trust.htm.

Gabreil Daveis Tavern: Built in 1756 to serve boatmen on Timber Creek, this 8-room tavern house was also used for colonial township meetings. Owners and occupants have included a licensed pirate, local Revolutionary leader, a man with a wooden leg, and a number of ghosts. Outside is a small stage used for concerts in July–Aug. **HOURS:** Apr.–mid-Dec., Sun., 1–4. **ADMISSION:** Free. **LOCATION:** 4th Ave., Glendora (Camden County). Off Black Horse Pike. **TELEPHONE:** 856-784-5243. **WEBSITE:** www.glotwp.com/about_us.

Woodruff House/Eaton Store: Built in 1735 and added onto in 1790 and 1890, the house captures the atmosphere of colonial and Victorian times with some nicely done furnishings from each era. An adjacent general store, built in 1900, displays typical goods from the period as well as an old ballot box with ballots for President Wilson. Out back is a reconstructed barn with old farming implements and a room of memorabilia dedicated to Yankee hall of famer Phil Rizzuto—much of it donated by the "Scooter" himself, who lives a few blocks away. **HOURS:** Third Sun. of month, 2–4. **ADMISSION:** Free. **LOCATION:** 111 Conant St., Hillside (Union County). Off Salem Ave. **TELEPHONE:** 908-353-8828. **WEBSITE:** www.woodruffhouse.org.

Hopper-Goetschius House: This Dutch Colonial farmhouse, built in the early 1700s, has been nicely restored and filled with interesting antique furnishings, with about half from the family that lived here for 150 years. The decor ranges from colonial to Victorian. Outside is a barn with an antique sleigh, carriage, and farming implements as well as a second house set up as a school room. Special events spring and fall. **HOURS:** June–Labor Day, Sun., 2–4. **ADMISSION:** Free. **LOCATION:** 245 Lake St., Upper Saddle River (Bergen County). **TELEPHONE:** 201-327-6354. **WEBSITE:** www.usrhistoricalsociety.org.

Garretson Forge and Farm: This early 1700s Dutch Colonial house was the home of six generations of Garretsons, until 1950. The first floor includes a jambless open-hearth kitchen, a museum display room, and a large parlor and sleeping area, where you get a demonstration on spinning. Herb, vegetable, children's, colonial flower, and butterfly gardens outside. Spring Festival last Sat. in Apr. and other events. **HOURS:** Mar.–June and Sept.–Nov., Sun., 1–4. **ADMISSION:** Donation. **LOCATION:** 4-02 River Rd., Fair Lawn (Bergen County). Off Rt. 4 or Rt. 208 to west on Morlot Ave. to River. **TELEPHONE:** 201-797-1775. **WEBSITE:** www.garretsonfarm.org.

Holmes-Hendrickson House: This farmhouse is interpreted in the style of the late 1700s, based on an inventory of Dutch Colonial furnishings from that time, with two kasten (Dutch armoires), rope beds, and an open-hearth kitchen. **HOURS:** May–Sept., Thu.–Sat., 1–4. **ADMISSION:** $. Discounts: Seniors, children. Under 6 free. **LOCATION:** 62 Longstreet Rd., Holmdel (Monmouth County). **TELEPHONE:** 732-462-1466. **WEBSITE:** www.monmouth.com/~mcha/historichouses. html.

Dr. William Robinson Plantation: This restored 1690 farmhouse contains artifacts, maps, and pictures in its museum section. Currently closed for restoration. **LOCATION:** 593 Madison Hill Rd., Clark (Union County). **TELEPHONE:** 732-381-3081.

NEARBY OUT-OF-STATE SITES
Van Cortlandt Manor

Set on a rise overlooking the Hudson and Croton Rivers, Van Cortlandt Manor is a prime example of the strong Dutch influence in the New York–New Jersey area. The Manor House, one of the better restorations in the area, is among several sites run by Historic Hudson Valley.

From the reception center, costumed guides lead tours through several buildings. At the Ferry House, travelers stopped for food, drink, and lodging. At the other end of a long brick walk is the Manor House. While not as elegant as Southern Colonial mansions, it is impressive—three stories high with a two-story porch wrapped around it. On the main floor, the atmosphere is one of burnished wood and quiet elegance. Delft tiles line the fireplaces. Chippendale and Queen Anne furniture fill the rooms, and English china rests in the Dutch cupboards. The property also includes a smokehouse, icehouse, tenant house, and a blacksmith forge.

HOURS: Apr.–Oct., daily except Tue., 10–4. Nov. & Dec., weekends only. **ADMISSION:** $$. Under 6 free. **LOCATION:** Croton-on-the-Hudson,

NY. Take Tappan Zee Bridge to Rt. 9 north to Croton Pond Ave., one block east to South Riverside Ave., turn right and go a quarter-mile to entrance. **TELEPHONE:** 914-631-8200. **WEBSITE:** www.hudsonvalley.org.

Philipsburg Manor

A large farm and gristmill, a wood-planked bridge that spans a tranquil stream, an old stone manor house, and a huge modern reception center filled with exhibits are all part of this Historic Hudson Valley restoration. The estate is set up as it was from 1680 to 1750, with authentic furnishings and costumed guides. Tours begin with a movie about the Philipse family, who managed 90,000 acres and shipped flour and meal down the Hudson but backed the losing side during the Revolution and lost their holdings.

Guided tours of the manor, a demonstration at the gristmill, and a walk through the barn are part of the outing. The Visitor Center includes a large, well-stocked gift shop and a glass-enclosed cafe that offers light lunches.

HOURS: Apr.–Oct., daily except Tue., 10–5; Nov.–Dec., 10–4. Weekends only in March. **ADMISSION:** $$. Discounts: Seniors, students. Under 6 free. **LOCATION:** Upper Mills, North Tarrytown, NY. Take Tappan Zee Bridge, then Rt. 9 north for 2 miles. Follow signs. **TELEPHONE:** 914-631-8200. **WEBSITE:** www.hudsonvalley.org.

Museums of All Kinds

"Were You Invited" by J. Seward Johnson is a 2001 sculptural rendition of Renoir's painting "The Boating Party" at Grounds for Sculpture. *(Photo by Patrick Sarver)*

ART AND SCIENCE MUSEUMS

Newark Museum

Newark Museum is twice the size it was a few years ago; it is open, airy, and convenient—a truly first-class museum. There is room to show off the collection—American paintings, Tibetan statues, African masks—plus plenty of space for the special exhibits. The center court is open for light lunches and teas, and there's a museum shop nearby. There's also a separate Science Shop in the museum.

The Asian Galleries on the third floor not only include the museum's fine Tibetan collection but also Indian, Chinese, and Korean treasures. The American Art Galleries covers two floors on the North Wing, tracing the development of art in the United States from the colonial to the contemporary. Works from major artists are displayed in separate galleries according to period and theme.

The Dynamic Earth, in the Victoria Hall of Science, adds a strong natural science angle to the museum's collections. It features seven galleries that cover forces shaping the natural world, an exploration of the world's ecosystems, and a look at New Jersey's natural setting. Hands-on activities are mixed with traditional exhibits for exploring volcanoes, earthquakes, and survival of the fittest. There's a Discover Field Station, where kids can do their own scientific investigations. You'll also find a real mastodon skeleton uncovered in a "dig," ancient insects trapped in amber, fluorescent minerals from New Jersey, and fossils in a re-created New Jersey cave. Science workshops and other programs are often held on weekend afternoons. There's also a Junior Gallery and minizoo with terrariums and aquariums, and a Native American Gallery offers costumes and artifacts.

The fifty-seat Dreyfuss Planetarium is near the garden entrance and offers sky shows to the general public on weekends and holidays (extra fee). The museum also includes a pleasant garden complete with several modern sculptures. A tiny one-room schoolhouse that dates to 1784 and a Fire Museum are also part of the garden scene.

Attended parking is available in an adjacent lot (corner of Central and Washington Avenues). Have your ticket stamped at the Information Desk, where you can also pick up floor plans. The Ballantine House (q.v.) is also accessible through the museum.

HOURS: 12–5, Wed.–Sun. Opens weekends at 10, Oct.–June. Closed major holidays. **ADMISSION:** Free, with donations welcomed. **LOCATION:** 49 Washington St., Newark (facing Washington Park). **TELEPHONE:** 973-596-6550; planetarium, 973-596-6609. **WEBSITE:** www.newarkmuseum.org.

Montclair Art Museum

A true art museum nestled in a town that was once an artists' center, the Montclair Art Museum reflects a high level of community support. Built in the early twentieth century, this solid, neoclassical stone edifice is dedicated to painting and sculpture, with a permanent collection of more than 15,000 works.

The collection consists entirely of American art, covering a period of three centuries. Many familiar names, such as Hopper, Nevelson, Sargent, Peale, Eakins, Copley, and Currier & Ives, are represented here along with other prominent American artists. One gallery is dedicated to the work of George Inness, the Hudson River School painter who did much of his work in Montclair. The museum is also a repository for the works and papers of Morgan Russell, originator of Synchromism, the first American modernist art movement. The paintings in the permanent collection are often used for changing exhibits, which are themed for a certain point of view.

Kids are likely to find the permanent Native American collection most interesting, but the collection is also used for adult-oriented exhibits. Costumes and artifacts highlight the Plains and Southwest Indians, including interesting displays of Sioux and Navajo dress. From time to time the museum also shows works by contemporary Native American artists. This is an active museum, with classes, children's programs, and lectures as well as gallery tours. Many traveling exhibits are shown throughout the year, all focusing on American art. A museum store and free parking lot behind the museum help make a visit a pleasant experience.

HOURS: Tue.–Sun., 11–5. **ADMISSION:** $$. Discounts: Seniors, students. Under 12 free. Free, Fri., 11–1. **LOCATION:** S. Mountain and Bloomfield Aves., Montclair (Essex County). **TELEPHONE:** 973-746-5555. **WEBSITE:** www.montclairartmuseum.org.

Zimmerli Art Museum

The Jane Voorhees Zimmerli Art Museum, on the Rutgers Campus in New Brunswick, keeps growing all the time. Once a small collection, there are now over 55,000 works (paintings, lithographs, drawings, photographs) in this museum. The lobby level is home to American art, a large Russian art collection, children's book illustrations, Soviet nonconformist art, and the museum store. Upstairs, on the mezzanine level, is the home of American prints and an environmental sculpture gallery. A spiral ramp leads to the lower level, where a maze of walls presents ancient art, modernist European and American art, Japonisme, European art, special exhibition galleries, and additional Soviet nonconformist works.

The American Art collection includes paintings and sculpture from the late eighteenth century to today, including nineteenth-century portraits and landscapes and American art influenced by surrealism and abstraction. Other American collections cover women artists, original illustrations for children's literature, and a regional stained-glass design. Kids will enjoy the Learning Center, which has computers and interactive learning materials on art for the entire family.

The Riabov Collection of Russian Art contains a wide variety of periods and media, including folk prints, sculpture, religious icons, landscapes, and stage designs, as well as Russian émigré art. The Dodge Collection of Non-conformist Art from the Soviet Union is the largest collection of its kind in the world, encompassing more than 17,000 works by dissidents.

The Zimmerli also has a large graphic arts collection from the nineteenth century. European modernism is represented through the graphic arts, displayed in the twentieth-century galleries. There is a small teaching collection of European paintings from the fifteenth to nineteenth centuries.

A Japonisme room also displays a permanent collection of European and American works on paper and ceramics—a selection that reflects the strong influence of Japan on Western art in the late 1800s and early 1900s. Plus, the museum features a number of traveling exhibits throughout the year.

HOURS: Tue.–Fri., 10–4:30; weekends, 12–5. Closed major holidays, Aug., and Tue. in July. **ADMISSION:** $. Under 18 free. Free the first Sun. of each month. **LOCATION:** 71 Hamilton St., New Brunswick (Middlesex County). At corner of George St. **TELEPHONE:** 732-932-7237. **WEBSITE:** www.zimmerlimuseum.rutgers.edu.

Grounds for Sculpture

For those who like to stroll on lush lawns and inspect large works of sculpture at leisure, this is the only major venue in New Jersey. Located on the former grounds of the New Jersey State Fair, the 35-acre site includes two large buildings dedicated to indoor exhibitions and an expanse of well-tended greenery that serves as a backdrop for the large sculptures. Although there are many abstract pieces, you will also find "lifelike" forms by such artists as J. Seward Johnson. Johnson was the founder of this facility, and a number of his works on the grounds interpret well-known Impressionist paintings as sculptures. Overall, dozens of artists' works in all manner of media are displayed at this art park. Special exhibits are offered several times a year, and there are guided tours May to October.

Walkways throughout the site are made of concrete and pebble, but there is no prohibition against walking on the grass. A large lake serves as backdrop for the grounds. One of the pleasant aspects of this place is the number of benches and Adirondack chairs, where you can sit and contemplate the lawn, ornamental trees, and heroic-sized sculptures. In fact, the grounds have so many plants and flowering bushes, it is as attractive to garden groups as it is to art lovers.

The Domestic Arts Building includes large spaces for rotating exhibits, a small cafe, and a museum shop. The cafe also offers an outdoor courtyard where you can sit at a bistro-style table next to bamboo trees and a three-dimensional rendition of a French cafe scene. A formal Water Garden, which features reflecting pools, concrete walkways, plantings, and outdoor "rooms" of sculpture, is next to the building. At the far side of the grounds is the Toad Hall shop and gallery and an upscale restaurant called Rats (open for lunch and dinner), which is accessible on foot or via a separate entrance.

HOURS: Apr.–Oct., Tue.–Sun., 10–8; Nov.–Mar., 10–6. Tours Sat. at 11, Sun. at 2, May–Oct. Closed major holidays. **ADMISSION:** $$ ($ on Tue.–Thu.) Discounts: Seniors, children. **LOCATION:** 18 Fairgrounds Rd., Hamilton Twp. (Mercer County). Rt. 295, Exit 65B. Follow signs. **TELEPHONE:** 609-586-0616. **WEBSITE:** www.groundsforsculpture.org.

Princeton University Art Museum

One of the leading university art museums in the United States, the Princeton University Art Museum is beautifully laid out with a modern, well-lit interior. The collection of 60,000 works range from ancient to contemporary, with concentrations on the Mediterranean, Western Europe, China, the United States, and Latin America.

The museum's greatest strengths are its collections of Greek and Roman antiquities from the university's excavations in Antioch, as well as Chinese and pre-Colombian art, most notably Olmec, Maya, and Aztec items. Medieval European works include sculpture,

The Medieval European collection at the Princeton University Art Museum focuses on architectural sculpture, metalwork, and stained glass, one of many galleries filled with artistic treasures.
(Photo by Patrick Sarver)

metalwork, and stained glass. Western European paintings encompass important examples from the early Renaissance through the nineteenth century, with a growing collection of twentieth-century and contemporary art. The American Gallery includes works by such artists as Copley, Peale, Eakins, Homer, and Sargent, while the Nineteenth-Century Gallery features works by Impressionist notables like Cezanne, Degas, Gaugin, Van Gogh, and Monet. The museum also has many old master prints and drawings as well as a wide collection of original photographs. Special exhibits show portions of these collections on a rotating basis. You'll also find a nice museum shop here.

HOURS: Tue.–Sat., 10–5; Sun., 1–5. Closed major holidays.
Several adult group tours are available; call 609-258-3043 for options.
ADMISSION: Free. **LOCATION:** Princeton University Campus, Nassau and Witherspoon Sts., Princeton (Mercer County). From Nassau St., walk past the left side of Nassau Hall. Museum is straight ahead.
TELEPHONE: 609-258-3788. **WEBSITE:** www.princetonartmuseum.org.

Liberty Science Center

Set in the middle of Liberty State Park, Liberty Science Center is just finishing a massive $100 million upgrade that has enlarged the entire center by 50 percent. Reopening in July 2007, the center now features enlarged lobby space and numerous new exhibits in a totally new configuration. As you enter the building, the first thing that strikes your eye is the aluminum Hoberman Sphere, which expands and contracts as it hangs in the expanded lobby. Nearby is the center's new exhibit on skyscrapers. This large gallery in the new wing of the center offers such displays as cutaway views of tall building interiors, displaying the design, operation, and ecology of modern high-rise structures.

On the second floor is the Times Square of Science and Technology, which surrounds one section of the floor with colorful screens and news on the latest findings in science. Young kids (6 and under) also have their own section here where they can learn about their bodies, their world, and their own talents.

Next floor up includes a new exhibition on communication, including electronic graffiti, language karaoke, and other exhibits on the nature of human communication. Other galleries here include Eat and Be Eaten, where you can explore the predator-prey life cycle, and Infection Connection, where you see the world of microbes and their role in the spread of disease.

On the very top level an exhibit called Our Hudson Home explores the relationship between people and nature along the nearby lower Hudson River. There's also a section on the Earth's energy resources, a traveling exhibition gallery, and two dozen favorite exhibits from the previous science center, such as the Resonance Tube, a rock-climbing wall, and brain teaser stations.

One of the few unchanged things is the IMAX Theater, housed in a geodesic dome that features an eight-story curved screen. Movies produced in the IMAX format are twice as large as feature films and use a six-channel sound system. Nature films are popular here. Reserve when you come in (or even ahead of time). Two or three different movies may be shown on a single day. The Joseph D. Williams Science Theater is unchanged. The 3-D shows here are also an extra expense, but they are usually very good. There is a large, redesigned gift shop on the first floor, and a new Skyline Cafe on the second.

HOURS: Mon.–Fri., 9–5; Sat., Sun., holidays, 9–6. Extended hours July–Aug. 2007. **ADMISSION:** Adults, $$$. Discounts: Seniors, children, teachers. Combination fee for IMAX & 3-D show available. **LOCATION:** Exit 14B, N.J. Turnpike, turn left, follow Liberty State Park signs, take Burma Road to the Science Center. **TELEPHONE:** 201-200-1000. **WEBSITE:** www.lsc.org.

New Jersey State Museum

It stands in Trenton, pristine and white against the backdrop of the Delaware River. The museum and adjacent planetarium are, however, both currently closed for renovation, with a planned reopening of both in late 2007 or early 2008. (Check the Website to confirm reopening dates.) In the meantime, the separate Museum Theater building, which offers a well-proportioned stage and comfortable seating, has two galleries open, one on the history of Trenton and the other devoted to changing exhibits. There's also a permanent display of Civil War flags and a changing exhibit in the State Archives building at 225 W. State St.

Set up as a family museum, with exhibits to interest both children and adults, the museum offers a balance among its various sections. The permanent collection galleries are being redesigned and will focus on fine art, cultural history, archeology, and natural history, with changing exhibits slated for the first floor. There will also be a gift shop and museum cafe on the first floor. As for the planetarium, a new schedule of public shows and laser concerts are planned following reopening.

ADMISSION: Free. Planetarium, $. **LOCATION:** 205 W. State St., Trenton. Use Rt. 29 along Delaware River or Rt. 1 into State St. **TELEPHONE:** Museum, 609-292-6464; planetarium, 609-292-6303. **WEBSITE:** www.newjerseystatemuseum.org.

Morris Museum

The Morris Museum of Arts and Sciences is a dependable bastion of culture great for any day. Housed in a lovely old mansion surrounded by large trees, it is small enough not to be too exhausting for young kids but varied enough to appeal to all ages.

One popular area is the rock and mineral exhibit (it comes complete with a darkroom for viewing fluorescent rocks). Another is the natural science section with its glass-encased exhibits of stuffed mammals and birds in their natural habitats. And since it is called a museum of arts and sciences, there is always at least one art exhibit on display that changes every few months. In recent years, major traveling exhibits have taken over much of the first floor. Sometimes, they are interactive and continue onto the outside terrace. Permanent exhibits include a collection of Victorian dolls, a model railroad, Native American artifacts, and a small dinosaur room. The gracious Dodge Room is kept as a reception room with some excellent paintings—including a Rembrandt and a Gainsborough—and decorative arts shown in a domestic atmosphere.

Also on site is the comfortable 300-seat Bickford Theater, which is the setting for dramas, musicals, comedies, and children's shows. The museum also offers art workshops for adults and fun crafts and other activities for kids as well as a museum shop with an interesting range of gifts.

HOURS: Tue.–Sat., 10–5; Sun., 1–5; Thu. until 8. **ADMISSION:** $$. Discounts: Seniors, children. Thu., 1–8, free. **LOCATION:** 6 Normandy Heights Rd., Morristown (Morris County). Off Columbia Turnpike. **TELEPHONE:** 973-971-3700. **WEBSITE:** www.morrismuseum.org.

Paterson Museum

Located near Paterson's Great Falls in the old Rogers Locomotive factory, the Paterson Museum takes up the first floor of this imposing red brick building. The museum contains a fascinating compilation of photographs, factory machines, old posters, and early inventions. Among other things, you'll find the great wheels that spun silk thread and ribbons, and jacquard-style punch-hole machines. There is also a collection of Colt pistols and other armaments made at the company's factory in Paterson. Although primarily a historical museum, there are other exhibits as well, including one on rocks and minerals, a model train set, Lou Costello memorabilia, and rotating art shows. One of the newest is the story of Automatic Data Processing, which started in Paterson.

Paterson seems to be the only community in New Jersey that does not equate the historical with the quaint. The great weaving machines, the metal shells of the first two submarines, and engines from the Wright Aeronautical Corporation all testify to the fact that the dominant thrust of the nineteenth century was the industrial revolution. The two Rogers locomotives that stand outside the building are symbols of the Iron Horse that opened up the plains.

For more on Paterson's history, walk around the corner and up the hill to the overlook of the **Great Falls**. A Visitor Center across the street offers a 20-minute film and lots of literature. A stop at the point overlooking the Great Falls to take a picture is de rigeur. These falls are quite majestic, and if Alexander Hamilton hadn't decided to harness their power for a new industrial city, they might have been a great tourist attraction.

HOURS: Tue.–Fri., 10–4; Sat., Sun., 12:3–4:30. **ADMISSION:** Adults, $. **LOCATION:** 2 Market St., Paterson (Passaic County). **TELEPHONE:** 973-321-1260.

Hiram Blauvelt Art Museum

Founded in 1957, this was the first museum in New Jersey concentrating solely on wildlife art. Mini-galleries on the main floor of this 1893 shingle and turret-style carriage house feature one of seventeen remaining original 1830s Audubon folios in the United States as well as extinct birds and an ivory collection. The permanent gallery presents works of wildlife art masters and contemporary artists. A former natural history gallery upstairs is no longer open, however. Outdoors, you'll find a pleasant sculpture garden featuring ten large bronzes. The museum offers programs on art for schools, and an artist-in-residence presents painting demonstrations from time to time.

HOURS: Wed.–Fri., 10–4; Sat. & Sun., 2–5. Closed holidays. **ADMISSION:** Free. **LOCATION:** 705 Kinderkamack Rd., Oradell (Bergen County). Garden State Parkway, Exit 165 to Oradell Ave., then left on Kinderkamack. On-site parking. **TELEPHONE:** 201-261-0012. **WEBSITE:** www.blauveltmuseum.com.

Other Art and Science Museums

Tenafly Museum of African Art: Run by the Society of African Missions (SMA) fathers and set inside a church complex, this smallish museum highlights West African art and artifacts. Its permanent collections, exhibited on a rotating basis, offer a chance to see sub-Saharan sculpture, painting, costumes, pottery, textiles, masks, and decorative arts as well as religion and folklore. There are also exhibits of collections on loan, often with well-done catalogs. Tours for school groups. Surrounded by 5 acres of beautifully landscaped grounds. **HOURS:** Daily, 9–5. **ADMISSION:** Free. **LOCATION:** 23 Bliss Ave., Tenafly (Bergen County). **TELEPHONE:** 201-894-8611. **WEBSITE:** www.smafathers.org/museum.

Stedman Gallery: A growing collection of art on paper and photography by contemporary American artists highlights this museum, supplemented by other works in other media and from different periods and places. There are also changing exhibits from other museums, private collectors, and artists. Special events include lectures, performances, video programs, and art performances throughout the year. **HOURS:** Mon.– Sat., 10–4. Closed major holidays and between exhibitions. **ADMISSION:** Free. **LOCATION:** Fine Arts Center, Rutgers Campus, Third and Pearl Streets, Camden (Camden County). **TELEPHONE:** 856-225-6350. **WEBSITE:** www.ruarts.org/info/venues/the_stedman_gallery/index.html.

Rutgers Geology Museum: A large room ringed by a balcony comprises this science museum on the second floor of the Geology Hall on the Rutgers campus. A mastodon skeleton from south Jersey looms in the center, while the walls hold charts of geological periods and cases of smaller fossils, including New Jersey dinosaurs. There's also an Egyptian mummy from 300 B.C. A mineral display includes Jersey's famous fluorescent rocks. The balcony—up a very narrow spiral staircase—offers rock samples taken from a cross section of New Jersey geological zones. Interesting lectures and demonstrations for school groups take place here. **HOURS:** Mon., 1–4; Tue.–Fri., 9–12. Call for weekend and summer hours. **ADMISSION:** Free. **LOCATION:** 85 Somerset St., New Brunswick. Enter parking lot through iron gates at George and Somerset Sts. **TELEPHONE:** 732-932-7243. **WEBSITE:** http://geology.rutgers.edu/museum.shtml.

Jersey City Museum: This art and history museum celebrates Hudson County's culture with eight galleries, a theater, classrooms, cafe, and a museum shop. All are in a 35,000-square-foot facility that opened in 2001. The collection includes regionally significant art and historical objects. There are drawings, paintings, prints, photos, sculpture, decorative arts, and industrial objects at the museum, including more than three hundred works by local artist August Will. Other established and emerging Hudson County artists are also showcased, with the emphasis on contemporary works. Many events are held throughout the year, including a music series, a film series, children's programs, lectures, symposia, and other events. **HOURS:** Wed. & Fri., 11–5; Thu., 11–8; Sat. & Sun., 12–5. **ADMISSION:** $. Discounts: Seniors, students. **LOCATION:** 350 Montgomery St., Jersey City

(Hudson County). On-street parking only. Near the Grove St. PATH station. **TELEPHONE:** 201-413-0303. **WEBSITE:** www.jerseycitymuseum. org.

Noyes Museum of Art: This striking, beach-style museum overlooks a lilypad lake on the edge of a national wildlife refuge. Inside, you'll find a dozen or more changing exhibits a year of contemporary paintings, photography, and sculpture by regional and national artists. It also has a growing collection of its own American fine and folk art, including a nice collection of vintage duck decoys. A special gallery for exhibits by students from area schools and community groups adds a nice touch. You'll also find an interesting shop in this museum, which was established by Fred W. Noyes, an academically trained painter and creator of nearby Smithville. **HOURS:** Tue.–Sat., 10–4:30; Sun., 12–5. **ADMISSION:** $. Discounts: Seniors, students. Under 7 free. **LOCATION:** Lily Lake Road, Oceanville (Atlantic County). Off Rt. 9. **TELEPHONE:** 609-652-8848. **WEBSITE:** www.noyes museum.org.

Ellarslie, the Trenton City Museum: Housed in a Victorian Italianate villa built in 1848, the museum offers a blend of changing and traveling art exhibits on the first floor and a permanent collection of fine and decorative arts, cultural history, and industrial artifacts from the area on the second. Included are exhibits of Trenton's renowned ceramic and porcelain companies, such as Boehm, Cybis, and Lenox. The museum also hosts many special events, musical programs, and art classes. Ellarslie is set in Trenton's Cadwalader Park, designed by Frederick Law Olmstead. **HOURS:** Tue.–Sat., 11–3; Sun., 1–4. Closed major holidays. **ADMISSION:** Free. **LOCATION:** Cadwalader Park, Parkside Ave., Trenton. **TELEPHONE:** 609-989-3632. **WEBSITE:** www.ellarslie.org.

Hunterdon Museum of Art: Housed in an 1836 stone gristmill across a picturesque dam from the Red Mill Museum, this historic structure has a rustic wood interior that forms a backdrop for changing exhibits of emerging and established contemporary New Jersey and other artists as well as a permanent collection of five hundred prints. The museum also offers art classes, workshops, lectures, tours, and a gift shop. **HOURS:** Tue.–Sun., 11–5. **ADMISSION:** Donation. **LOCATION:** 7 Lower Center St., Clinton (Hunterdon County). **TELEPHONE:** 908-735-8415. **WEBSITE:** www.hunterdonartmuseum.org.

Bergen Museum of Art and Science: A new museum gallery on the lower level of the Bergen Mall displays works by regional artists as well as scientific and historic artifacts, including two mastodons.

There is also a variety of smaller changing exhibits, from Holocaust art to doll houses. The museum also sponsors special programs, including art classes, in the mall auditorium. **HOURS:** Tue.–Sat., 10–5. **ADMISSION:** $. Discounts: Children and students. Free on Wed. for seniors. **LOCATION:** Bergen Mall, Rt. 4 East, Paramus (Bergen County). **TELEPHONE:** 201-291-8848. **WEBSITE:** www.thebergenmuseum.com.

CHILDREN'S MUSEUMS

New Jersey Children's Museum

This museum is dedicated to the proposition that children learn through play and experience. Set in a reconditioned industrial building in Paramus with 15,000 square feet of space, the museum is 100 percent hands-on. Children from ages 3 to 8 can touch, climb, put on clothes, and play-act to their hearts' content. The walls are brightly painted, the floor is carpeted, and the place may remind you of a giant nursery school. But the exhibits are far more expansive than what you would find at a local preschool. There is a real helicopter, for instance. It has been simplified so that a child can climb inside and pretend to fly. There is a genuine backhoe with a hard hat to match, and a fire engine that comes complete with fire hose and bell. Each of the thirty interactive exhibits is designed around a theme, including a fantasy castle, a prehistoric cave where kids can scribble their own "cave paintings" on a blackboard, and a garage where they can repair a jeep. The huge space is divided into sections devoted to dance, music, medicine, construction, and so forth. The "office" has real computers, and the pizzeria keeps the kids busy for hours.

The museum is not a drop-off spot. Parents must supervise their children, and they are welcome to join in the play. There are assistants around to help. No food is allowed. Birthday parties can be arranged by reservation. And there's a gift shop.

> **HOURS:** Daily, 10–6; weekends May–Sept., 10–5. **ADMISSION:** $$. Under 1 free. **LOCATION:** 599 Valley Health Plaza, Paramus (Bergen County). Off Ridgewood Avenue between Rt. 17 and Garden State Parkway, Exit 165. Call for directions. **TELEPHONE:** 201-262-5151. **WEBSITE:** www.njcm.com.

Garden State Discovery Museum

This interactive children's museum serves the southern part of the state. The 15,000-square-foot center has painted murals on the walls and fifteen large interactive exhibit areas. The theme is New Jersey, so there's a diner complete with chrome and red vinyl seats and a kitchen where kids can whip up plastic hamburgers. A "Down the Shore" exhibit lets kids fish off a boat or send rubber ducks down a stream.

Other areas include a rock-climbing wall and the hundred-seat theater where the kids can put on costumes and act. A flowered Volkswagen "bug" and a house construction complete with gravel pit and junk musical instruments are also on hand. One section is devoted to the science of sports. The museum directors have included a snack area where you can eat your own sandwiches and augment them with vending-machine items. There is a child-centered gift shop. Geared for childen up to 10 years old—and parents must accompany them. Family memberships available, as are overnights and birthday parties.

> **HOURS:** Tue.–Sun., 9:30–5:30; Sat. until 8:30. **ADMISSION:** $$.
> Discount: Seniors. Under 1 free. **LOCATION:** 2040 Springdale Rd.,
> Cherry Hill (Camden County). Not far from N.J. Turnpike, Exit 4,
> or Rt. 295. Call for directions. **TELEPHONE:** 856-424-1233.
> **WEBSITE:** www.discoverymuseum.com.

Monmouth Museum

This is a three-part museum, with one section a museum for adults and two sections devoted to exhibits for children. The Lower Gallery features changing exhibits in art, history, science, and nature. The Becker Children's Wing is geared toward 7- to 12-year-olds and mounts major exhibits on school subjects related to science and cultural history (such as the Western frontier) that run for two years. The third section, the WonderWing, is designed for the six-and-under set. It contains interactive play areas, including a tree house, pirate ship, whale slide, and kelp forest in an under-the-sea setting. A lot of activities are packed into a small setting. Also note that, while the Monmouth Museum is on a public college campus, it is a private institution.

> **HOURS:** Lower Gallery, Tue.–Sat., 10–4:30; Sun., 1–5. Becker Children's
> Wing, Tue.–Fri., 2–4:30; Sat., 10–4:30; Sun., 1–5. WonderWing, Fri.,
> Sat., 10–4:30; Sun., 1–5; Tue.–Thu., call for hours. **ADMISSION:** $$.
> Under 2 free. **LOCATION:** Brookdale Community College, Lincroft
> (Monmouth County). Garden State Parkway, Exit 109, then west on
> Newman Springs Road (Rt. 520). **TELEPHONE:** 732-747-2266.
> **WEBSITE:** www.monmouthmuseum.org.

Imagine That!!!

A discovery center with forty hands-on activities. Ballet/tap area, computers, art and music rooms, shadow play, VW Bug, real Piper plane. There's also a TV newsroom, a real fire truck, a grocery store, train exhibit, a post office, computer room, simulated space shuttle, science area, and a Dr./Dentist office. There are lots of crafts here, too. Food is available at an in-house cafe.

> **HOURS:** Daily, 10–5:30. **ADMISSION:** $$ for kids (under 1 free), $ for adults. **LOCATION:** 4 Vreeland Rd., Florham Park (Morris County). **TELEPHONE:** 973-966-8000. **WEBSITE:** www.imaginethatmuseum.com.

Other Children's Museums

Jersey Explorer Children's Museum: Inside an East Orange Library, this noncommercial museum is dedicated to bringing the Afro-American heritage alive for children, including older kids. **HOURS:** Open to groups only, by reservation, Tue.–Fri. Open to the public, Sat., 10–3. Includes Time-Traveler Theater, arts and crafts, interactive storytelling, and some exhibits. **ADMISSION:** $$ for adults and kids. Under 3 free. **LOCATION:** 192 Dodd St., East Orange (Essex County). **TELEPHONE:** 973-673-6900. **WEBSITE:** www.jerseyexplorer.org.

Community Children's Museum: This smaller museum features such exhibits as stepping into a painting at Van Gogh's bedroom and exploring Nancy's Lake House and John Glenn's Space Capsule. There's also a portrait studio, an electricity exhibit, art studio, homes around the world, theater area, and more. **HOURS:** Thu.–Sat., 10–5. **ADMISSION:** $. Discount: Seniors. **LOCATION:** 77 E. Blackwell St., Dover (Morris County). **TELEPHONE:** 973-366-9060. **WEBSITE:** www.communitychildrensmuseum.org.

Jersey Shore Children's Museum: A smaller museum, with sixteen exhibits, such as a TV newsroom, hospital emergency room, construction zone, car factory, post office, puppet corner, country store and more. Summer and family memberships available. **HOURS:** Mon.–Sat., 10–5; Sun., 12–5. **ADMISSION:** $$. Under 1 free. **LOCATION:** Shore Mall, 6725 Black Horse Pike (Rt. 40/322), Egg Harbor Township (Atlantic County). Garden State Parkway, Exit 36 N or 37 S. **TELEPHONE:** 609-645-7741. **WEBSITE:** www.eht.com/childrensmuseum.

SPECIALTY MUSEUMS

Yogi Berra Museum and Learning Center

Yogi Berra was not only a famous catcher for the New York Yankees and a famous manager for the New York Mets, he is just as famous for his funny sayings. This is an interesting, well-done museum that adjoins the Yogi Berra Stadium on the campus of Montclair State University. The Berra family lives in Montclair, which is a major reason that this New York baseball star is honored in New Jersey.

The museum not only has loads of memorabilia about Yogi but also lots of general baseball lore. Exhibits on the evolution of the catcher's glove and the qualities of wood and aluminum bats are typical. Plus, there are cases of trophies, World Series rings, and newspaper clippings about the Yankees and other teams, as well as a permanent exhibit on the history of the Negro Leagues.

In the 125-seat auditorium you can watch a movie about the glory days of the Yankees. The front area allows for unobstructed viewing from wheelchairs. The museum is open late on days when a baseball game is played, and you can visit the souvenir shop then, too. From a special "group" area you can overlook the outdoor stadium where both the Montclair State baseball team and the minor-league New Jersey Jackals play. If you have a kid who memorizes baseball statistics or a relative who remembers the 1961 World Series—take them here! Special programs for school and scout groups.

HOURS: Wed.–Sun., 12–5 (until 7 on N.J. Jackals game nights).
ADMISSION: $$. Discount: Students. Under 5 free.
LOCATION: 8 Quarry Rd., Little Falls (Passaic County).
North end of Montclair State campus. **TELEPHONE:** 973-655-2378.
WEBSITE: www.yogiberramuseum.org.

Golf House Museum

Set among the posh country estates of Far Hills, the Golf House, home of the United States Golf Association, includes a stately house-museum, an administration building, an interesting research lab, and a gift shop. Two floors of exhibit space include a history of the game itself, plus there are rooms devoted to golfing costumes, golf clubs, and the evolution of the golf ball.

Some of the prized mementos are the golf clubs of presidents Wilson, Franklin Roosevelt, and Eisenhower. Also on view is the Moon Club used by Alan Shepard to play on the lunar surface. Specific exhibits are also devoted to such golfing greats as Ben Hogan and Gene Sarazen and a room is devoted to Bobby Jones.

The house is currently closed while a large addition is built. To be known as the Arnold Palmer Center for Golf History, it will feature a Hall of Champions, exhibits on the USGA, and a research center. The enlarged facility is due to reopen in 2008.

LOCATION: Rt. 512, east of Rt. 202, Far Hills, Somerset County.
TELEPHONE: 908-234-2300. **WEBSITE:** www.usga.org.

Vietnam Era Educational Center

The New Jersey Vietnam Veterans Memorial is set on a green hillock only a short way from the PNC Arts Center and features a circular black wall engraved with the names of the fallen. A short distance behind it stands the Vietnam Era Educational Center, a beautifully constructed building. It is dedicated to the whole Vietnam era—not just the war. It was designed by the same firm that created the Holocaust Museum in Washington, D.C., and refurbished Ellis Island. The museum captures the tempo of the 1960s and early 1970s without taking sides in the debate of those times. It is an evenhanded presentation of the events behind the war. The history of Vietnam, the history of communism, the French colonization of Indochina, and the Japanese occupation in World War II are all covered.

A double timeline runs along the walls of the circular building. On top, there is a montage of photos of the era's culture. Scenes from 1950s and 1960s television shows, pictures of Marilyn Monroe and JFK, Elvis and the Beatles, the 1970s disco era, presidential conventions and moonshots are featured. Below that, there are pictures and text on America's growing involvement in the war: the French defeat at Dien Bien Phu, the Red Scare in this country, and the Domino Theory.

For a personal touch, there are handwritten letters to mothers, wives, and sweethearts back home—many from soldiers who never returned. Interactive TV sets allow you to call up a scene from a specific year—the murder of a Vietnamese official or a college anti-war rally. The tone of the TV narration changes over time from brisk reports to "up close and personal" views of battle scenes and burning villages. In the central theater a continuous movie shows "testaments" from various viewpoints—dog soldiers, officers, commanders. From the museum you can walk directly to the Vietnam Veterans' Memorial through a row of stately trees.

HOURS: Tue.–Sat., 10–4. **ADMISSION:** $. Discounts: Seniors, students. Under 10, veterans, and military free. Guided tours available for groups of fifteen or more. **LOCATION:** Holmdel (Monmouth County). Exit 116 on Garden State Parkway to PNC Arts Center. Follow signs. **TELEPHONE:** 732-335-0033. **WEBSITE:** www.njvvmf.org.

New Jersey State Police Museum

For mystery buffs, the exhibits in this $2 million edifice offer information about the role of the State Police as well as insights into crime detection. In fact, you'll feel like Sherlock Holmes just trying to locate the place—the museum is tucked inside the grounds of the New Jersey State Police Headquarters. At the entrance gate you will be checked in by a state trooper who will point out the way to the museum.

The museum buildings include a refurbished log cabin that once was the dormitory for state troopers. It now houses a 1930 Buick touring car, early motorcycles, and other exhibits of early transportation. You learn that the State Police was established in 1921 and that Colonel H. Norman Schwarzkopf—father of the Gulf War commander—was the first superintendent.

The main building is full of interactive exhibits and easy-to-read posters. The 911 exhibit, for instance, lets the viewer decide whether to send an incoming call to the police, fire, or medical emergency unit. Most interesting is the exhibit called "Scene of the Crime." Through a window you see a murder scene. A man is lying on the floor of a kitchen in a pool of blood. Flour is spilled on the counter. Is the dead man the owner of the premises, or is he an intruder? He was shot, but where is the murder weapon? An overhead video walks you through the preliminary investigation and the procedures for collecting and preserving evidence.

But the pièce de résistance is the exhibit on the Lindbergh case. The kidnapping of the baby son of Charles and Anne Lindbergh took place in 1932 from an estate just outside Hopewell. The State Police played a major role in the investigation. Some of the evidence used to convict Bruno Hauptmann of the crime, such as the kidnap ladder, is on display. There are also videos made from old newsreels on the trial, and you can see the baby's sleeping suit that was sent to the Lindberghs along with a ransom note. Reward posters, pictures, and memorabilia of the "trial of the century," which took place in Flemington in 1935, are here.

HOURS: Mon.–Sat., 10–4. **ADMISSION:** Free.
LOCATION: Rt. 175 (River Rd.), West Trenton (Mercer County). Near Exit 1 on Rt. 95 south. **TELEPHONE:** 609-882-2000, ext. 6400.
WEBSITE: www.njsp.org/about/museum.html.

Franklin Mineral Museum

New Jersey is both the zinc mining and fluorescent rock capital of the world. While this may not be on the same level as a financial or entertainment capital, it does provide a mecca for rock hounds: Sussex County. Here, you will find both the Franklin Mineral Museum and the Sterling Hill mine (q.v.).

Children seem to have a fascination with rocks—as any mother can attest—and they can find plenty here. The museum itself is divided into several sections: a fluorescent rock display, a general exhibit on zinc and other local minerals, exhibits of 6,000 worldwide mineral specimens, and a replica of an actual mine.

As part of the tour you are ushered into a long, narrow room where you face a row of gray, ordinary rocks behind a glass case. The guide flicks off the lights, and—lo and behold—the rocks turn into an extraordinary array of shining colors. Green, purple, red, and blue luminous rocks glow behind the glass. Next is a tour of the mine replica, which is a plaster labyrinth, filled with mock-ups of miners and ore carts. You can also check out the annex, dedicated to dinosaur footprints and Indian artifacts. At the gift shop you'll find a good selection of rocks, gemstones, and necklaces.

For many, the highlight of the trip is the chance to go prospecting in the rock dump at the back of the museum, although the possibility of finding a real specimen is slim. Check with the museum about equipment and age requirements. There is a picnic area out back as well.

HOURS: Apr.–Nov., Mon.–Fri., 10–4; Sat., 10–5; Sun., 11–5. Weekends only in March. **ADMISSION:** $$. Discount: Children. Same rate applies for mineral dump. **LOCATION:** 32 Evans St., Franklin (Sussex County). Rt. 80 to Rt. 15 to Sparta, then Rt. 517 north to Franklin. One mile north on Rt. 23. **TELEPHONE:** 973-827-3481. **WEBSITE:** www.franklinmineralmuseum.com.

American Labor Museum

Also known as the Botto House, this is a combination historic house/museum with an emphasis, for a change, on the working class. This family home of an Italian immigrant worker became a rallying place for striking union members during the 1913 Paterson silk strike. Since Haledon had a socialist mayor at the time and Paterson itself had banned group assemblies, workers gathered here to hear John Reed and Big Bill Hayward during the bitter strike.

The Botto House is a sturdy, well-built wooden structure in the center of a middle-income neighborhood. It has been restored to the era of 1903–1913 to reflect the time when Italian immigrants lived here. The kitchen, dining room, front parlor, and bedrooms reflect the lifestyle of a skilled worker of the time. The family took in boarders, grew vegetables, and lived frugally but not poorly. There is even a bocce court in the yard.

The museum section of the Botto House on the second floor offers a video and displays about the labor movement. These include photographs of the unsafe and unsanitary working conditions in turn-of-the-century factories, and the 1913 silk strike. There are also changing exhibits that emphasize more recent immigrant groups, racial problems, and other aspects of working life. Labor Day parades sometimes start or end here.

HOURS: Wed.–Sat., 1–4. **ADMISSION:** $. **LOCATION:** 83 Norwood St., Haledon (Passaic County). Call for directions.
TELEPHONE: 973-595-7953.
WEBSITE: www.geocities.com/labormuseum.

New Jersey Aviation Hall of Fame

Located on one edge of Teterboro Airport is a museum filled with aviation memorabilia with a focus on the Garden State. There are loads of model airplanes, a section devoted to women pilots, and photos of all sorts of early air machines. Hanging from the ceiling are models of satellites and astronaut uniforms. There is also a small helicopter you can try out, and a balloon basket that children can climb into. At the sixty-seat theater you watch a film on the history of aviation in New Jersey. In the tower room you can listen in on pilot-control tower conversations. There's also an X-1 rocket engine, the aircraft used by Chuck Yeager to break the sound barrier; an X-15 engine, a rocket plane that was the first aircraft in space; a 48-cylinder reciprocal engine built by Curtis Wright; and a Hindenburg display with a piece of the ill-fated airship's frame.

Outside, you can climb aboard an old-fashioned propeller plane and see how the folks in the 1940s and 1950s used to ride. (At least the seats were wider!) And behind the building, a Bell helicopter and a M.A.S.H. unit with jeeps and a truck re-create a Korean War scene. There is even a mess tent for lunch. This is a fun place for those who remember when a Sunday outing with the kids was a jaunt to the airport, and for air force veterans.

HOURS: Tue.–Sun., 10–4. Closed major holidays. **ADMISSION:** $. Discounts: Seniors, children, military. Under 5 free.
LOCATION: 400 Fred Wehran Dr., Teterboro Airport, Teterboro (Bergen County). Off Rt. 46 at the eastern edge of the airport.
TELEPHONE: 201-288-6344. **WEBSITE:** www.njahof.org.

Air Victory Museum

Set within a hangar in the South Jersey Regional Airport, this museum celebrates American air power and the technology and engineering behind it. The large collection of major aircraft on display includes an F-14A Tomcat, F-4A Phantom II, F104G Starfighter, F-86 Sabrejet, A-4 Skyhawk, and A-7B Corsair II. There are also a number of small helicopters in the hangar, such as the Bell helicopter. Small replicas of famous planes (such as the Spirit of St. Louis) as well as wooden and plastic models of a large variety of aircraft can be found throughout the museum. There is also a full display of flight suits, bombardier jackets, and other memorabilia.

The Air Victory Museum in Burlington County displays a hangar filled with aircraft, engines, and other aeronautical memorabilia. *(Photo by Patrick Sarver)*

Kids can try the Flight Trainer 150 and other interactive exhibits and visit a special area devoted to astronauts and space flight. The museum also contains a cafe and a gift shop. Outside, you can inspect a full-sized helicopter, capable of carrying fifty-five soldiers.

HOURS: Wed.–Sat., 10–4; Sun., 11–4. Closed Sun., Nov.–Mar. Check winter hours. **ADMISSION:** $. Discounts: Seniors, children. Under 4 free. **LOCATION:** South Jersey Regional Airport, 68 Stacy Haines Rd., Lumberton (Burlington County). Rt. 38, south on Ark Rd., then left on Stacy Haines Rd. **TELEPHONE:** 609-267-4488. **WEBSITE:** www.airvictorymuseum.org.

Naval Air Station Wildwood Aviation Museum

There are lots of planes here, honoring the World War II naval air training facility. Planes include an F-14 Tomcat, A-4 Skyhawk, MiG-15, Vietnam-era Huey helicopter, 1940s biplane, TBM Avenger torpedo bomber, and many others inside Hanger #1. There's also an exhibit room, orientation room with a video, and an interactive aviation technology exhibit.

HOURS: Daily, 9–4. Winter, weekdays, 8–4; weekends, 8–3. **ADMISSION:** $. Discount: Children. Under 3 free. **LOCATION:** Cape May County Airport, Rio Grande. Garden State Parkway, Exit 4 onto Rt. 47 west, left on Seashore Rd. then right on Breakwater to airport. **TELEPHONE:** 609-886-8787. **WEBSITE:** www.usnasw.org.

Millville Army Air Field Museum

This museum honors the 1,500 pilots who received advanced fighter training in P-47 Thunderbolts and P-40 Warhawk fighter planes during World War II. It displays a large collection of aviation artifacts, memorabilia, and exhibits on Millville's role in aviation history. It also hosts the Millville Wheels & Wings Airshow in late spring, featuring military jets, classic planes, and classic cars (Admission, $$$).

> **HOURS:** Tue.–Sun., 10–4. **ADMISSION:** $. **LOCATION:** Millville Airport (Cumberland County). **TELEPHONE:** 856-327-2347.
> **WEBSITES:** www.p47millville.org and www.millvilleairshow.com.

Other New Jersey Specialty Museums

New Jersey Museum of Agriculture: Part of Rutgers University's Cook College, this huge museum features early farming equipment, a seventeenth-century trading post, tractors, milk carts, plows, buggies, kitchen utensils, and displays of land-clearing in its surrounding research farm. Here you'll find everything from egg sorters to apple pickers, plus the history of New Jersey chicken and produce farms. There are also early crafts shops, such as those of a tinker, blacksmith, and carpenter. Weekend family specials once a month may include live farm animals. Lots of elementary school programs are offered during the week. **HOURS:** Tue.–Sat., 10–5. **ADMISSION:** $. Discounts: Seniors, students, children. Under 4 free. **LOCATION:** Off Rt. 1 on College Farm Rd., Cook College, New Brunswick. **TELEPHONE:** 732-249-2077. **WEBSITE:** www.agriculturemuseum.org.

Afro-American Historical Society Museum: The museum concentrates on the African-American experience in America. Exhibits include posters and mementos of the civil rights movement, pictures of athletes, quilts, a typical kitchen, and African artifacts. The collection of black dolls goes back to 1860 and numbers in the hundreds. The 4,000-square-foot exhibit space is on the second floor of Greenville Library. **HOURS:** Mon.–Sat., 10–5. Closed Sat. in summer. **ADMISSION:** Free. **LOCATION:** 1841 Kennedy Blvd., Jersey City (Hudson). **TELEPHONE:** 201-547-5262.

U.S. Bicycling Hall of Fame: The museum features bicycles, trophies, jerseys, photos, and other memorabilia of famous cyclists and mementos of the Velodrome in Newark. More than eighty significant notables have been included to date. Nearby Somerville also hosts the Tour of Somerville, the oldest bicycle race in the United States, every Memorial Day. Currently closed pending relocation. (908-393-9384; www.usbhof.com).

Snowmobile Barn Museum: With a collection of more than three hundred sleds and thousands of related collectibles, this private museum covers snowmobiling history from the early 1900s to today. There's more than just snowmobiles, including such unique snow machines as a wooden replica of a 1924 Eliason motorized toboggan and a twelve-passenger vehicle built in 1951 as a schoolbus/emergency vehicle. The museum also includes farm animals, a short nature trail, and a gift shop. **HOURS:** Sat., Sun., 10–4. **ADMISSION:** $$. Discount: Children. **LOCATION:** Dixon Rd., Fredon (Sussex County). Rt. 94 to Fairview Hill Rd., then right onto Fredon-Marksboro Rd. Take the first left on Dixon Rd. **TELEPHONE:** 973-383-1708. **WEBSITE:** www.snowmobilebarn.com.

Toms River Seaport Museum: Devoted to small-craft restoration and maritime artifacts, especially relating to Barnegat Bay, the museum is located in the 1868 Carriage House of the estate of Joseph Francis, developer of the Lifecar. The museum also includes forty indigenous watercraft, boat sheds, and a specialized library. A workshop is used for boat restoration, educational programs, and teaching maritime and boat-building skills. **HOURS:** Tue., Thu., Sat., 10–2. **ADMISSION:** Donation. **LOCATION:** Water St. & Hooper Ave., Toms River. **TELEPHONE:** 732-349-9209. **WEBSITE:** www.tomsriverseaport.com.

American Indian Heritage Museum: The Powhatan Renape Nation's museum provides an inside look at Native American culture. Visitors will learn about history, culture, and traditions from guides who gear group tours to visitors' ages. The American Indian staff interprets displays that contain tools, musical instruments, clothing, weapons, and decorative arts. You'll find large dioramas, a gallery of contemporary artwork by American Indian artists, and a Native American gift shop. Outdoors, you can explore a re-creation of a traditional woodland village, walk down nature trails, or see the live bison. There are also American Indian arts festivals here in May and October. **HOURS:** First and third Sat. of month, 10–3. Call first. **ADMISSION:** $. Discounts: Seniors, children. **LOCATION:** Rankokus Indian Reservation, Rancocas Rd., Westampton (Burlington County). I-295, Exit 45A to Rancocas Rd. **TELEPHONE:** 609-261-4747. **WEBSITE:** www.powhatan.org.

Seabrook Educational and Cultural Center: This museum explains the history of the Seabrook Company and the Japanese-Americans recruited from internment camps in 1944 during World War II. After the war, many continued on as company employees and formed the basis of the area's Japanese-American community. Exhibits depict the settlement history and community life, including a large-scale model of the village in the 1950s and photos and artifacts of life in the company village. **HOURS:** Mon.–Thu., 9–2. **LOCATION:** Upper Deerfield Twp. Municipal Bldg., 1325 Rt. 77, Seabrook (Cumberland County). **TELEPHONE:** 856-451-8393. **WEBSITE:** www.co.cumberland.nj. us/tourism/seabrook_museum.

Hungarian Heritage Center: Used as a meeting place for programs and activities for Hungarian Americans, the center includes 10,000 feet of exhibition space. Folk art and immigrant life plus special exhibitions by Hungarian artists are featured here. Upstairs is a library on Hungarian culture, including rare books. There's also a special festival in early June. **HOURS:** Tue.–Sat., 11–4, Sun., 1–4. **ADMISSION:** $. **LOCATION:** 300 Somerset St., New Brunswick. **TELEPHONE:** 732-846-5777. **WEBSITE:** www.ahfoundation.org.

Whippany Railway Museum: A small museum here exhibits railroad and ocean liner memorabilia amid a railroad yard with a restored steam loco, a railbus, and numerous passenger cars in various states of restoration. **HOURS:** Apr.–Oct., Sun., 12–4. **ADMISSION:** $. Discount: Children. **LOCATION:** Rt. 10 West at Whippany Rd., Whippany (Morris County). **TELEPHONE:** 973-887-8177. Call first. **WEBSITE:** www.whippany railwaymuseum.org.

New Jersey Firemen's Museum: This two-story museum in the New Jersey Firemen's Home features early fire engine models, tools, hats, and other memorabilia. Most notable is sizable collection of early fire vehicles, including horse and hand-pulled pumpers from the 1800s as well as early 1900s powered vehicles. The museum also hosts a Fire Apparatus Muster in late September. **HOURS:** Daily, 8–4. **ADMISSION:** Free. **LOCATION:** 565 Lathrop Ave., Boonton. **TELEPHONE:** 973-334-0024. **WEBSITE:** www.njstatefiremensrelief.com/nj_ firemens_home/museum.htm.

HISTORICAL MUSEUMS

Museum of Early Trades and Crafts

Housed in a handsome Richardson Revival building that once was the Madison Public Library, this museum serves two purposes. The refurbished building, brought back to its circa 1900 glory, with brilliant stained glass windows, bronze chandeliers, and wrought iron balcony, is an architect's delight. And it houses a major collection of tools for the thirty-four trades that existed in New Jersey in 1776 on revolving display. Some of these concern more common trades like coopering (barrel making), printing, and so forth from the colonial period onward, while others include the more specialized, such as making musical instruments.

Downstairs, the development of local craft businesses from their early origins is traced. For instance, the town funeral home is still owned by a family whose patriarch was a carpenter. He made coffins as a sideline, but when funeral parlors came into vogue, he expanded his business. Docents are on hand, and there is a children's "activity" room here.

HOURS: Tue.–Sat., 10–4; Sun., 12–5. Closed major holidays.
ADMISSION: $. Discounts: Seniors, children. Under 6 free.
LOCATION: Main Street (Rt. 124) and Green Village Rd.,
Madison (Morris County). **TELEPHONE:** 973-377-2982.
WEBSITE: www.rosenet.org/metc.

Ocean City Historical Museum

Life in the 1890s is graphically depicted in this small historical museum, which takes up one whole section of the Community Cultural Center (which also houses the library and art center). Mannequins in costumes and sections of nineteenth-century family rooms depict the heyday of the Jersey Shore when Victorian families headed for Ocean City, the quiet and sober neighbor of Atlantic City. A stained glass window and a complete exhibit are devoted to the wreck of the *Sindia,* which sank on a sandbar beyond the beach in 1901 and is forever embedded in the sand. Oriental plates and vases as well as other items and photos are on display.

HOURS: Mon.–Fri., 10–4; Sat., 11–2. Shorter winter hours.
ADMISSION: Free. **LOCATION:** 1735 Simpson Ave., Ocean City (Cape May County). **TELEPHONE:** 609-399-1801. **WEBSITE:** www.ocnjmuseum.org.

New Jersey Historical Society

In 1997 the society moved into its new home (the former Essex Club), across from Military Park and only half a block from the NJPAC (q.v.). This handsome townhouse contains three floors of exhibits about the Garden State. An extensive collection of books and manuscripts is in the library. Permanent holdings include furniture, paintings, sculpture, and an incredible number of items covering 300 years of history: music, quilting, ship making, and what-have-you.

Changing exhibits emphasize different periods or themes based on New Jersey history. The opening exhibit in the new building was called "From Sinatra to Springsteen" and traced the evolution of teenagers in the Garden State from the 1940s to the 1980s. Another exhibit followed the life of Paul Robeson, and a later one on the popular Jersey diner. Various interactive exhibits are geared for school-age children to keep them involved, but there's plenty for adults here, too.

HOURS: Tue.–Sat., 10–5. **ADMISSION:** Free. **LOCATION:** 52 Park Place, Newark. **TELEPHONE:** 973-596-8500. **WEBSITE:** www.jerseyhistory.org.

Ocean County Historical Society Museum

Located in the Pierson-Sculthorp House, the rooms of this museum are set up in comfortable nineteenth-century fashion. A music-library room with an Edison cylinder phonograph and Victor Talking Machine and a well-set Victorian dining room set the tone. The Victorian kitchen is of particular interest since it is full of useful, old-fashioned gadgets. A gizmo for softening corks had the curators mystified until a tourist told them what it was. Upstairs, the Jeffrey Child's room features a toy and doll collection. The Charles A. Morris School Room, which includes a one-room schoolhouse replica as well as a magic lantern, impresses the youngsters. Downstairs, in the basement, are museum-type exhibits covering the history of the Lakehurst Naval Air Station during the age of dirigibles as well as a diorama of the nearby Blockhouse Fight during the Revolution. Other exhibits include Revolutionary War memorabilia, fossils, Native American artifacts, and Barnegat Bay duck decoys. The Myrtle A. Moore Room is dedicated to early Ocean County industries like cranberry production, boat building, and charcoal and glass making. There are also changing exhibits during the year. The museum also contains a research library with 8,000 volumes on local history.

HOURS: Tue. & Thu., 1–3. **ADMISSION:** $. Under 12 free. **LOCATION:** 26 Hadley Ave., Toms River (Ocean County). Rt. 9 to Washington St., then four blocks to Hadley. **TELEPHONE:** 732-341-1880. **WEBSITE:** www.oceancountyhistory.org.

Hopewell Museum

This combination historic house/museum features rooms done up in particular periods as well as a number of specialty exhibits. The house itself is Victorian, built in 1877, but the rooms display Colonial, Empire, and Victorian furnishings. An 1880 organ and a Joseph Bonaparte sideboard are prized possessions here. In the back of the mansion, an addition houses a large collection of Indian artifacts and many costumed mannequins. The costumes include ball gowns, wedding dresses, and other finery worn in the nineteenth century. Upstairs, you'll find a World War I and II memorabilia room, a Hopewell Fire Department memorabilia room, a country kitchen, a glassware room, two children's rooms, a quilt exhibit, and a Civil War room. Guided tour.

HOURS: Mon., Wed., Sat., 2–5. **ADMISSION:** Free (donations accepted). **LOCATION:** 28 E. Broad St. (Rt. 518), Hopewell (Mercer County). **TELEPHONE:** 609-466-0103.

Cape May County Museum

This museum in the 1704 Robert Morris Holmes House is operated by the Cape May County Historical and Genealogical Society. The museum includes the 1704 kitchen, a pre-1820 dining room all set up, a children's room with antique toys, and much glassware and china. The Victorian Room includes a unique organ with an inlaid clock. There's a military collection from the Revolution to today, including the flag from the Civil War ironclad, the *Merrimac*. The Doctor's Room shows changes in surgical instruments from the Revolution to 1900. Across the yard, the barn features maritime and whaling exhibits; a Native American Room with an extensive arrowhead collection and other Lenni-Lenape artifacts; and a room containing a stagecoach, peddler's wagon, and a restored doctor's sulky. Here also is the original Fresnel lens from the 1847 Cape May Point Lighthouse. A Genealogy Room is of interest to many historians because of the number of Mayflower descendants in the Cape May area. There is also a gift shop in a room adjoining the house.

HOURS: June–Aug., Tue.–Sat., 10–4; Thu.–Sat. in Sept.; Sat. only, Oct.–May. Last tour at 2. **ADMISSION:** Adults, $. Discounts: Seniors, children. Under 4 free. **LOCATION:** 504 Rt. 9 North, Cape May Courthouse (Cape May County). **TELEPHONE:** 609-465-3535. **WEBSITE:** www.cmcmuseum.org.

Camden County Historical Society

Three buildings at the society's complex on the eastern edge of Camden include a museum, library, and Colonial-style mansion. The two-story Museum of County History showcases life in the region during the past three centuries. It includes early American glass, Civil War artifacts, and the tools of early handicrafts set up in "shops" of cobblers, blacksmiths, carpenters, coopers, etc. There's also a one-room schoolhouse as well as a harness and storage area for sleighs and a hand pumper from an early 1800s fire company.

Pomona Hall is an excellent example of early Georgian architecture, furnished as it would have looked when it was the home of a prominent colonial Quaker family. The guided tour will take you through many well-furnished rooms, including the plantation office, dining room set for a holiday feast, dowager's bedroom, a parlor set for tea, and kitchen, where demonstrations of open-hearth cooking are held for special events from September to May.

The library has 20,000 books and pamphlets, manuscripts, and newspapers dedicated to the history and genealogy of South Jersey and the Delaware Valley. In addition to its permanent exhibits, the society also has numerous special events throughout the year, from festivals and special tours to historical talks and art exhibits.

> **HOURS:** Wed.–Fri., 12:30–4:30; Sun., 12–5. **ADMISSION:** $. Under 16 free. **LOCATION:** 1900 Park Blvd., Camden (Camden County). **TELEPHONE:** 856-964-3333. **WEBSITE:** www.cchsnj.com.

Monmouth County Historical Association

Another combination of museum and society headquarters is housed in a three-story Georgian-style house not far from the scene of the Battle of Monmouth. Besides its permanent exhibit on the battle, the museum has an impressive collection of mahogany furniture, old china, glassware, and paintings within its historical rooms. The Discovery Room is devoted to a "hands-on experience." Here children can try on period clothes, play at carding wool, and do other colonial tasks. Temporary exhibits on all aspects of Monmouth County can be found here, from steamboats on the Shrewsbury River to Jersey shore memorabilia. The Historical Association also administers several historic houses in nearby towns, including the Allen House, Marlpit Hall, Covenhoven House, and Holmes-Hendrickson House (q.v.).

> **HOURS:** Tue.–Sat., 10–4. Call first. **ADMISSION:** $. Discounts: Seniors, children. Under 6 free. **LOCATION:** 70 Court St., Freehold. **TELEPHONE:** 732-462-1466. **WEBSITE:** www.monmouth.com/~mcha.

Other Historical Museums

Meadowlands Museum: This small museum in a 200-year-old Dutch Colonial farmhouse focuses on area history and fine arts. Permanent exhibits include the Homespun Kitchen and Pre-Electric Kitchen on the first floor. Upstairs you'll find an Antique Toy and Game Room plus a Fluorescent Mineral Room containing fossils and minerals, including fluorescents from the Franklin Mine. Changing exhibits range from quilts to art to history. **HOURS:** Mon., Wed., Sat., 1–4; Sun., 2–4. Also open Tue. & Thu. in July and Aug. **ADMISSION:** $. Discount: Children. **LOCATION:** 91 Crane Ave., Rutherford (Bergen County). **TELEPHONE:** 201-935-1175. **WEBSITE:** www.meadowlandsmuseum.org.

Fort Hancock Historic District: Until 1974 Fort Hancock on Sandy Hook served as part of the coastal defenses. The district contains

eighteen Georgian Revival officer homes and other military buildings. The remains of late 1800s concrete fortifications, used to
defend New York Harbor, have fallen into disrepair, but there are a
few scattered points where you can see them close up. Tours are
held in summer (see the park's program guide at the Visitor Center
for dates and times). Fort Hancock is also the site of the Fort Hancock Museum, where you can learn about the history of the fort,
including displays of military memorabilia. HOURS: July–Aug., daily,
1–5; Sept.–June, weekends, 1–5. History House, a restored home of
Officer's Row, can also be toured, weekends, 1–5. A brochure and
map are available at the Visitor Center. LOCATION: Sandy Hook,
Gateway National Recreation Area (Monmouth County). TELEPHONE:
732-872-5970. WEBSITE: www.nps.gov/gate/shu/shu_home.htm.

Middlesex County Museum: Set in a handsomely restored 1741 Georgian mansion (also known as the Cornelius Low House), the
museum offers changing exhibits. A one-theme exhibit (about
some aspect of the Raritan Valley, its history, or population or on a
larger aspect of New Jersey) takes up the entire house and usually
lasts a few months. Entrance is most easily attained through the
Busch Campus of Rutgers University. An interpretive path from the
back parking lot here offers a history of the local area. There's also
a small parking lot right off River Road. HOURS: Tue.–Fri. and Sun.,
1–4. Closed the last Sunday of the month. Tours at 11:30 and 1:30.
ADMISSION: Free. LOCATION: 1225 River Rd., Piscataway. TELEPHONE:
732-745-4177. WEBSITE: www.co.middlesex.nj.us/culturalheritage/
museum.asp.

Edison Memorial Tower and Museum: The tower is shaped like an
electric light with a bulb on top and commemorates the site of Edison's Menlo Park laboratory, birthplace of the practical incandes-
cent light. There is a popular story that the actual laboratory was
moved to Greenfield Village, Michigan, by Henry Ford for his Americana museum. But Curator Jack Stanley says that it had actually
fallen into ruins and that Ford created a replica. There's a model of
the lab, created from pieces of the original. For a long time the tower
itself has not been open to tourists. However, there is a small
museum adjacent to it, which is filled with lightbulbs, phonographs,
and other mementos of Edison's achievements. HOURS: Tue.–Sat.,
10–4. ADMISSION: Free. LOCATION: 37 Christie St., Menlo Park (Middlesex County). Off Rt. 27 in Edison State Park. TELEPHONE: 732-549-3299.
WEBSITE: www.menloparkmuseum.com.

Heritage Glass Museum: This museum, located in an old bank building, is dedicated to the local glassblowing industry, with blowing

tools and displays of bottles, vases, other glassware, and lots of local memorabilia. There's also a display on novelty glass. Upstairs, there's a small library on glass-related topics. **HOURS:** Sat., 11–2 and fourth Sun. of the month, 1–4. Groups by appointment. **ADMISSION:** Free. **LOCATION:** 25 E. High St. (at Center), Glassboro (Gloucester County). **TELEPHONE:** 856-881-7468.

Fort Lee Museum: The museum is at the Judge Moore House, operated by the Fort Lee Historical Society. This museum and adjacent Monument Park offer exhibits on local history, from Revolution history to Fort Lee's days as America's pre-Hollywood movie-making capital. The museum grounds served as an encampment area for Washington's troops. **HOURS:** Open weekends, 12–4. **LOCATION:** 1588 Palisade Ave. **TELEPHONE:** 201-592-3580. **WEBSITE:** www.fortleenj.org/departments/museum.html.

PLANETARIUMS

Aside from the planetariums in major museums, there are a number of places star-seeking New Jerseyans can visit for sky programs. Children under six are sometimes not admitted to programs for good reason—once those doors shut in darkness, there is no escape. Luckily, many planetariums feature special "Stars for Tots" shows. Admission fees run about $5 for adults at college sites. County college planetariums may close down when the college is not in session. Here's what is available.

Ocean County College: The Robert J. Novins Planetarium is located in Toms River on a large campus. The planetarium not only schedules public shows year-round but also has a special astronomy curriculum for school grades 1–6 during the school year. Weekend shows (Friday nights and several Saturday and Sunday viewings) are well attended. They do shut down every once in a while to prepare a new show, so call first. The planetarium holds 117 people and is quite modern. **ADMISSION:** Adults, $$. Discounts: Seniors, children. **LOCATION:** College Drive, Toms River. **TELEPHONE:** 732-255-0342. **WEBSITE:** www.ocean.edu/campus/planetarium/index.htm.

Raritan Valley College: The newest planetarium in New Jersey seats one hundred people and hosts many school shows plus two public showings on Saturdays. Special preschool shows are featured. The staff uses both the "canned" slide shows, and their own give-and-take lecture-style sky show. Nighttime laser shows are popular. There is a nice little astronomy museum before you go in. Reservations are required. It is at the top of a long set of stairs, but you can use the elevator in the adjoining building. **ADMISSION:** $. **LOCATION:** Lamington Rd. & Rt. 28, North Branch (Somerset County). **TELEPHONE:** 908-231-8805. **WEBSITE:** www.raritanval.edu/rvcc/frameset/planetarium.html.

Morris County College: This automated eighty-seat planetarium offers not only several programs to the local citizenry but also courses for those who really want to delve into the subject. Shows for school and other groups are scheduled during the week and early Saturday. Public showings take place one Saturday per month usually while the college is in session. Since they fill up, reserve beforehand. **ADMISSION:** $$. **LOCATION:** Rt. 10 & Center Grove Rd., Randolph. **TELEPHONE:** 973-328-5076. **WEBSITE:** www.ccm.edu/planetarium.

Trailside Planetarium: At the Watchung Reservation's Trailside Nature and Science Center, Mountainside (Union County) (908-789-3670). The planetarium is currently closed.

NEW YORK MUSEUMS

Metropolitan Museum of Art

This huge Beaux Arts building on New York's Fifth Avenue is still the grande dame of museums this side of the Atlantic. At one time the museum was so Old Europe centered that it admitted neither American nor "modern" art. All that has changed. With the American Wing, you get a museum and a half. The wing encompasses American furniture and decorative arts, re-created seventeenth- and eighteenth-century rooms, paintings, and sculpture. To view it chronologically you must take an elevator and start at the top, descend through the restored rooms, pass the paintings of George Washington and the Frederic Remington sculptures, and end up on the first floor with large canvases by James Whistler and John Singer Sargent.

One traditional rule of thumb at the museum is that, from the front lobby, it's Greeks and Romans to the left, Egyptians to the right, and Europeans upstairs. If you are with children you might go for the mummies and the Egyptian section. The medieval armor on the first floor is another child's favorite. The second floor houses the European paintings, which start with the medieval period. From there you wander through Italian Renaissance, Dutch masters, English portraits, and French landscapes. Other sections of the museum include Asian Arts, fashion design, New Guinea primitives, and modern art.

HOURS: Tue.–Thu., Sun., 9:30–5:30; Fri., Sat., 9:30–9.
ADMISSION: Suggested donation, $$$. Discounts: Seniors, students.

Under 12 free. **LOCATION:** 1000 Fifth Ave. at 82nd St., New York City.
TELEPHONE: 212-535-7710. **WEBSITE:** www.metmuseum.org.

American Museum of Natural History

The Rose Center for Earth and Space, a seven-floor wonder that
opened in 2000, gave this nineteenth-century museum a new
look. Its centerpiece is an 87-foot sphere that appears to hover
within a cube of glass, like the Earth in space. This sphere houses
both the planetarium upstairs and a space theater below in which
visual and audio effects simulate how the universe began. Within,
the Hall of the Universe looks like a futuristic space terminal and
the Cosmic Pathway that leads down from the planetarium is a spiral walkway that covers 13 billion years of cosmic evolution. Inside
the Rose Center is the Black Hole Theater, the Galaxies Zone, the
Star Zone, and the Planet Zone, with its 15-ton Willamette Meteor-
ite. Visitors walk through to the Hall of Planet Earth, which has all
sorts of rocks, astrophysics exhibits, videos of earthquakes, and the
usual interactive computers. The Rose Center added some such
extras as a parking garage, a huge cafeteria, and several museum
shops. Reserve your tickets to the planetarium show by phone or
Internet.

As for the main part of the museum, you might want to go to the
fourth floor to see the dinosaur collection first. The skeletons are
arranged in poses that today's scientists believe these ancient reptiles would assume. On the first floor there are gems and minerals.
A Discovery Room for children offers scientific hands-on exhibits.
The museum also hosts an IMAX theater and a butterfly conservatory in season.

> **HOURS:** Daily, 10–5:45. **ADMISSION:** Combination space show
> and museum: $$$$. Discounts: Seniors, children, members.
> **LOCATION:** Central Park West at 79th St., New York City.
> **TELEPHONE:** 212-796-5100. **WEBSITE:** www.amnh.org.

The Cloisters

High on a tree-covered bluff minutes from bustling Washington
Heights, the Cloisters are a world apart. Built in the style of a
fourteenth-century monastery, this branch of the Metropolitan
Museum displays the art and architecture of the Middle Ages in a
setting completely devoted to the twelfth to fifteenth centuries in
Europe. It includes both religious and secular art and geographical
variety. The red tile roof of the building reflects the style of southern Europe. But inside there are stones of a Romanesque chapel and
a Gothic hall complete with arched ceiling and flying buttresses.

The Cloisters gets its name from the covered walkway around an enclosed garden that was typical of a medieval monastery.

A star attraction is the Unicorn Tapestries. Remarkable in color, preservation, and realism, these panels tell a story that you read by moving from one to the other. The story of the hunt, killing, and resurrection of the Unicorn shows the life of the medieval aristocracy as well as the symbolism of the age. Other top exhibits include illuminated manuscripts and the Chalice of Antioch.

> **HOURS:** Tue.–Sun., 9:30–5:15; Nov.–Feb., 9:30–4:45.
> **ADMISSION:** Suggested donation, $$$$. Discounts: Seniors, students. Includes same-day admission to the Metropolitan Museum of Art. Under 12 free. **LOCATION:** George Washington Bridge to Henry Hudson Parkway north. Take first exit to Fort Tryon Park. Follow signs. **TELEPHONE:** 212-923-3700. **WEBSITE:** www.metmuseum.org.

Frick Collection

This little jewel of a museum, housed in a former mansion, is a must for art lovers. The European paintings and furniture display a heavy emphasis on both the Renaissance and eighteenth century. The Fragonard Room with panels painted for Madame Du Barry and the Boucher Room with panels commissioned by Madame de Pompadour have the appropriate French furniture and ambience. Medieval paintings, enamels, Rembrandts, and lots of British portraits and landscapes abound. Since this was once a home, the paintings are hung much as they would have been in the days of opulence. Gainsborough ladies and Turner landscapes decorate the comfortable halls, and a lovely inner courtyard provides an atrium for contemplation. Only the first floor is open, but this is a formidable collection, so allow at least an hour. Children under 10 are not admitted, and those under 16 must be accompanied by adults. Admission includes artphone guide.

> **HOURS:** Tue.–Sat., 10–6; Sun., 11–5. **ADMISSION:** Adults: $$$. Discounts: Seniors, students. **LOCATION:** One East 70th St. (at Fifth Ave.), New York City. **TELEPHONE:** 212-288-0700. **WEBSITE:** www.frick.org.

PENNSYLVANIA MUSEUMS

Philadelphia Museum of Art

It is a Greek temple that surveys the town and the river from an imposing height, with a magnificent flight of steps leading up to its classical columns. The steps, in fact, are as famous as the museum ever since Sylvester Stallone ran up them in the movie *Rocky*.

Inside the pillared entrance (you can avoid most of the steps by parking in the back lot), one of the best collections of art in North America awaits. Galleries of European art include the Johnson Collection on the first floor, which is heavy in Renaissance paintings. Twentieth-century art comes next and includes Marcel Duchamp's famous "Nude Descending a Staircase." There are also a medieval cloister, an Indian temple, a Chinese palace hall, and a Japanese teahouse.

Kids will find the collection of armor fascinating. And one whole wing, devoted to Americana, includes paintings and period rooms filled with Philadelphia-style bonnet-and-scroll bureaus, secretaries, and chests. There is also plenty of early silverware, urns, and other examples of decorative arts. Tours are offered by volunteer guides at no extra cost. They leave at specific times from the West Entrance hall. Downstairs, there is a pleasant restaurant, cafeteria, and gift shop.

HOURS: Tue.–Sun., 10–5; Fri. to 8:45. **ADMISSION:** $$$. Discounts: Seniors, children. Under 13 free. Sunday, pay what you want.
LOCATION: Benjamin Franklin Parkway, & 26th St., Philadelphia.
TELEPHONE: 215-763-8100. **WEBSITE:** www.philamuseum.org.

Barnes Foundation

The best collection of Impressionist and post-Impressionist paintings in America can be found in this museum, set in suburban Philadelphia. Visiting hours at this Renaissance-style mansion are somewhat limited. There's also the unusual way the pictures are hung. Paintings cover some walls and even hang over a door transom. African statues and medieval ironwork are interspersed with nineteenth- and twentieth-century art. No biographical data or dates are shown. For visitors conditioned to gallery arrangement based on geography and showing dates of the works, Dr. Barnes's ideas about presentation can require some mental adjustment. He certainly had his own ideas about art appreciation, with color and form paramount. Luckily, the names of painters and titles of paintings are available.

This said, the museum contains two floors filled with a formidable collection: more Matisses than you would expect, including a huge piece entitled "The Piano Lesson," more Renoirs than you can count, huge Navajo patterned baskets, Cezannes, El Grecos, African masks, and wood sculptures. Downstairs, you can rent audio guides or visit the gift shop. And you can visit the 13-acre arboretum that surrounds the museum. The number of visitors allowed is limited, and reservations are required.

HOURS: Sept.–June, Fri.–Sun., 9:30–5; July–Aug., Wed.–Fri., 9:30–5.
ADMISSION: $$. Audio tour costs extra. Reserved parking, $$.
LOCATION: 300 North Latch's Lane, off City Ave. (Rt. 1), Merion, PA.
TELEPHONE: 610-667-0290. **WEBSITE:** www.barnesfoundation.org.

Franklin Institute

The venerable Franklin Institute has always been a pioneer in hands-on exhibits. The museum has four main sections: Science Center, Mandell Futures Center, Fels Planetarium, and Tuttleman IMAX Theater. There are computer terminals in the halls that can answer your questions about what is where.

Science Center: This is the original museum, which still has many of its popular exhibits. There's a 36-times-life-size heart you can walk through, a steam locomotive in the basement that chugs along for 10 feet every hour, and a giant lever you can swing on. Space Command features an astronaut's suit and interactive tools of the astronauts plus a space academy. And there's a T-33 air force jet trainer you can "fly," plus lots of exhibits on physics, printing, and such.

Fels Planetarium: The 340-seat planetarium is outfitted with a state-of-the-art Digistar projection system and seamless 60-foot dome that give viewers a three-dimensional feel to their star-gazing. Special laser shows, too.

Mandell Futures Center: This brave new world is divided into several permanent exhibits with names like FutureSpace, FutureEarth, and FutureComputers. You will find such things as a fiberglass model of a human cell a million times its actual size, a computer that lets you "age" yourself, a model of a NASA space station, a 10-foot globe with fiber-optic lights to show population growth shifts, and an artificial forest and displays involving cyberspace.

Tuttleman IMAX Theater: Large reclining seats arranged in steeply angled rows face the movie screen, 79 feet across and four stories high in a hemispheric dome. This is the place for nature films that roar and soar.

3-D Theater: The Stearns Auditorium presents a changing schedule of 15-minute education films. 3-D glasses included.

The museum has underground parking and two restaurants, a huge atrium for resting (unless you want to pay extra to ride the SkyBike 28 feet above the atrium floor), and an outdoor science park (in summer). Expect to spend at least four hours here.

HOURS: Daily, 9:30–5. Closed major holidays. IMAX and planetarium, see schedule for hours. **ADMISSION:** Science and Future Centers, $$$. Discounts: Seniors, children. Under 4 free. Extra for IMAX. **LOCATION:** 20th St. and Benjamin Franklin Parkway, Philadelphia. **TELEPHONE:** 215-448-1200. **WEBSITE:** www.fi.edu.

Please Touch Museum

For younger children, this place is sure to be a hit. One of the first hands-on, interactive museums to cater to children under 8, it is also one of the most copied. It is ensconced in a multifloored space in the center of the city's museum district, directly across from the Franklin Institute.

One display is set up to re-create the city's bus system—there's even the front of a bus on the floor. There's also an outdoors "set" for boats that go down a river, a TV studio, and the standard kitchen and fruit market areas where kids can re-create grownup activities. A unique stop is the Russian nursery school for an introduction to other cultures. Another exhibit is based on Maurice Sendak's most popular books and includes a giant bed, giant mixing bowl, lots of pots and pans for creating a rumpus, as well as other scenes from the book. Alice in Wonderland is another book that is translated into interactive play elements.

During summer, you can visit Science Park, a joint venture with the Franklin Institute that is a family-centered, outdoor park with such interactive "elements" as a sky bike, Jumping Fountain, Bubbling Volcano, and so forth. Admission to the park (which is right behind the Franklin Institute) is free with admission to either museum.

HOURS: July 1–Labor Day, daily, 9–5; rest of year, 9–4:30.
ADMISSION: $$. Discount: Seniors. Under 1 free.
LOCATION: 210 North 21st St. (across from Franklin Institute), Philadelphia. **TELEPHONE:** 215-963-0667.
WEBSITE: www.pleasetouchmuseum.org.

Rosenbach Museum and Library

Located two blocks from Rittenhouse Square, this 1860s townhouse was the home of rare-book collectors. The books and furnishings of the Rosenbach brothers are at once a paean to the good life and a paradise for collectors. Since one brother searched for antiques while the other concentrated on books, the home is a treasure trove of decorative arts. It is also an important research library. Stored here are 130,000 manuscripts and 30,000 rare books, which range from medieval illuminated manuscripts to letters written by George

Washington and Abraham Lincoln. Lewis Carroll's own edition of *Alice in Wonderland* and the manuscript of James Joyce's *Ulysses* together with hundreds of first editions are shelved in what is essentially a home with beautiful and delicate furniture.

The dining room features an Empire-style table, Venetian Grand Canal scenes, and Chippendale chairs. A painting by Thomas Sully and a scrolled fireplace adorn the cozy parlor. Upstairs is the re-created Greenwich Village living room of poet Marianne Moore. Now that the museum has acquired the house next door, it has more room to display its large collection, which includes illustrations by children's book author Maurice Sendak and ancient Judaica. The annex is also used for temporary exhibits and for tour introductory lectures.

HOURS: Tue.–Sun., 10–5, Wed. until 8. Closed national holidays.
ADMISSION: $$. Discounts: Seniors, children. Under 5 free.
LOCATION: 2010 Delancey Place, Philadelphia.
TELEPHONE: 215-732-1600. **WEBSITE:** www.rosenbach.org.

Brandywine River Museum

From the front, it's a century-old gristmill; from the back it's a strikingly modern glass tower overlooking the Brandywine River. Altogether, it is a pleasant museum where the setting and structure are almost as interesting as the paintings within.

Inside, the atmosphere belongs to the Brandywine River artists (a group that formed around Howard Pyle and N. C. Wyeth) and to Wyeth's talented progeny, particularly Andrew and his son Jamie. Both Pyle and N. C. Wyeth were famous illustrators and many an older edition of *Treasure Island* or *King Arthur* contains their realistic works. They are still among the most respected painters in America. Pyle began a summer teaching center in the Brandywine Valley in 1898. The artists from this center include Maxfield Parrish, Peter Hurd, and the elder Wyeth. But Andrew Wyeth, whose painting *Christina's World* is world famous, holds the most interest for viewers. The strong emotional impact of his canvases dominates the collection. You'll find a small number of Jamie's paintings in the permanent collection, plus special exhibits that emphasize other Brandywine artists, American landscapes, and still-lifes. After viewing the exhibits, you can lunch at the cafeteria and view the meandering river and wildflower garden below. There are also trips by shuttle bus from the museum to the N. C. Wyeth house and studio and to the Kuerner Farm from April to November. Reservations are recommended. Each tour costs extra.

HOURS: Daily except Christmas, 9:30–4:30. **ADMISSION:** $$. Discounts: Seniors, children. Under 6 free. **LOCATION:** Rt. 1 (at Rt. 100), Chadds Ford, PA. **TELEPHONE:** 610-388-2700. **WEBSITE:** www.brandywinerivermuseum.org.

Note: Also see museums that are part of a larger entity, such as the Museum of American Glass (Wheaton Arts and Cultural Center) and West Point Museum (West Point).

The Classics

This evening view looking toward Lower Manhattan from atop the Empire State Building is one of several dramatic scenes that draw people to this landmark from all over the world. *(Photo by Patrick Sarver)*

Statue of Liberty

Things have changed since 9/11, but now, more than ever, you may want to take the ferry trip to this icon of freedom. These days, visitors are allowed to the top of the statue's pedestal. Bartholdi, the French sculptor who created Lady Liberty, actually assumed it would be filled with sand and admired from the exterior only. Time pass reservations are now required for visiting the inside of the monument.

New Jersey residents can embark from Liberty State Park for the short ride over. Backpacks may be searched, and you'd be well advised to take as little as possible along. After stopping at Ellis Island, the ferry gives you a view of the statue from all angles as it makes port.

Liberty Island is larger than you might expect. On its 12½ acres are administration buildings, a snack shop, a gift and souvenir shop, a pleasant tree-shaded picnic area, and walking esplanades that rim the island. As a visit to a national shrine and a pleasant day's outing, a trip to the Statue of Liberty is a must. The summer is quite busy, and so are the Christmas holidays. Check the Website for updates on access, which may be affected by security closures.

HOURS: Daily, 9:30–5; ferry, Liberty State Park, daily, 9:15–3:45; schedule expands in summer, shortens in winter.
ADMISSION: Ferry fee, adults, $$. LOCATION: Liberty State Park (take the N.J. Turnpike to Exit 14B). Parking fee if taking the ferry.
TELEPHONE: Ferry, 866-STATUE-4; Liberty State Park, 201-915-3400; Liberty Island, 212-363-3200.
WEBSITES: www.nps.gov/stli and www.statuereservations.com.

Ellis Island

If a visit to the Statue of Liberty is inspiring, a visit to its neighbor, Ellis Island, is absolutely fascinating. Since you get both islands for the same ferry price, allow enough time to explore both—up to five hours for the exhibits.

Ellis Island is a museum commemorating the peopling of America, not just those who set foot on this island (one section is for that). It is the story from the beginning, with emphasis on the late nineteenth and early twentieth centuries. A movie, shown in two theaters, recounts the experience of those who left troubled homelands to take the sea voyage to the new land.

Earlier immigration sites, greed, corruption, and the one-day processing of thousands of people are all covered in the movie as well as the displays. But there is also an amassing of hundreds of trunks, shawls, tickets, flyers, and other mementos of the immigrant experience. A play about typical immigrants is also offered.

Newspaper cartoons depict the rising tide of intolerance against the newcomers, which finally culminated in a restrictive law in 1924 ending mass migration. Ellis Island was closed in 1954. In its refurbished state it is a wonderful learning experience, and an emotional one as well for anyone who has immigrated or is descended from all those who arrived on these shores.

HOURS: 9:30–5:15, daily except Christmas. Longer hours in summer.
TELEPHONE: Ferry, 201-435-9499; Ellis Island, 212-363-3200.
WEBSITE: www.nps.gov/elis.

United Nations Headquarters

The first thing you notice as you approach the United Nations complex is the line of colorful flags half-circling the entrance. The next thing you notice is that this place is clean. In the spring, the gardens in back of the buildings sport daffodils and cherry trees, while the rose garden blossoms in June. Outside sculpture includes a gigantic abstract next to the circular fountain and the Japanese Peace Bell.

Tours of the U.N. are still popular, although now you must enter through an airport-type security system. The tours combine a short history of the United Nations with a description of the building's art and architecture. The number of chambers you enter during the tour depends on whether the various councils are meeting or not. The General Assembly, which is usually open, is a huge hall with high-domed ceiling and more than 2,000 seats. This is the hall most often seen on television.

Various member donations are also pointed out, such as a crimson Peruvian ceremonial cloak, an intricate Chinese ivory carving, and a wall mosaic based on Norman Rockwell's *The Golden Rule.* The famous Chagall stained glass mural is in the huge public lobby. The tour ends in the Public Concourse, where you can proceed to the bookstore, gift shops, or postal counter. Handicraft items from around the world, flags, and dolls of all nations are available.

HOURS: Mon.–Fri., 9:30–4:45; weekends, 10–4:30; no weekends Jan. & Feb. **ADMISSION:** Free; for tours, $$. Children under 5 not admitted on tours. **LOCATION:** 1st Ave. between 45th & 46th Sts., New York City. **TELEPHONE:** 212-963-8687. **WEBSITE:** www.un.org/tours.

Empire State Building

For those who want to view New York City from a skyscraper, the place to go is this 1931 Art Deco building. When it was first built, the

Empire State was the tallest building in the world. There is only one entrance, on Fifth Avenue, and you must go through an airport-type security check. You can purchase tickets beforehand (by phone or Website) and skip the ticket line, but everyone must go through security. You then are sent on two different elevator rides to the 86th floor (the lines can be long).

At 1,050 feet above the street, the 86th floor observatory has both an enclosed area and an open promenade. High-powered binoculars are available for a fee. You will also find a small snack bar and souvenir shops. On a clear day, you can see up to 80 miles in all directions. The view to the west offers New Jersey and the Hudson; to the north you get Midtown, Central Park, and beyond; to the east there are the U.N. and Chrysler buildings and Queens; and to the south is Lower Manhattan. The 102nd floor observatory has reopened (extra cost, $$$). Views are similar but from higher up, but through enclosed windows only.

A virtual-reality movie called New York Skyride that features a flight-simulator helicopter ride over the city can be seen on the second floor of the building (daily, 10–10; www.skyride.com.), and there is a combination ticket for the ride and the observatory. Throughout the year, concerts and art exhibits take place in the lobby, as well as holiday decorations and shows. The location is walkable from the PATH station at 33rd Street and 6th Avenue or from Penn Station.

HOURS: Daily, 8 a.m.–midnight. Until 2 A.M. in summer.
ADMISSION: $$$; combo ticket with Skyride, $$$$$. Discounts: Seniors, children. Under 6 free. **LOCATION:** 34th St. and 5th Ave., New York City. **TELEPHONE:** 212-736-3100. **WEBSITE:** www.esbnyc.com.

South Street Seaport

Boston has its Quincy Market, Baltimore has its Inner Harbor, and New York has the South Street Seaport. The "museum" (as it is called) is a restoration of eleven square blocks that were the nucleus of New York's earliest seaport. It has some of the few remaining federal-style townhouses in the big city, which have been beautifully restored and now contain shops and restaurants. At the water's edge several ships are available for touring. Tours of the lightship *Ambrose,* the four-masted barque *Peking,* and the *Wavertree* can be fascinating with the right docent. The talks really give you a feeling for the hard work, danger, and close quarters of the old ships.

A more fanciful view of the sea may be obtained from a ride on the Seaport Liberty Cruise Line, a one-hour bay cruise, or the narrated harbor cruise run by N.Y. Waterways. In warm weather you can also book a two-hour sail on the schooner *Pioneer*, where you have the chance to help raise the rigging. Ship tours and rides cost extra, of course, as does entrance to the formal exhibit galleries (the museum part of the Seaport), the Children's Center, and the guided tour of the historic area. Tickets may be purchased at the Pier 16 ticket booth or the Museum Visitor Center at 12 Fulton St.

But the main attraction at the Seaport is the food, shops, and street entertainment. Many of the early quaint shops have been replaced by high-class chains. Pier 17, a large building that juts out into the water, is just like a New Jersey mall inside. As for the Fulton Market, it has gone through many changes as a food emporium and still has not found an identity. The large plaza at Pier 16 attracts performers and musicians, both for impromptu sessions and formal entertainment—one reason that tourists love the spot. Some well-known seafood restaurants are around, and the open-air cafes also seem popular. Shops and restaurants are open daily.

HOURS: Tue–Sun., 10–6, Apr.–Oct.; Fri.–Mon., 10–5, Nov.–Mar.
ADMISSION: $$. Discounts: Seniors, students, children.
Excursion boats extra. **LOCATION:** Fulton & South Sts., just off
FDR Drive, New York City. **TELEPHONE:** Museum, 212-748-8600.
WEBSITE: www.southstseaport.org.

New York Insider Tours

Since New Yorkers are traditionally preoccupied with being "in," it is only natural that some of the most popular tours here are of the behind-the-scenes variety. **Lincoln Center,** for instance, runs escorted tours throughout its whole complex. That means you get a peek at the Vivian Beaumont Theater, the opera, and the State Theater on one ticket. Buy tickets at the Tour Desk in the downstairs concourse; there are four tours daily. Call 212-875-5350 for information and reservations. For the 1½ hour backstage tour of the Metropolitan Opera (3:45 P.M. on weekdays and 10 A.M. on Saturday) you don't have to be a phantom, but you do have to make reservations. It is highly supervised, but you get to see everything from scenery and costume rooms to a view of the Met stage from the wings and the orchestra seats. Call 212-769-7020 for registration.

NBC Television tours are also extremely popular. You get to see a few studios and hear a lot of history and inside information on how television actually works. A newer tour offers a viewing of HDTV on a 130-degree screen and a chance to "interact" with Jay Leno on a blue screen. Tours run every 15 minutes from 9:30 to 4:30 and leave from the main floor of 30 Rockefeller Plaza. Children under 6 are not permitted. Get your tickets as early as possible; better yet, reserve beforehand. Price is way up (adults, $$$$). Telephone 212-664-3700 or go to www.studioaudiences.com/tvstudios/nbcexperience.asp for information and tickets.

Sports lovers and kids will enjoy the All-Access behind-the-scenes tours of **Madison Square Garden,** which are run frequently at the 7th Avenue and 33rd Street site. The arenas, team locker rooms, and suites are covered in this one-hour tour, and you also get a look behind the scenes of the theater section. Tickets are available at the box office and online. **TELEPHONE:** 212-465-5800. **WEBSITE:** www. thegarden.com/inandaroundgarden_allaccess.html.

West Point

West Point has a beautiful view of the Hudson River, gray collegiate Gothic buildings that rise from rocky inclines, parades of cadets on Saturday mornings, and football games in the fall. The tour begins at the Visitor Center, which is several blocks outside of the actual gates (take a photo ID). The Visitor Center has plenty of interesting displays, including a mock-up of a cadet's room, a movie about army life, and a busy gift shop. Narrated bus tours leave regularly during warm weather for a 50-minute tour of the campus. Stops include the magnificent Gothic chapel, the old chapel, the Battle Monument, and Trophy Point with its great scenic views.

Also check out Olmstead Hall behind the Visitor Center. Here is the fascinating **West Point Museum,** with three floors of exhibits, models, mock-ups, and memorabilia. The decisive battles of the world are re-created here. The point of view here is military history, rather than social or political events. You'll see lots of armor and costumes, with everything from a Roman foot soldier with a bear-skin headress to a modern astronaut. Another section is devoted to West Point history and trivia. There was that incident when Benedict Arnold tried to allow the British fleet to sail up the Hudson, but did you know that James Whistler dropped out because he couldn't pass the chemistry course?

> **HOURS:** Visitor Center, daily, 9–4:45; museum, 10:30–4:15. **ADMISSION:** Fee for bus tour, otherwise, free. **LOCATION:** Palisades Parkway to Rt. 9W north to Highland Falls, NY. **TELEPHONE:** 845-938-2638; tours: 845-446-4724. **WEBSITES:** www.usma.edu/visiting.asp and www.westpointtours.com.

Independence National Historic Park

This national park in Philadelphia covers several square blocks and includes twenty-four different sites. You can drive right off I-95 and into the historic area (via Rt. 676). First stop should be the Visitor

Center on 6th Street. A thirty-minute film will give you the necessary background for your tour. Special exhibits are also on view, and sometimes costumed characters are on hand. And there are plenty of maps and brochures.

The two most important sights are the **Liberty Bell** and Independence Hall. The bell is in a large glass pavilion, with more space to read the information panels than in its previous home. A Park Service person may give a talk on the strange history of this particular icon (and how it got its crack) at specified times.

Independence Hall is shown only by a guide. Tickets are sold ahead of time at the Visitor Center, and there is a wait to pass through security. The hall is impressive, although not very large by today's standards. You can see the inkstand used by the signers of the Declaration of Independence, benches, and so forth. The guide gives a very full explanation of the events surrounding the adoption of the Declaration. There is a crush to see the hall during the heavy tourist season, so make reservations ahead for a specific time by telephone (800-967-2283) or through the Internet at http://reservations.nps.gov.

Other buildings in the historical park include Carpenters Hall, the Army-Navy Museum, Old City Hall, and several other sites of importance. All have informative displays and are worth visiting. Also see **Franklin Court** (at Market and 4th Streets). This complex includes a steel outline of the original Franklin house (which was torn down) plus an interesting underground museum. As you descend a winding ramp, you pass many displays of Benjamin Franklin's inventions and furniture, until you come to a center with interactive exhibits the kids will like, and a film about Franklin. The square outside features a replica of a colonial printing shop and an authentic old-time post office.

The new **National Constitution Center,** now part of Independence Mall, is the first museum devoted exclusively to that important national document. You start with a multimedia presentation with a live actor, then head upstairs to an extensive exhibit on the Constitution and its impact on American life and history. There is also a section where you wander through life-size bronze statues of all the delegates. **HOURS:** Daily 9:30–5, until 6 on Sat. **ADMISSION:** $$. Discounts: Seniors, students, children. Under 4 free. **TELEPHONE:** 866-917-1787. **WEBSITE:** www.constitutioncenter.org.

> **HOURS:** Some buildings may be closed in winter. Otherwise, daily, 9–5. **ADMISSION:** Free. Small charge for advance reservations.
> **TELEPHONE:** Visitor Center, 215-265-2305.
> **WEBSITE:** www.nps.gov/inde.

Betsy Ross House

While it's not a proven fact that Betsy sewed the first stars and stripes, historical evidence points in that direction. What's not in doubt, however, is that the house at 239 Arch Street is a top attraction in Philadelphia. This small red brick building with its narrow staircase is always so crowded that you have little time to glimpse the mannequins who represent Betsy and other colonial ladies busy at their needlework. In fact, the small house is almost overpowered by the adjacent gift shop. Here you can stock up on Liberty Bells, facsimiles of the Declaration of Independence, and, of course, the thirteen-star flag that Betsy is reputed to have sewn.

HOURS: Open daily, 10–5. Closed Monday, Oct.–Mar.

ADMISSION: $. Discounts: Seniors, children. Audio tour extra.

TELEPHONE: 215-686-1252. **WEBSITE:** www.betsyrosshouse.org.

Penn's Landing

When William Penn first landed at this curve of the Delaware River he envisioned a "greene, country towne." What Philadelphia developers envisioned with Penn's Landing was a recreational/educational/entertainment complex that would bring a fading waterfront district back to bloom.

Penn's Landing is a ten-block-long "district" that includes a museum, a Visitor Center, an amphiteater for small shows or fireworks watching, historic naval vessels, a pier for excursion boats, numerous restaurants, and space for more attractions in the future. Within walking distance is the South Street area of Philadelphia, which is a sort of Greenwich Village with interesting shops and lots of street traffic.

Of the vessels on the Philly side, you have a choice of different warships. The largest is the *Olympia,* which was Admiral Dewey's flagship during the Battle of Manila Bay (Spanish-American War) and is the oldest steel-sided warship in existence. The other is a World War II submarine named the *Becuna.* Both are available for self-guided tours through the **Independence Seaport Museum.** Inside are exhibits on the *Olympia,* Delaware River waterfront history, and lots of boats and interactive exhibits. A single ticket (adults, $$) includes admission to the museum and the ships outside. (215-925-5439; www.phillyseaport.org).

Penn's Landing also includes the pier for the *Spirit of Philadelphia,* an excursion boat that does lunch and dinner cruises (215-923-1419; www.spiritcitycruises.com/ph/index.jsp); the dock for the Riverlink, a ferry that crosses to the Camden waterfront; and new condos and a hotel. The Festival Pier, part of Penn's Landing, but several blocks north, has an ice-skating rink and an amphitheater for shows and fireworks. More development is expected. In the meantime, between the new amphibious "Ducks" (which take tourists around town and then plunge into the river for a waterside view), the planned water commutes, and the restaurant-ship *Moshulu*, the Delaware River is swimming with activity.

HOURS: Daily, 9–5 for museum. Vary for other attractions.
LOCATION: Columbus Blvd. and Walnut St. (parking lot).
TELEPHONE: 215-928-8801. **WEBSITE:** www.pennslandingcorp.com.

Theme Parks, Water Parks, and Amusement Parks

The Buccaneer Pirate Ship in the Pirate's Cove water park at Land of Make Believe in rural Warren County is one of many attractions that make this a popular amusement destination. *(Photo by Patrick Sarver)*

Six Flags Great Adventure

There seems to be an unwritten law for theme parks that each year there is a new and scarier thrill ride, and each year the price goes up. So what's the story with Six Flags Great Adventure, which combines a theme park with a drive-through safari? (See Animal Kingdom chapter for the safari.) There seem to be more children's rides on the one hand, and bigger and faster roller-coasters to attract the teenagers and young adults on the other. For example, there is Kingda Ka, at 456 feet the tallest and fastest coaster on Earth, and El Toro, at 188 feet high the second tallest wooden coaster in the U.S. On the other hand, there's Bugs Bunny National Park, Great Adventure's third children's area.

Great Adventure never had much of a real theme, but it is moving in that direction. Because the park is owned by Warner Brothers, one whole area is called Movietown. First came the Batman Ride (an upside down roller-coaster with decor from the second film). Then there was the Chiller, a double-track inverted coaster based on the Batman and Robin movie. A Hollywood "commissary" nearby dispenses the usual fast food. Another section is called "Midway," featuring an all-American amusement park theme. Here are the games of chance, some small rides, and "Superman, The Ride" (a gravity-defying pretzel-shaped monster of a coaster). At the other end of the park, "Frontier Adventures" has a vague Western theme. The section encompasses the Super Teepee for gifts, the Runaway Mining Train, and a barbeque palace next to the splashing log flume. The Northern Star Arena here hosts large concerts with rock and pop acts.

For those who hate thrill rides (like grandparents) there are variety shows, festivals, and the central Fort Independence arena where the dolphin show reigns. There are also tiger and other wild animal shows as well as the original carousel, a large Ferris wheel, and a few other tame entertainments that are still around. And acrobat and circus acts are usually on hand. The Grandstand at the Lake hosts fireworks (when the park is open until 10 P.M.). For young kids there is the Looney Tunes Seaport, with expanded kiddie rides and some interactive play areas.

Patrons who want spend their time on rides and not in lines have a better chance if they choose smaller, midway-style ones. And the classic wooden Rolling Thunder and the Great American Scream Machine are quicker to board than the newer Medusa, a "floorless" model with seven loops and sharp curves, and Nitro, a favorite of roller-coaster critics.

As for food, don't expect gourmet fare (although prices are up there). Veteran visitors bring picnics in their coolers and just tailgate it in the parking lot. (You are not allowed to bring food inside the park except to the designated picnic area near the Safari section.) Bring along towels—there are still flume rides that drench you! Lockers are available. And of course there are plenty of shops, drink vendors, and concession stands. Six Flags also has elongated the season with a Halloween Fright Fest that takes place in October. The rides, ghoul shows, and the atmosphere are strictly for teenagers.

> **HOURS:** Early Apr.–mid-June, call or check the Website for hours.
> Late June–Labor Day, daily, 10–10; safari, 9–4. Open weekends,
> Sept., Oct. **ADMISSION:** $$$$$$ (safari included). Discounts: Disabled,
> children 54 inches & under. Under 4 free. Parking extra. Season tickets
> available. **LOCATION:** Jackson Twp. (Ocean County). N.J. Turnpike,
> Exit 7A, then Rt. 195 to Exit 16. **TELEPHONE:** 732-928-1821.
> **WEBSITE:** www.sixflags.com.

Hurricane Harbor

In 2000 Six Flags Great Adventure opened up Hurricane Harbor, a separate water park with its own hours and prices. The entrance is on the left-hand side of the Six Flags parking lot. This place is large, and you can buy a combo ticket to both parks even though you may not be able to handle both parks in a single day,

Hurricane Harbor consists of 45 acres of wave pools, high-flying water slides, and roving rivers. Six Flags has spent a lot of money on the "look" of a tropical hideaway. One section has a theme of a shipwrecked inventor on a tropical island. For families there is Discovery Bay, a large wading pool that features a giant bucket that pours 1,000 gallons of water onto the waiting crowd below. As for the thrill seekers, the park keeps adding more multicolored, sky-high water slides each year. These include slides for passenger rafts and body surfers plus chutes for the popular enclosed rides. And the big wave pool lets everybody get into the act—it actually has some tranquil moments before the wave machine starts.

Adventure River is a long, meandering tube ride that has a bit more swirls and eddies than the usual ones. It also acts as a transportation river between one part of the park and another, so it is a way to get around without getting your feet sore. For younger kids, there are all sorts of climbing nets and water gadgets. Also there are 1,400 lounge chairs in the park for parents who are ready to flop. No outside food or drink is allowed, but bring suntan lotion, hats, towels, and swim sneakers if you have them. Changing rooms and showers are provided; lockers are extra.

HOURS: Late June–Labor Day, daily, 10–7. Weekends, Memorial Day–mid-June and until mid-Sept. **ADMISSION:** Adults, $$$$$: Discount: Children 48 inches & under. Under 4 free. **LOCATION:** See Six Flags entry for location and telephone.

Mountain Creek

In the old days, Action Park was a thrill-seeking park that appealed to teenagers and young adults. It was transformed into Mountain Creek in the 1990s, with a family orientation. Now it's back to action again with two different areas: a water park and a mountain biking park (as well as a ski area for winter sports).

At Mountain Creek Waterpark, there are more than two dozen rides, slides, and pools. Adventurous rides are emphasized, although there are moderate rides as well. The Wild River Canyons area includes the Colorado River Ride, a 1,600-foot whitewater adventure. Thunder Run and the Gauley are major whitewater tube rides. Adventure Ridge features the Vortex and Vertigo tube speed coasters in the dark. And then there's the H2-Oh-No!, a speed slide that drops you down 99 feet in mere seconds, and High Anxiety, a two-to four-passenger tube ride that drops you down four stories.

Moderate rides include an area called Kids World, featuring the Spraygrounds, an interactive water play fort, the relaxing Lost Island River, and, of course, a wading pool. Elsewhere, there are rubber tube rides that twist and turn, straight slides that jackknife you into the water, closed chute rides, and the Tarzan Swing water hole, where you just jump in from a swinging rope. The High Tide wave pool is comparatively tame except when it gets overcrowded, and there's a beach club above it for sunset drinks.

Diablo FreeRide Park is a separate area for mountain biking, with forty downhill trails. You take the same gondola to the top of the mountain like skiers, only you go down on a bike. The trails travel mostly in the wooded areas between the ski runs. Lessons and rentals are available. **HOURS:** Daily, July–Labor Day. **ADMISSION:** $$$$$. Weekends, mid-May–June and Sept.–Oct. **TELEPHONE:** 973-209-3388. **WEBSITE:** www.diablofreeridepark.com.

HOURS: Varies for water park and mountain biking. Call.
ADMISSION: Waterpark, people 48 inches & taller, $$$$$.
Discounts: Seniors, children 48 inches and under. Under 3 free.
LOCATION: Rt. 94, Vernon (Sussex County). Rt. 80 to Rt. 23 north to Rt. 94; go north for 4 miles. **TELEPHONE:** 973-827-2000.
WEBSITE: Water park, www.mountaincreekwaterpark.com.

Clementon Park

Set on 40 acres about 12 miles southeast of Camden, this venerable amusement park established in 1907 has rides that range from an old-fashioned carousel to a large log flume for families. Newer rides include the Thunderbolt, Sea Dragon, Chaos, Chance Inverter, Samba Tower, and Turtle Whirl. There is an interactive playport for kids, plus traditional kiddie rides. More relaxing rides include the Clementon Belle mini-steamboat, the C. P. Huntington Train, and the ten-story Giant Ferris Wheel. The biggest ride by far, though, is the new J-2 wooden roller-coaster, one of the largest in the state.

Splash World, a 13-acre water park alongside the amusement park, has a separate entry, so you can enter it alone or buy combination tickets. Splashworld includes a Pirate Ship, set in a 10,000-square-foot pool for the little ones. Caribbean Cove is a 5,000-square-foot activity area for kids, including new pint-sized slides. For the more adventurous, there are the 700-foot enclosed chutes of the Black Viper or the Sky River Rapids, with their three sets of water slides and three splash pools. Besides the other curling and straight slides, one can always find the level 1,200-foot Endless River, a tube ride that eddies through scenic waterfalls and rock formations. Changing rooms, showers, and lockers available.

> **HOURS:** Late May–June, Thu.–Sun., 12–9; June, Thu.–Sun., 12–10 (Splashworld, 12–8); July–Labor Day, daily, 12–10 (Splashworld, 12–8). Times vary in May, June, and late Aug. Closed occasionally for private parties. Check seasonal schedule on the Website.
> **ADMISSION:** Combination pass, $$$$$. Individual parks, $$$$; after 5, $$$. Free parking. Discount: Children under 46 inches tall. Under 36 inches free. **LOCATION:** 144 Berlin Rd. (Rt. 534) off Rts. 30 or 42, Clementon (Camden County). **TELEPHONE:** 856-783-0263. **WEBSITE:** www.clementonpark.com.

Land of Make Believe

For years this was a simple, down-home amusement park, set in rural Warren County, next to Jenny Jump State Park. It catered to children under 12 at a time when most parks were geared toward teenagers. There were a few mechanical rides and a miniature train ride, as well as such simple attractions as a talking scarecrow, a haunted house with a few scary exhibits, and an old-fashioned hayride.

The park is now more than a half-century old and encompasses 30 acres. Every year, Chris Maier, who took over from his father, adds bigger and new attractions. He has also expanded the range of activities. There are two sections: the water park and the amusement rides, but the place is small enough that you can easily do both in a day. And many of the dry rides are definitely for the younger kids.

The Pirate's Cove water park includes a lazy river ride and several midsized water slides. There is a giant wading pool for youngsters, with a life-sized pirate ship in the middle. This one squirts water and has a simple slide. Parents can sit on lounge chairs around the pool and watch. The river tube ride can be used by children and parents alike and is fairly mild. A covered water slide called the Black Hole is geared to older kids (you must be at least 8 years old to use it), while other new water slides like Pirate's Plunge and Pirate's Cannonball seem geared to the faster crowd. Lockers and changing rooms are available.

On the amusement park side there is a carousel, Frog Hopper, Tilt-A-Whirl, miniature train ride, hayride, and a number of small kiddie rides. There is a trend to newer, faster coasters, although not the gigantic types you find in the large parks. Still, many young children prefer putting on costumes and becoming part of the show at the Middle Earth Theater, or going to simple attractions like the petting zoo and the maze. The park still offers free parking and a picnic area plus the usual hamburger, ice cream, and concession stands.

HOURS: Mid-June–Labor Day, daily, 10–6. Call for May, Sept. hours. **ADMISSION:** Children, $$$$; adults, $$$$. **LOCATION:** Rt. 80, Exit 12. Two miles south to Hope (Warren County), then follow signs. **TELEPHONE:** 908-459-9000. **WEBSITE:** www.lomb.com.

Wild West City

This northern New Jersey version of a Western "Dodge City" comes complete with marshal, cowboys, the Sundance Kid, shootouts, and a posse of kids. Run by the Stabile family for many years, it is still going strong. On a dusty street flanked by stores and a blacksmith shop, you can lean on the hitching post and watch cowboys twirl ropes and go through a series of lasso tricks. But the big deal of the day is when the bad guys rob the bank or the stagecoach on its way down Main Street. The sheriff "deputizes" all the kids to help round up the villains. Once the bad guys are caught, will they be strung up from the nearest tree? Not if these actors are expected to show up for the next go-round of cowboy activities!

For the last few years, the management has added more educational shows, such as a frontier cooking demonstration, Native American dances, mountain men get-togethers, and other nonviolent, politically correct events. However, the main theme here is the Wild West as it was imagined in dime novels and by Hollywood.

The Golden Nugget saloon offers food, but it also has some simple shows inside at scheduled times. There are two other eateries, and many of the stores along the street sell real Western goods and plenty of toy guns. There are others that display relics of the Old West, such as an old-time barber shop, a working blacksmith shop, and a real jail cell. You can take an authentic stagecoach ride down the main street or the miniature train ride that circles the town (extra fee for these). And don't be surprised if there's a hold-up on the way. You can also "pan" for gold or visit the petting zoo or the chuck wagon. Picnicking allowed in a shady grove off the main street, but pizza and other snacks are also available. Miniature golf and pony rides are extra.

> **HOURS:** Mid-June–Labor Day, daily, 10:30–6. Shows start at 11.
> Open weekends, May to Columbus Day. **ADMISSION:** Adults, $$;
> kids, $$. **LOCATION:** I-80 to Rt. 206 north (exit 25) to 50 Lackawanna
> Dr., Netcong (Sussex County). **TELEPHONE:** 973-347-8900.
> **WEBSITE:** www.wildwestcity.com.

OTHER AMUSEMENT PARKS

Blackbeard's Cave: This recreation park south of Toms River includes a variety of activities, from a miniature golf course and bumper boats that travel through caves to batting cages and a driving range. For small kids, there's the Adventure Station, a park with numerous kiddie rides and activities, including a mini-Ferris wheel, a mini-coaster, and a mini-train ride. Older kids have an archery range, Water Wars (water balloons), and a quarter-mile Formula 1 Go-Kart track. An unusual form of jousting and Splatter Zone (a paintball arena) are also on hand, as well as an arcade and restaurant. **HOURS:** May–Oct., daily, 10 a.m.–midnight; hours vary rest of year. **ADMISSION:** Pay per ride. **LOCATION:** 136 Rt. 9, Bayville (Ocean County). **TELEPHONE:** 732-286-4414. **WEBSITE:** www.blackbeardscave. com.

Bowcraft Amusement Park: Set down alongside busy Rt. 22 in urban Union County, this small park has been modernizing over the years. It includes a swing carousel, a miniature train ride, and several other kiddie rides such as a minicoaster, bumper cars, Tilt-a-Whirl, and Frog Hopper. A video arcade and game room keep older kids busy. With a larger coaster and a flume ride, the trend here is to provide more for younger teens. Fast food is available. Free parking and admission—you pay per ride. Convenient for area people who don't have to battle beach traffic to get here. **HOURS:** June–Aug., daily 10–9; weekends, Apr.–May and Sept.–Oct. **LOCATION:** 2545 Rt. 22 West, Scotch Plains (Union County). **TELEPHONE:** 908-233-0675. **WEBSITE:** www.bowcraft.com.

Storybookland: This well-known children's park has small structures in the shape of the Gingerbread House, the Old Woman's Shoe, Noah's Ark, etc. The petting zoo, miniature train ride, antique car ride, and numerous kids' rides are included in the admission price. It was built for the summer crowd, but now special events also include a Halloween event, and a large, popular Christmas light display from mid-November to Christmas. Picnic area, snack bar. Ten miles west of Atlantic City. **HOURS:** July–early Sept., 10–5:30; shorter hours, spring and fall. Special afternoon and evening Christmas hours. **ADMISSION:** Children & adults, $$$$. Under 1 free. **LOCATION:** 6415 Black Horse Pike (Rt. 40/322), Egg Harbor Twp. (Atlantic County). **TELEPHONE:** 609-641-7847. **WEBSITE:** www.storybookland.com.

Tomahawk Lake: This old-fashioned family picnic lake, with tables, ice-cream stand, hamburgers, and catering facilities for groups is combined with a new-fashioned kiddie water park, making for an interesting combination. The setting is an 18-acre freshwater lake with sandy beach. The low admission fee includes parking, lake use, and a tot-sized water world. Several larger water slides, the bumper boats, and miniature golf are available for an extra fee. There is also an area for those who simply want to swim. **HOURS:** Memorial Day–mid-June, weekends only; mid-June–Labor Day, daily. **ADMISSION:** Adults, $$. **LOCATION:** Tomahawk Trail (off Rt. 15) Sparta (Sussex County). **TELEPHONE:** 973-478-7490. **WEBSITE:** www.tomahawklake.com.

The Funplex: There are actually two locations, one in East Hanover and another in Mount Laurel. Both are similar, with a few more activities at the Mount Laurel location. There's an arcade, laser tag, motion simulator, bumper cars, electric go-karts, a small Ferris wheel, bumper boat ride, miniature golf, batting cages, outdoor go-karts, and the like. Both sites are very geared to parties for youngsters. **HOURS:** Daily, 10–7. Until 10 on Fri. **ADMISSION:** Pay per ride or a variety of wristband packages. **LOCATION:** 3320–24 Rt. 38, Mount Laurel (Burlington County) and 182 Rt. 10 West, East Hanover (Essex County). **TELEPHONE:** 856-273-9666 and 973-428-1166. **WEBSITE:** www.thefunplex.com.

BOARDWALK AMUSEMENTS

There are small arcades, video game rooms, and miniature golf places all up and down the Jersey Shore. The major amusement centers are concentrated at the boardwalks in a few towns. Although they could use more bathrooms, and sometimes you'll find bubble-gum stuck on the boards, these are fun places to visit. The larger amusement piers have become more sophisticated over the years. Rides seem to be larger each year, and now there are huge roller-coasters, swinging pirate ships, and taller rides than ever.

Many boardwalks now offer water parks that can compete with theme parks. They also have plenty of lifeguards around. You'll find lazy river rides for kids (and lazy adults), slides that are partially or fully enclosed (to give you a scarier feeling), slides with mats, and slides where the only cushion on the water is your backside. The only difference from large theme parks is that the rides have been compressed into a smaller space.

At boardwalk amusements you generally pay per ride. With the water park you usually buy a bracelet that allows you a certain number of hours. Often there are specials on less-crowded weekdays. Amusement rides aren't the only boardwalk experience, of course. There is always cotton candy, saltwater taffy, pizza slices, soft ice cream, games of chance, and lots of T-shirts. Starting from the north, here is a list of major amusement parks.

Keansburg: This is an older area that has been resurrected with new rides. The boardwalk runs about four or five blocks and includes plenty of kiddie rides, plus several arcades and a growing number of adult rides, such as the 100-foot-high Double Shot and the Wildcat coaster. There are also concessions and an arcade.

Across from the amusement area is a block-long water park called **Runaway Rapids** that definitely gives class to the area with its large water chutes and slides. A high-speed slide and double-wide slides for tubes make the 12-year-olds happy. A new corkscrew slide puts a new twist on the downhill motion. The park also advertises a huge hot tub. A lazy river ride and a kiddie pool with giant bucket and lounge chairs for parents offer an alternative to the slides. You buy bracelets for two- or three-hour sessions. Grandmas can buy a "dry" spectator bracelet at half price. **LOCATION:** Garden State Parkway to Exit 117, then Rt. 36 to Laurel Ave. Open seasonally, beginning in late March. **TELEPHONE:** 732-495-1400. **WEBSITE:** www.keansburgamusementpark.com.

Point Pleasant Beach: Jenkinson's Amusements at 300 Ocean Ave. dominates the boardwalk here, featuring four indoor arcades and three miniature golf courses for the family crowd. The amusement ride section includes around thirty rides, with half strictly for the kiddies. The adult rides vary but none are overwhelming. The rides are mostly midsize, for both kids and adults, and they cover several blocks. A large food pavilion that juts out onto the beach has everything from a fast food buffet to sit-down service plus a very active bar.

On the northern end of the amusement area, Jenkinson's Aquarium (q.v.) is open year-round and offers something for rainy days. Special events, such as fireworks and concerts, take place on the beach, usually Wednesday or Thursday nights. **LOCATION:** Garden State Parkway to Exit 98 south to Rt. 34 south to Rt. 35. **TELEPHONE:** 732-892-0600. **WEBSITE:** www.Jenkinsons.com.

Seaside Heights: New Jersey's version of Coney Island has one of the largest boardwalk amusement centers, with lots of amusements and concessions along the boardwalk and the piers. The beaches are free on Wednesday and Thursday, and weekly fireworks go off on Thursday nights.

The **Casino Pier** features forty rides, including many large ones like the Ferris wheel, Skyscraper, and the Pirate Ship, plus an assortment of bumper cars, a log flume, and kiddie rides as well as a Haunted House ride. The indoor section features an authentic 1910 American-made wooden carousel. Along the quay are numerous indoor arcades, such as Coin Castle, that include air hockey games and food stands along with the usual Skeeball and video games. Rides are active all day. **LOCATION:** 800 Boardwalk. **TELEPHONE:** 732-793-6488. **WEBSITE:** www.casinopiernj.com. Just north of the pier is a half-mile long skyride (fee, $) that takes you to the far northern end of the boardwalk.

Across from Casino Pier is **Jenkinson's Breakwater Beach.** This is a full-sized water park that offers water slides, Patriots Plunge, Krazy Krick, the Cannonball, and an interactive children's play area called the Perfect Storm. **ADMISSION:** $$$$. 3-hour and twilight admissions are less. Discount: Children (under 42 inches) and seniors. **LOCATION:** 800 Ocean Terrace. **TELEPHONE:** 732-793-6488. **WEBSITE:** www.casinopiernj.com/breakwaterbeach.

About a mile down the boardwalk is **Funtown Pier.** Rides here include the Tower of Fear and a looping coaster that join the old Giant Wheel on the pier. All together there are more than forty rides and attractions, and special all-day (12–6 P.M.) prices on summer weekdays. **LOCATION:** 1930 Boardwalk, Seaside Park. **TELEPHONE:** 732-830-7437. **WEBSITE:** www.funtownpier.com.

LOCATION: Garden State Parkway to Exit 82 to Rt. 37 east through Toms River to bridge; keep left for Seaside Heights. **WEBSITE:** www.seasideheightstourism.com.

Beach Haven: A small cluster of amusements caters to families on Long Beach Island. On the square block at Bay and Taylor Avenues, you'll find **Thundering Surf,** which is a combination of six curling water slides, the Crazy Lazy River, and a small kids area called Squirtworks. Next to it is Settler's Mill, a fancy miniature golf complex complete with waterfall (609-492-0869; www.thunderingsurf waterpark.com). A block away, at 7th Street, there is the Victorian-themed **Fantasy Island,** which includes a small coaster, kiddie rides, Ferris wheel, carousel, arcades, and an old-fashioned ice-cream parlor. The most adventurous ride here is Max Flight, a flight simulator that rotates 360 degrees in all directions (609-492-4000; www.fantasyislandpark.com).

Atlantic City: Directly across from Trump's Taj Mahal (Virginia & Boardwalk) is the **Steel Pier,** which is open during the warm-weather season (609-345-4893; www.steelpier.com). Coasters, flume ride, go-karts, Ferris wheel, carousel, a roller-coaster with spinning cars, and many kiddie rides combine with cotton candy, hot dogs, and sporadic thrill shows (such as high-wire walking) from time to time. There's also a real helicopter ride (admission, $$$$$) at the end of the pier.

The venerable **Central Pier** (1400 Boardwalk) looks a little worn but hosts a large video arcade, go-karts, and Shoot the Geek paintball. And across from the centrally located, newly renovated Boardwalk Hall, you'll find a landscaped miniature golf course that overlooks the ocean (609-347-1661). There's a memorial pavilion and gazebo for concerts here also. Most casino hotels keep at least one video arcade room available for their guests' children and outsiders.

Ocean City: The piers here are a little different: they are actually on the inland side of the boardwalk. A giant Ferris wheel dominates the skyline at **Gillian's Wonderland Pier** (Boardwalk & 6th; 609-399-708; www.gillians.com). This amusement park has a few adult rides, such as a log flume and a small coaster, but the majority are for the smaller set. There's also an indoor area with monorail and kiddie rides for inclement weather. **Playland's Castaway Cove** (Boardwalk & 10th; 609-399-4751; www.boardwalkfun.com) offers arcade games and more than thirty rides, mostly for younger children, but there is a flume ride and a paintball gallery. **Gillian's Island Waterpark**

Gillian's Wonderland Pier in Ocean City is one of the many popular boardwalk amusement piers in a number of Jersey Shore towns. *(Photo by Patrick Sarver)*

(Boardwalk at Plymouth Place) has a wide range of water slides and other standard waterplay activities packed into a seemingly small space. And at Playland's Pier 9 (Boardwalk and 9th), there is a go-kart track under the boardwalk.

The 2-mile boardwalk here also includes a movie theater, karaoke parlor, several restaurants, and the usual beach stores and ice cream stands. The more sedate Music Pier provides popular concerts and shows for the family crowd. There are a record number of miniature golf courses in this town (www.oceancitynj.com).

Wildwood: The boardwalk stretches almost 2 miles from North Wildwood through Wildwood itself. It includes games of chance, arcades, food stands, and T-shirt and souvenir shops. A tram ride goes up and down the boardwalk for those who get tired. Start with **Morey's Surfside Pier** (Boardwalk & 25th St., N. Wildwood) at the northern end. It's the most visible of the Morey Organization's three piers because of the really high AtmosFear and Condor rides. This pier offers all sorts of thrill rides and amusements, including the Great Nor'Easter, a looping, twisting coaster in which you ride suspended; a double log flume; and the Doo Wopper coaster with spinning cars. There are go-karts, too, as there are on all the Morey piers. There's also a complete water park (OceanOasis) at the end of the pier. It includes a kids' area with a dumping water bucket, an endless river, and plenty of turning, twisting waterslides. Parents can watch while hanging out at the beach club area.

The middle pier, **Mariner's Landing** (Boardwalk & Schellenger), includes a Raging Waters park with water slides, raft run, endless river, activity pool, and other water fun for kids. The awesome coiling Sea Serpent coaster highlights dozens of thrill rides and smaller rides that are all packed onto this pier.

The **Adventure Pier** (Boardwalk & Spencer) has the fewest rides, but these include notable ones, such as the Great White, a 110-foot-high wooden coaster, one of the largest on the East Coast. Or you can get a different perspective—upside down—on the Inverter. Or be flung into the sky on the Spring Shot. There are a dozen other rides here as well. **HOURS:** The piers are open on weekends in late March and run until early October. Open daily in summer. **ADMISSION:** Pay as you go with tickets or get passes for rides on all 3 piers (fee, $$$$$$), a waterparks-only pass, or a combination pass. **TELEPHONE:** 609-522-3900. **WEBSITE:** www.moreyspiers.com.

Across the boardwalk from Mariner's Landing is a separate water park, **Splash Zone**. It has speed slides and chutes, body flumes, giant water blasters, and a big raft ride as well as a shaded wading pool and a lazy river. Hurricane Island is an interactive play area with blasters, sprays, and other fun stuff. **ADMISSION:** $$$$. Other limited-time rates available. **TELEPHONE:** 609-729-5600. **WEBSITE:** www.splashzonewaterpark.com.

For general information, check out the town's Website: www.the-wildwoods.com.

OUT OF STATE

Sesame Place

When Sesame Place first opened, it was the first activity park devoted directly to the younger set. Children from 3 to 13 were supposed to stretch their minds and muscles in a series of innovative "play concepts," such as swimming in thousands of plastic balls and climbing up cargo netting. While these activities still exist, the park is now more commercially oriented, with enough grown-up rides to interest the rest of the family. A mild roller-coaster called "Vapor Trail" is designed for a kid's first coaster experience.

As for the water rides—they come in large and small sizes. There's Big Bird's Rambling River, a level waterway for rubber tubing. Ernie's Waterworks is a mix of fountains and water-spraying mazes. The larger water rides are exactly like the ones at the Jersey Shore—metal structures where you chute down on a cushion of water. Some twist and turn, some are partially enclosed, and some are straight down; you end up in a small pool of water all the same. The lines are long, but they move in an orderly fashion. There is also a simple fountain in the center of the park where everybody can just jump around and get wet. Lockers are available for a fee as well as changing rooms.

For landlubbers, there are shows: one features bird or animal acts; another is a song-and-dance revue starring Bert, Ernie, Elmo, and company. Every afternoon a musical parade by costumed characters rocks down Sesame Street. There are a few eateries—but expect lines. You can no longer bring picnics into the park. When is the best time to visit Sesame Place? Because season tickets are bought by nearby families and daycare buses come in droves on weekdays, this park is often crowded. Try early morning and late afternoon.

HOURS: June–Aug., daily, 10–8; May, Fri.–Sun., 10–5; Sept.–Oct., weekends, 10–5. **ADMISSION:** $$$$$$. Under 2 free. Parking fee. **LOCATION:** Rt. 1 south through Trenton to Oxford Valley Mall, Langhorne, PA. Turn right at New Oxford Valley Rd. just before the mall. **TELEPHONE:** 215-752-7070. **WEBSITE:** www.sesameplace.com.

Dorney Park and Wildwater Kingdom

When Cedar Faire bought Dorney Park in 1992 they started souping it up with new rides and attractions. There's now a 200-foot-high megacoaster called "Steel Force" and a huge Dominator that drops you down twin towers. Every year there have been more thrill rides, such as the green, double-looping Laser, and Talon, the tallest inverted coaster in the region.

For nostalgia buffs, Thunderhawk is an old-fashioned wooden coaster left over from Dorney's old days. A replica steam engine train takes passengers around the park, and the Center Stage features acts and song-and-dance revues. There's also Camp Snoopy, which includes costumed characters, easy rides, and some interactive play elements.

The other side of Dorney park is Wildwater Kingdom, a popular water park with almost twenty rides, including water slides of all variations. You will find looping, speeding inner tube and kiddie water slides here. The taller rides include the Aquablast, which features a raft for four or six people that hurtles down a slide. The giant wave pool has two sections: one for those who ride plastic surfboards and mattresses and one for those who stand and jump. The park does provide plastic sun chairs and lounges so parents can sit and sun while their offspring surf and slide. Locker rooms and showers are available, as are surfboard rentals.

HOURS: Daily, 10–10, full season. Shorter hours May to mid-June & Sept.–Oct. **ADMISSION:** Combo ticket, adults, $$$$$$. Discounts: Seniors, children 3 and older to 48 inches tall. Under 3 free. Season ticket available. Parking extra. **LOCATION:** 3830 Dorney Park Rd., Allentown, PA. Rt. 78 past Allentown to Exit 16B. **TELEPHONE:** 610-395-3724; 800-551-5656. **WEBSITE:** www.dorneypark.com.

OTHER OUT-OF-STATE AMUSEMENT PARK

Camelbeach Waterpark

The Camelback Ski area in the Poconos is transformed each summer into a water park, complete with a wave pool and plenty of water slides. The Titan, which parallels the mountain, is eight stories tall and 819 feet long, a world's record. There are also lazy river tube rides, a swimming pool for grownups, bumper boats, miniature golf, and a "skyride" (the ski lift) for a scenic view.

HOURS: Memorial–Labor Day: daily, 10–7. Closes at 6 until mid-June. **ADMISSION:** Adults, $$$$$$. Discounts: Seniors, children. Under 2 free. **LOCATION:** Tannersville, PA (off Rt. 80). **TELEPHONE:** 570-629-1661. **WEBSITE:** www.camelbeach.com.

The Jersey Shore

Beaches up and down the coast offer fun in the sun and surf all along the Jersey Shore. *(Photo by Patrick Sarver)*

There are 127 miles of beach along the coast of New Jersey, offering swimming, boating, and fishing. But for most people, going to the shore means visiting one particular portion of that coastline. Here's a quick look at the various types of shore resorts that await the newcomer or old-timer.

First of all, there are the beaches. Some are narrow and some are wide, but few are free except off-season. Sandy Hook (run by the U.S. Park Service) charges a parking fee during season but can become crowded nevertheless. Atlantic City and the beaches of the Wildwoods are free. Island Beach State Park charges a per-car admission. Most other beaches require beach badges (which you buy at the beach or town hall) or admission through a private bathhouse. The price of badges varies depending on whether you buy per day, week, or season. If you stay at a hotel that owns its own beachfront, you don't have to bother with all this. Guest houses and motels usually provide beach tags to clients. There are a few select beaches that are accessible to club members only. No matter where you go in the summer, parking can be hard to find, and none too cheap in many towns.

Cottage and beach-house rentals vary according to size, closeness to beach, and the social status of the town. Guest houses remain the cheapest accommodation, especially if you don't mind walking a few blocks to the beach. Bed & Breakfasts charge more than motels but offer much more charm. Most motels offer efficiency apartments for those who want to cook in. Motel rates compare well to other beach areas along the Atlantic Coast. Major amusement areas are found at Point Pleasant, Ocean City, Seaside Heights, and Wildwood. Otherwise, arcades and miniature golf are in close proximity to beachgoers, even in towns where boardwalks are noncommercial.

THE UPPER SHORE

Sandy Hook to Island Beach State Park

The closest and most accessible to the urban and suburban areas of northern New Jersey, the upper shore is naturally very popular for daytime and weekend trips as well as vacations. Sandy Hook is part of the Gateway National Recreation Area and is run by the National Park Service. The beach is free, but there are parking fees mid-June to Labor Day. Sandy Hook also offers the oldest lighthouse in the United States, a nature center, Visitor Center, tours of Fort Hancock, and surf fishing.

Below Sandy Hook begins a string of beachfront communities, each with a slightly different personality. Some, like Belmar and Manasquan, cater to a young, singles crowd who share cottages and guest houses. Others, like Deal, are quiet and rich and interested primarily in full-time residents and full-summer rentals. (It does have one admission-free beach, though.) Avon, with its lovely hotels and guest houses, has a pleasant, tasteful boardwalk. Long Branch has a spa-hotel, a public beach called Seven Presidents Park (small admission fee), lots of new high-rise condos, and an upscale shopping and dining area with a beachfront promenade called Pier Village.

Asbury Park is an older resort that's a faded remnant of its former self. It is best known for its rock clubs, including the Stone Pony, where Bruce Springsteen began his career. The boardwalk is practically deserted, although a renaissance always seems to be just over the horizon. Separated from Asbury by a canal, Ocean Grove is quiet, reserved, and has lots of Victorian homes as well as a well-known auditorium. These turn-of-the-century houses remain from the early religious camp meeting days.

To the south is the so-called Irish Riviera, towns from Bradley Beach and Avon to Belmar, Sea Girt, and Manasquan, where many of North Jersey's Irish traditionally spent their summers in years past. You can find Spring Lake here, with its turreted late-Victorian homes.

Farther south is Point Pleasant and Point Pleasant Beach, towns with a large fishing fleet and residential areas, including an increasing number of condos. Summer rentals, popular boardwalk amusements, and several marinas keep this area bustling. Lots of seafood restaurants are here, also. Point Pleasant has a classical concert on summer Wednesday nights and fireworks on certain nights, too. But for the young single crowd, Jenks nightclub on the boardwalk is the place to be.

From Bay Head south to Ortley Beach, things get pretty residential—almost suburbia-by-the-sea. Things get more down to earth by the time you reach Seaside Heights, Seaside Park, and Dover Township. There are hundreds of guest cottages here, some of them minimal-comfort types with just two rooms and a couple of screened windows. Almost one hundred motels also service the many vacationers who come to this popular area, with its large amusement center. Island Beach State Park at the southern end of this long peninsula has pristine beaches that draw many daytime visitors (the park often closes its gates on summer weekends when the lots get full).

Long Beach Island

For many middle-executive families the place to go is Long Beach Island, only an hour and a half or so from North Jersey's affluent suburbs and an hour from Cherry Hill. A long, narrow strip of beach that extends from Barnegat Light to Holgate, the island is a series of little towns connected to the mainland by the Rt. 72 bridge, the only access. You will find lots of beach houses from the simple to those featured in design magazines, as well as a few motels. Since most people rent beach homes or apartments for at least two weeks, not to mention all the second homes, there is an air of leisure and permanence about Long Beach Island.

Courses in art photography, yoga, and such are offered at both the Foundation of Arts and Sciences and at St. Francis Center in

Beach Haven. The Surflight dinner theater assures visitors there's more to summer life than basking on the beach. An amusement area and boutique shopping center also attract both teenagers and families with kids.

Of course, a trip to Long Beach Island would not be complete without a visit to Barnegat Lighthouse State Park (q.v.). The park allows picnicking, surf fishing, and a panoramic view from atop the red-and-white nineteenth-century lighthouse. For a different side of the island, visit **Historic Viking Village**, a small crafts shopping area next to a commercial fishing dock at 19th and Bayview Avenues in Barnegat Light. One-hour tours of the dock are offered by reservation, Fridays at 10 from late June through August (609-494-7211).

THE JERSEY CAPE

Ocean City to Cape May

Like Atlantic City, this southernmost strip of coastline is often thought of as the "Philadelphia shore." However, people from all over come to these beaches, especially Canadians. Ocean City, the next island south of Atlantic City, bills itself as America's oldest family resort. It has never allowed liquor to be sold in its environs, the beach is wide and clean, and the long boardwalk is filled with stores, arcades, major amusement centers, a water park, and a movie house. There's also a Ghost Tour at 8 P.M. nightly in July and August and on weekends Memorial Day to October (609-814-0199).

South of there is Sea Isle City, largely residential. Then comes Avalon, with a growing number of upscale condos and a beautiful beach. On the same island is Stone Harbor, which has rental houses and apartments plus a bustling main boulevard filled with boutiques and bistros. Good restaurants are a major attraction here.

The Wildwoods have the largest number of boardwalk amusements at the shore. Wildwood Crest may have the advantage of getting the biggest family crowd, but the beaches all along this area are very wide and clean and are able to handle the huge crowds on weekends. The surf is definitely milder down here and shallow enough for a toddler to wade a little. And the beach is free—no badges required. North Wildwood, Wildwood, and Wildwood Crest are solid motels from top to bottom with guest houses and rental houses a block behind. Wildwood also prides itself on its "Doo Wop" atmosphere and the 50s-style designs of its motels. There's a Doo Wop District, a Fabulous 50s Weekend in the fall, a 50s tour (609-884-5404), and even a 50s-theme Bed & Breakfast. It also has the boardwalk amusements and the nightclub crowd, while the Crest is more family centered.

At the very tip of New Jersey lies Cape May. This is a beautiful Victorian town with colorful Victorian gingerbread houses and green lawns set against a placid shore. The beaches here are generally narrow, even after periodically receiving new sand (the jetty at the Cape May Canal traps the natural flow of sand in Wildwood). Automobile congestion can be a real problem in the town—or trying to get into it—because of the narrow streets and the town's popularity. Cape May has one of the largest collections of Victorian houses in the country, along with quaint boutiques, gaslight lamps, and brick walkways. The arts and crafts shops lining Washington Mall offer an evening's entertainment in themselves.

West of town, Cape May Point offers a wide beach, a refurbished lighthouse at Cape May Point State Park, and those little pieces of clear quartz known as Cape May diamonds at Sunset Beach. And the sunsets themselves can be quite impressive there, too. A little north on the Delaware Bay side, there's the Cape May–Lewes Ferry, which takes you to Delaware for outlet shopping or the beach at Rehoboth.

SIGHTSEEING AND EXCURSION BOATS

River Belle and *River Queen:* The *River Queen,* a simplified version of a Mississippi River sternwheeler, cruises for lunch, afternoon sightseeing, etc., from Bogan's Basin in Brielle (Monmouth County). Its sister ship, the *River Belle,* leaves from Broadway Basin in Point Pleasant (Ocean County). Both are popular with groups, especially senior citizens. The boats cruise the inland waters of the Manasquan and Metedeconk Rivers and Point Pleasant Canal to Barnegat Bay, so the water is calm and sightseeing is mostly of the docks of shore homeowners plus an occasional bridge. Luncheon, brunch, dinner, and sightseeing cruises are available. Sightseeing cruises offer narration. Dinner cruises feature a DJ. Late June through Labor Day. **TELEPHONE:** 732-528-6620. **WEBSITE:** www.riverboattour.com.

Cape May Whale Watcher: Summer cruises include morning Cape Island dolphin watch cruises, afternoon ocean whale and dolphin watches, and sunset dolphin watches and dinner cruises. Daily, 10, 1, and 6:30 in summer; May, Sept., & Oct., 10 and 1. Late Mar.– early May and Nov., weekends at 1. Under 6 free with adult. Also, special three- and five-hour Delaware Bay lighthouse cruises. Docked at Miss Chris Marina, 2nd Ave. & Wilson Dr. (across Rt. 109

from Lobster House), Cape May (Cape May County). **TELEPHONE:** 800-786-5445. **WEBSITE:** www.capemaywhalewatcher.com.

River Lady: This old-time riverboat sails on Barnegat Bay and Toms River. Lunch cruises, extended lunch cruises, historical sightseeing cruises, dinner and dance cruises, and early-bird dinner cruises. Cruises May–Sept., Tue., Thu., Sat. and second and fourth Wed. Advance purchase required. Docked at 1 Robbins Pky., Toms River (Ocean County). Off E. Water St. **TELEPHONE:** 732-349-8664. **WEBSITE:** www.riverlady.com.

Black Whale Cruises: One-hour evening bay cruises are available daily on the *Crystal Queen,* a riverboat paddlewheeler, as well as day-long trips from Long Beach Island to Trump Marina casino in Atlantic City. Operates May–Oct. Docked at the Black Whale Dock, Centre St. & Bayfront, Beach Haven (Ocean County). Reservations required for the Atlantic City cruise. **TELEPHONE:** 609-492-0333. **WEBSITE:** www.blackwhalecruises.com.

Atlantic Star: Two and a half hour sunset buffet cruises daily around the Cape May area. Sights include dolphins, Cape May Canal, Cape May Light, marinas, a Coast Guard base, and Delaware Bay. Operates May–Sept. from the Starlight Fleet dock at 6200 Park Blvd., Wildwood Crest (Cape May County). **TELEPHONE:** 609-729-3400. **WEBSITE:** www.jjcboats.com.

Atlantic City Cruises: *Cruisn 1* is a double-deck boat that carries one hundred passengers and has an enclosed bar and galley as well as plenty of open-air seating. Cruises range from morning skyline tours and marine mammal cruises to a harbor tour, cocktail cruise, and moonlight dance party. Operates May–Oct. Docked at Gardner's Basin, 800 N. New Hampshire Ave., Atlantic City (Atlantic County). Fares vary by cruise type. **TELEPHONE:** 609-347-7600. **WEBSITE:** www. atlanticcitycruises.com.

Cape May–Lewes Ferry: The ferry now offers a new $27 million, four-deck ship that makes the trip across Delaware Bay to Lewes in 70 minutes. Boats run about every 40 minutes in peak season. As ferries, their main business is transportation. However, the new ships resemble cruise liners in that they have elevators, modern decor, fancy restaurants, and can cater to groups. Older ferries also make regular runs (and sometimes have special events), so call first if you want the "fast" ferry. The terminal is at the Delaware Bay end of the Cape May Canal, where Rt. 9 ends (Cape May County). **TELEPHONE:** 800-643-3779. **WEBSITE:** www.capemaylewesferry.com.

LIGHTHOUSES

Sandy Hook: The pure white column and red top of the oldest working lighthouse in America is familiar from hundreds of postcards and calendars. The 103-foot-high lighthouse stands on a small grassy rise inside Fort Hancock, not by the ocean, in the Gateway

The Sandy Hook Lighthouse, built in 1764, is the oldest working lighthouse in America. You can climb to the top for a view of the New York skyline in the distance. *(Photo by Patrick Sarver)*

National Recreation Area. When it was built in 1764 it was 500 feet from the tip of Sandy Hook. Today, because currents have added more and more sand, that distance is now 1½ miles. **TOURS:** 12–4:30 on weekends, Apr.–mid-Dec.; daily in July and August. There's a sign-up sheet for tours at the building adjacent to the lighthouse. A maximum of eight people at a time is led to the top, where the views include the New York skyline, the Verrazano Bridge, and the Highlands. There's a height minimum of 4 feet, so smaller children won't be able to accompany you. **ADMISSION:** The lighthouse is free, but there's a $10 parking fee for the park in summer, and if you're not headed for the beaches, you'll have a better chance of finding parking near the lighthouse off-season. **LOCATION:** Take Garden State Parkway, Exit 117, to Rt. 36 east to Sandy Hook exit. **TELEPHONE:** 732-872-5970. **WEBSITE:** www.nps.gov/gate/shu/shu_home.htm.

Twin Lights: An unusual brownstone building that looks more like a castle than a lighthouse, Twin Lights is perched on a bluff in Highlands with a sweeping view of Sandy Hook and the ocean. The "twin" lights (one is square and one octagonal) are towers on either side of the main building. The first Fresnel lights were used here in 1841. The present fortress-like structure was built in 1862 and was the scene of many "firsts." The museum inside includes exhibits on early life-saving equipment and Marconi's demonstration of the wireless from this site. Part of the enjoyment is also the climb up the stairs. The spiral staircase involves only sixty-five steps and leads to an excellent view. Next to the museum is a small gift shop; outside are a picnic area and several historical markers. **HOURS:** Daily, 10–4:30 in summer. Closed Mon. & Tue. rest of year. **ADMISSION:** Donation requested. **LOCATION:** Lighthouse Rd., Highlands (Monmouth County). Rt. 36 east; make right turn just before Highlands Bridge, then right onto Highland Ave. Follow signs. **TELEPHONE:** 732-872-1814. **WEBSITE:** www.twin-lights.org.

Sea Girt: This lighthouse stands atop a four-story square brick tower in an L-shaped Victorian brick house in a residential area of Sea Girt. The interior has been restored and furnished according to the 1890s, when it was first commissioned. **TOURS:** Sun., 2–4, Apr.–Nov. Call first. **ADMISSION:** Free. **LOCATION:** Beacon Blvd. and Ocean Ave., Sea Girt (Monmouth County). Rt. 71 to Beacon Blvd. Left at end to Ocean Blvd. **TELEPHONE:** 732-974-0514. **WEBSITE:** www.seagirtboro.com/sglighthouse.html.

Barnegat: Probably the most famous New Jersey lighthouse, "Old Barney" guards the northern tip of Long Beach Island. It was built by

General George Meade of Civil War fame (who also constructed Absecon and Cape May lights). Its classic red-and-white design stands against a backdrop of ocean and bay in a state park of the same name. You can climb the 217 steps to the top (small fee in summer; under 12 free) or simply walk around the esplanade and view the tip of Island Beach State Park across the inlet. The park also includes some nature trails among the dunes, a maritime forest, a picnic pavilion, and a small Visitor Center with exhibits on the lighthouse and nature at the park. A private Barnegat Light Museum several blocks away at 5th and Central is open in the summer and has lots of material on the lighthouse and its Fresnel lens. **HOURS:** Lighthouse, daily, 9–4:30 in summer; weekends Nov.–Apr. Call for spring and fall hours. **ADMISSION:** Free. **LOCATION:** Take Garden State Parkway, Exit 63, to Rt. 72 to Long Beach Island, then 9 miles north to Barnegat Light (Ocean County). **TELEPHONE:** 609-494-2016. **WEBSITE:** www.state.nj.us/dep/parksandforests/parks/barnlig.html.

Absecon: Just northwest of the casino strip, this recently restored lighthouse stands on a sandy inland block surrounded by a fence. Painted pale yellow and black, it features a wrought-iron spiral staircase with 228 steps. Absecon, at 171 feet, is the tallest of the Jersey lights, and the view up top encompasses the beach, inlet, and ocean as well as the town. There's also a reconstructed keeper's house with displays of photos and artifacts about the lighthouse as well as a gift shop. **HOURS:** Thu.–Mon., 11–4; daily 10–5 July and Aug. **ADMISSION:** $. Discounts: Seniors, children. Under 4 free. Museum free. **LOCATION:** Pacific and Rhode Island Aves., Atlantic City. **TELEPHONE:** 609-441-9272. **WEBSITE:** www.abseconlighthouse.org.

Hereford Inlet: This is a true lighthouse, in that it is a house with a short tower for the light. Surrounded by lovely gardens and a park, this building in North Wildwood sports a furnished interior and Victorian architecture that make it a landmark worth seeing. Originally built in 1874, it has been restored to its Swiss Gothic style. The gardens are landscaped in the English "cottage" style and include two hundred varieties of flowers. There's a fee for a half-hour tour of the furnished "house" section, which includes exhibits on lighthouse history, shipwrecks, and the lifesaving service as well as furnished rooms from the days when keepers lived there. **HOURS:** Daily, 9–5, mid-May–mid-Oct.; spring and Oct., Wed.–Sun., 11–4. Call for Jan.–Mar. hours. **ADMISSION:** $. Discount: Children. Combo with Cape May Point lighthouse: $$. **LOCATION:** 1st & Central Aves., North Wildwood (Cape May County). **TELEPHONE:** 609-522-4520. **WEBSITE:** www.herefordlighthouse.org.

Cape May Point: Lovingly restored a few years ago, this 1859 lighthouse is the center of a state park well known for bird-watching, a beach, and a nature center. There are several historic plaques on the way up the 199 steps of the black spiral staircase. The view from the top includes Delaware Bay, Sunset Beach, Cape May, and the amusement rides at Wildwood. The lighthouse is maintained by the Coast Guard, but the Mid-Atlantic Center for the Arts operates guided tours for a small fee. **HOURS:** Daily, Apr.–Nov., 9–8; limited times rest of the year. At various times during the season the "keepers on duty" allow you to meet the last keepers of the light at the top and ask questions about their life and times in the 1920s. There's also a museum shop in the original oil house. **LOCATION:** Off Sunset Rd., Cape May Point. **TELEPHONE:** Park, 609-884-2159; tours, 609-884-5404. **WEBSITE:** www.capemaymac.org.

East Point Lighthouse: This Delaware Bay lighthouse stands atop a two-story red brick structure built in 1849 at the mouth of the Maurice River. The interior is being restored as a museum of local maritime heritage by the Maurice River Historical Society. **HOURS:** Open third Sun. of month, Apr.–Oct., 1–4. Also open for Bay Days, first weekend in June; Lighthouse Challenge Weekend in mid-Oct.; and annual open house the first Sat. in Aug. Groups by appointment. **LOCATION:** East Point Rd., Heislerville (Cumberland County). Off Rt. 47. **WEBSITE:** www.co.cumberland.nj.us/tourism/east_point_lighthouse.

The Animal Kingdom

At the Lakota Wolf Preserve near the Delaware Water Gap, you can get an up-close look at several packs of wolves. *(Photo by Patrick Sarver)*

ZOOS

Safari at Six Flags

The largest safari outside of Africa takes about an hour to drive through and covers 5 miles and eleven theme areas and features more than 1,200 animals. Some, such as camels, elk in heat, jealous giraffes, and short-tempered rhinos can get almost too close for comfort. The brochure warns that you should keep car windows closed at all times, so take an air-conditioned vehicle if you're visiting on a 90-degree day. The road through the safari is three lanes wide, and you can travel at your own speed. Each area is separated from the other by wire fences, so you must wait for guards to open the gates between one habitat and another. Camels seem like the beggars here; they sidle up to cars looking for handouts. Surprisingly, a number of cars may have open windows and people who nuzzle deer and feed popcorn to camels despite park rules and signs warning you not to feed the animals. Ostriches, on the other hand, are very surly and would just as soon peck at your finger as your window. In the African Plains section you can watch herds of elephants eat and socialize. And nothing can make you feel smaller than to sit knee-high to a giraffe as he nudges up against your car. The animals have right-of-way here, so if you get in real trouble, honk for a safari guard. The Australian section is unique: kangaroos, wallabies, wallaroos, and the flightless emu strut, waddle, and bound across the hilly terrain. The Asian section features animals from Central Asia like the yak and shaggy-haired ox.

As you drive slowly from one section to the next, you will see a Bengal tiger in its own Indian pavilion and, later on, brown bears that are usually up a tree or taking a dip in the stream. For those with metal-topped cars, the ride through monkey territory is always of interest. These curious simians will scamper all over your car, check on the occupants, pull on hood ornaments, knock your grillwork, and then pass on to the next car. If you want to avoid these monkeyshines, you can use the by-pass road to the exit. An air-conditioned bus ride through the whole park is an alternative to driving your own car, but there is an extra charge for that.

HOURS: Mid-May–Aug., daily, 9–4; Apr.–mid-May, Sept.–Oct., open weekends. **ADMISSION:** Safari, \$\$\$\$. Under 4 free.
Combo: Free with Six Flags/Great Adventure admission.
LOCATION: Jackson Twp.
(Ocean County). N.J. Turnpike, Exit 7A, then Rt. 195 east to Exit 16.
TELEPHONE: 732-928-1821. **WEBSITE:** www.sixflags.com/parks/wildsafari.

Cape May County Zoo

Cape May County has poured a lot of money into this 85-acre zoo, and the landscape is attractive. Various animal enclosures are arranged along meandering paths with pleasant foliage all about. Some of the enclosures simulate the natural terrain of the animals. Others are traditional cages. But the zoo is in a park filled with tall scrub pine and sandy soil, so the general effect is of seeing animals in their natural environments.

Among the many species here you will find llamas, tigers, chee-tahs, alligators, bears, spider monkeys, a lion, bison, and even white-maned and other tamarins. Quite a variety of birds are on hand also, including cockatoos, toucans, flamingos, peacocks, eagles, hawks, and barnyard fowl. The World of Birds is a two-story atrium filled with numerous species of tropical birds. There's also a reptile house.

This is one of the best-looking zoos in New Jersey, with colorful plantings and bridges over ponds. It offers a complete African savannah where giraffes, zebras, and oryx roam and visitors can watch from a shaded gazebo. Outside the zoo there is a lunch concession and farther on, a children's playground and a picnic area. All in all, a very pleasant outing. Still free, but during tourist season, there's a man at the park entrance taking "donations." A few dollars should do, and it's well worth it. *Note:* the parking lot gets really crowded on summer weekends!

HOURS: Daily, 10–4:45, winter, 10–3:45, weather permitting.
LOCATION: Rt. 9 & Crest Haven Rd., Cape May Court House.
TELEPHONE: 609-465-5271. **WEBSITE:** www.co.cape-may.nj.us. Click on the zoo icon.

Space Farms Zoo

This is a private zoo (in itself an endangered species) in a rural area that can approximate the natural surroundings of many of the animals housed here. It lies amid the farms and hills of northern Sussex County. The family name here is Space, and it was a farm before it became a zoo. The granddaughter of the original owner has a degree in animal biology and now administers the place. The entrance building includes a Museum of Americana (everything from Indian arrowheads to old clocks) and the stuffed Goliath, a twelve-foot-high grizzly that was the world's largest and once the main attraction here. There's also a full snack shop with booths and the inevitable gift shop. Buy your entrance tickets here (and perhaps some munchies for the animals).

Space Farms is set up for family outings, with many picnic tables, swing sets, and other attractions available for youngsters. A hundred hilly acres are devoted to rather simple cages of bears, lions, tigers, hyenas, monkeys, and such. A large pond at the center of the acreage allows ducks and geese to paddle about while pens of yak, llamas, buffalo, and goats dot the surrounding hills— 500 animals altogether. There is a separate den for snakes and a special enclosure for otters.

On the hills to the left of the zoo are the museums: several buildings filled with antique cars, sleighs, old buggies, tractors, dolls, farm machinery, toys, and everything else but the kitchen sink. The antique car collection is surprisingly large. Between the animals, the museums, the swings, and the slides you can make a day of it. Picnic lunches allowed.

> **HOURS:** Daily, 9–5, May–Oct. **ADMISSION:** $$$. Discounts: Seniors, children. Under 3 free. **LOCATION:** 218 Rt. 519, Beemerville (Sussex County), 7 miles north of Rt. 206 or 5 miles south of Rt. 23. **TELEPHONE:** 973-875-5800. **WEBSITE:** www.spacefarms.com.

Turtle Back Zoo

There are new walls, walkways, and entrance at this zoo, and the animal collection is returning to what it used to be. The zoo has a new walk-through reptile house, as well as renovated river otter and alligator exhibits. The Wolf Woods is a naturalistic exhibit where you can watch a family of wolves from behind a see-through shield. Penguins have taken over the old seal pond, and a peacock struts freely around. The Essex Farm petting zoo, which has been renovated and is always popular with kids, is open April to November with goats, pigs, and lambs. There are also pony rides at the farm, and a miniature train travels through the surrounding South Mountain Reservation. You'll also see a few large cats, such as cougars and bobcats, in cages. There are also black bears, bison, llamas, bald eagles, wallabies, and monkeys. And, of course, there are always birds, turtles, and deer. Food and gift concessions (except in winter) and a covered picnic area are available, along with a new playground.

> **HOURS:** Mon.–Sat., 10–4:30 (until 6 on Wed); Sun., 11–5:30; winter, Thu.–Sun., 11–3. **ADMISSION:** $$. Discounts: Seniors, children. Under 2 free. **LOCATION:** 560 Northfield Ave., West Orange (Essex County). Behind South Mountain Arena. **TELEPHONE:** 973-731-5800. **WEBSITE:** www.turtlebackzoo.com.

Bergen County Zoological Park

This popular small zoo in Van Saun Park exhibits animals from North and South America, so you won't see any tigers, giraffes, or elephants here. There is a North American Great Plains exhibit plus Central and South American animals and a North American Wetlands Aviary. Some large cats, including mountain lions, are on display. The two hundred animals here include elk, bison, alligators, bobcats, eagles, and more exotic species like the golden lion tamarin and spider monkeys. In the Discovery and Education Center, there's a touch tank with starfish, a tropical aquarium, and a 50-minute nature film.

Favorites with young children are the miniature train ride and an 1890s farmyard with its sheep, goats, and chickens as well as pony rides and a carousel across the park road from the zoo entrance. A gift shop and snack bar are also on hand. The zoo is part of a 140-acre park that features picnic tables, a fishing pond, and biking and hiking trails.

> **HOURS:** Daily, 10–4:30, Fri.–Sun. and holidays, May–Oct.
> **ADMISSION:** $. Discounts: Seniors, children. Under 3 free.
> Free, Mon.–Tue. and Nov.–Apr. **LOCATION:** Forest Ave., Paramus
> (Bergen County). Off Rt. 4. **TELEPHONE:** 201-262-3771.
> **WEBSITE:** www.co.bergen.nj.us/parks/Parks/Zoo.htm.

Lakota Wolf Preserve

This preserve at Camp Taylor near the Delaware Water Gap is home to more than twenty-four tundra, timber, and arctic wolves as well as some foxes and bobcats. Co-owner and handler Jim Stein presents wolves in their natural surroundings. The preserve is a scenic walk from the campground (rides are also available). The observation area is in the center of four packs of wolves. You'll talk with people who raised the wolves and will learn about the social structure of wolf packs, their eating habits, interaction with humans, and many other aspects of the animals' lives. You'll also learn that wolves respond to their names and be able to see them interact with each other, play, and perhaps howl. Guided photo sessions are also available from $125 to $300.

> **HOURS:** Open Tue.–Sun. Admission only at guided tour times,
> 10:30 and 4 during daylight savings time; 10:30 and 3 rest of year.
> Tours also by appointment. **ADMISSION:** $$$. Discount: Children.
> **LOCATION:** 89 Mt. Pleasant Rd., Columbia (Warren County). Rt. 80,
> Exit 4 to Rt. 94 north, 2½ miles to Mt. Pleasant turnoff.
> **TELEPHONE:** 908-496-9244 or 877-733-9653.
> **WEBSITE:** www.lakotawolf.com.

Other Zoos

Cohanzick Zoo: New Jersey's first zoo, founded in 1934, is set in an 1,100-acre park that borders the Cohansey River in Bridgeton. The more than two hundred animals include Asiatic bear, leopard, monkeys, white tiger, llama, alligator, reindeer, eagle, falcon, owls, and many others. You can find some unusual species—many in modern, naturalistic settings—as well as a walk-through aviary. The zoo also includes a "zoovenir" shop and concession area. The surrounding park contains plenty of picnic areas, nature trails, and lots more. **HOURS:** Spring/summer, daily, 9–5; fall/winter, daily, 9–4. **ADMISSION:** Free. **LOCATION:** City Park, Bridgeton (Cumberland County). Rt. 49 to Atlantic St. Follow to Mayor Aitken Dr. **TELEPHONE:** 856-455-3230, ext. 242. **WEBSITE:** www.co.cumberland.nj.us/tourism/cohanzick_zoo.

Popcorn Park Zoo: This is a 7-acre licensed zoo that caters strictly to injured, abandoned, and unwanted fauna, ranging from goats to lions, tigers, and llamas. (There are also kennels of abandoned pets waiting for adoption.) There's a small reptile house; domestic animals like pot-bellied pigs, sheep, and draft horses; and a monkey house as well as a Bactrian camel, bears, emus, and deer. Most animals are given cute names like Cindy Lou Cougar, Boo-Boo the Bear, and Holly the Sicilian Donkey. The facility is run by the Associated Humane Society. **HOURS:** Daily, 11–5. **ADMISSION:** $. Discounts: Seniors, children under 12. **LOCATION:** Humane Way and Lacey Rd., Forked River (Ocean County). **TELEPHONE:** 609-693-1900.

NEARBY OUT-OF-STATE ZOOS

Bronx Zoo

This is the largest urban zoo in America. Although there are still some old-fashioned ornate zoo houses, most of the acreage is devoted to open landscapes that allow the animals to roam free while visitors watch from across moats or behind plastic shields. Since there are more than 5 miles of terrain to cover, it's a lot easier to take the skyride or monorail in season. There is also a tram that transports visitors from the entrance plaza to JungleWorld, an indoor tropical forest, on the other side.

The zoo is divided into geographical sections. There is Wild Asia (open only in warm weather), a 40-acre habitat where elephants, rhinos, deer, and antelope roam free. Visitors view them from the glassed-in monorail. In Africa, lions, gazelles, antelopes, zebras, and gnus roam the grassy slopes. You can view them from surrounding walkways and bridges or from the slow-moving safari ride. The Congo Gorilla Forest is the current star attraction. You can get up close (through glass) with a lowland gorilla family, as well as view mandrills, colobus monkeys, and okapi.

Tiger Mountain is a new major exhibit, where you can also get up close with Siberian tigers. The World of Darkness offers a top-notch display of bats, owls, and other nocturnal animals. The World of Birds is housed in an ultramodern concrete cylindrical building. Other houses include the Sea Bird, Aquatic Bird, and Reptile Houses plus the Zoo Center. The Children's Zoo offers a host of fun things for kids. Giant rope "spider webs" to climb, snail "shells" to ride in, and prairie dog burrows to explore make this an educational amusement park.

HOURS: Weekdays, 10–5; weekends, 10–5:30; winter hours, 10–4:30. **ADMISSION:** Adults, $$$. Discounts: Seniors, children. Wed.: Donation. Parking fee. **LOCATION:** George Washington Bridge to Cross Bronx Expressway east to Bronx River Parkway north. Take exit marked "Bronx Zoo." **TELEPHONE:** 718-367-1010. **WEBSITE:** www.bronxzoo.org.

Central Park Zoo

If you are in Manhattan with children, a good place to stop is the Central Park Zoo on the east side of the park. This is a small zoo. The largest exhibit is the indoors Rain Forest, a transported tropical rain forest with chattering monkeys and colorful toucans moving along the three stories of foliage. Even tiny animals like leafcutter ants and other jungle insects are displayed. The sea lion pool is always popular at feeding time. The polar bears have limited space but seem to enjoy splashing in their vertical pool. An adjoining indoor "cave" is devoted to penguins. You can watch these funny creatures dive-bomb through the water when they aren't waddling about. There is also a small children's zoo with interactive play areas and some small animals about. A snack bar, tables, and a gift shop are also available.

HOURS: Apr.–Oct., weekdays, 10–5, weekends until 5:30. Nov.–Mar., daily, 10–4:30. **ADMISSION:** $$. Discounts: Seniors, children. **LOCATION:** 830 Fifth Ave. (at 64th St.), New York City. **TELEPHONE:** 212-439-6500. **WEBSITE:** http://nyzoosandaquarium.com/5719085.

Philadelphia Zoo

This is America's oldest zoo, but, like most others, it is quickly changing into modern landscaped habitats. The outstanding Peco Primate Reserve features lowland gorillas, orangutans, gibbons, and lemurs in a lush habitat of 2.5 acres. There is also Carnivore Kingdom, a big draw with a rare white lion as one of its stars. African Outpost re-creates the African veldt, featuring giraffes, zebra, sable antelope, and secretary birds, while Bear Country specializes in bruins. Elephants and rhinos, giraffes and zebras are always on hand.

Besides the lions, tigers, and hooved animals, you can also find kangaroos and wallabies, plus a Rare Animal Conservation Center filled with some unusual varieties of monkeys and other species. The newest attraction is Big Cat Falls, the home to endangered cats from around the world. The Children's Zoo's exhibits let kids interact with animals and their keepers. There are also several specialized zoo houses and a baby animal nursery where you can watch the newborns. Other features include a mini-train ride (extra fee), the ZooBalloon (extra fee), and the swan boat rides.

HOURS: Open daily, Mar.–Nov., 10–5; Dec.–Feb., 10–4. **ADMISSION:** $$$$. Discounts: Seniors, children. Under 2 free. Parking: $$. **LOCATION:** 34th & Girard in Fairmount Park, Philadelphia. Girard Ave. exit off Rt. 76. **TELEPHONE:** 215-243-1100. **WEBSITE:** www.phillyzoo.org.

AQUARIUMS

Adventure Aquarium

The New Jersey State Aquarium has undergone a major expansion, virtually doubling in size, and changed its name to the Adventure Aquarium. In the process, it changed from a nonprofit to a commercial enterprise, increased fees, moved its main entrance to the north side of the new addition, and eliminated the combination ticket with the adjacent Camden Children's Garden (q.v.).

The huge 760,000-gallon Ocean Realm tank houses over 2,000 fish, including tuna, stingrays, and sea turtles. From a theater you can watch volunteer scuba divers go into the big tank and answer questions or wave to a turtle. Altogether there are eighty freshwater and saltwater exhibits, including a special exhibit on South American fish and birds upstairs. The aquarium also features a mangrove lagoon, a Caribbean beach, and the replica of an ironclad mail ship that sank in 1867. At the touch tanks, children can feel the surface of sharks, sting rays, sea stars, and crabs. There's also a new Deep Sea 4D Theater, which features a 20-minute special effects program on the undersea world, with 3D video and chairs that move (extra fee).

At the new section, you'll encounter the West African River, where there are hippos, crocodiles, and fish in the water and birds flying above. A presentation at an underwater observation area and a video explain the life of African rivers. There's also a Jules Verne Gallery that has moon jellyfish, giant spider crabs, and octopi. But the main attraction is the new 550,000-gallon Shark Realm tank, which has thirty sharks as well as stingrays that you can see from underwater observation points—and more impressively when you

The West African River exhibit, complete with hippos, crocodiles, and fish, is one of the major exhibits at the expanded Adventure Aquarium on the Camden Waterfront. *(Photo by Patrick Sarver)*

walk through the Shark Tunnel. This clear passageway through the center of the tank makes the toothy predators appear to be "flying" just over your head.

If you have a sense of adventure (and $115), you can also don a wetsuit, get a snorkeling lesson, and then go for a swim in the Shark Realm tank. The Swim with the Sharks program lets you get up close and personal with the sharks and feed the stingrays in a two-hour program that starts at 9:30 A.M. and 12:45 and 2:45 P.M.

Outside, at the Seal Shores section, a daily "training session" allows visitors to watch as gray seals take on such audience-pleasing chores as catching Frisbees and leaping to touch a suspended ball. Meanwhile, over at Penguin Island, a colony of African black-footed penguins waddles around. This exhibit includes a beach, rocks, and a pool with an underwater viewing area so you can also watch the birds swim.

The aquarium also offers a cafe on the first floor. It has an outdoor deck with a nice view of Philadelphia across the river and a large gift shop filled with stuffed animal versions of whales and penguins and other aquatic-themed souvenirs.

HOURS: Daily, 9:30–5. **ADMISSION:** Adults: $$$$. Discounts: Seniors, students, children. Under 2 free. **LOCATION:** 1 Riverside Dr., Camden (Camden County). Parking lot across street (fee).
TELEPHONE: 856-365-3300. **WEBSITE:** www.adventureaquarium.com.

Pequest Trout Hatchery

This modern concrete building complex has three purposes. One is to raise the trout that are used to stock the state's streams and lakes. The second is to introduce youngsters to proper fishing techniques and educate them on wildlife conservation. The third is to manage this huge acreage and the wildlife that lives in it. Outside, there is a run with breeder trout that you can feed with special trout food. The Visitor Center includes a large room with many hands-on exhibits. There are also charts, displays, and a tank of adult trout so that even those who do not fish can get a look at these big specimens. In another room a continuous video shows how the fish are bred, fed, and finally transported by truck to freshwater streams as well as displays on various habitats. Then you can go outside to see the tanks where the young fish are. A look into the glass-sided building will allow you to see hundreds of tiny fingerlings swimming about. About 600,000 brown and rainbow trout are raised here.

This is a popular place for school and scout groups, because during the group tour, kids often get to wield a fishing rod. There are also special Saturday classes on fishing techniques and environmental classes for kids. Individuals don't get a tour but can visit the exhibits, hike the trails in the surrounding 1,600 acres, or picnic at the nearby tables.

HOURS: Daily, 10–4. **ADMISSION:** Free. **LOCATION:** 605 Pequest Rd., Oxford (Warren County). Off Rt. 46. **TELEPHONE:** 908-637-4125. **WEBSITE:** www.state.nj.us/dep/fgw/pequest.htm.

Atlantic City Aquarium

Atlantic City once had an aquarium on the boardwalk. Now it has one at Gardner's Basin on the inlet, which is much larger and more environmentally correct. This multimillion dollar aquarium/marine learning center—which recently changed its name from Ocean Life Center—is meant to anchor the quaint maritime park of Gardner's Basin.

The center includes seventeen large tanks of fish, both tropical and local, including giant moray eels, and a diorama showing local species. A larger aquarium tank features fish of the Jersey Coast, such as nurse sharks, sea bass, and a 100 pound loggerhead sea turtle. There's also a touch tank with horseshoe crabs and other sea creatures. The maritime section upstairs includes a diving suit, a captain's wheel, and lots of explanations about barrier reefs and life along the sea. Kids will like the many computer stations here. There is also a nice open deck on the upper floor where you can walk out and watch the boats. The jitney now stops at Gardner's Basin, so you can visit from the boardwalk area.

HOURS: Daily, 10–5. **ADMISSION:** $$. Discounts: Seniors, children. Under 3 free. **LOCATION:** 800 N. New Hampshire Ave., Atlantic City. **TELEPHONE:** 609-348-2880. **WEBSITE:** www.atlanticcityaquarium.com.

Other Aquariums

Jenkinson's Aquarium: This popular spot on the boardwalk near Ocean Avenue in Point Pleasant Beach (Ocean County) is about a block north of the amusement rides. It is roomier than you would expect inside, and it includes tanks of small sharks and rays, a penguin area, an alligator pit, a Pacific Coast tank with a mini kelp forest, and some hard-working seals. The centerpiece is the sunken ship, the *Bounty,* with freshwater tropicals flitting in and around it. Coral reef fish and colorful parrots are here as well, and you can walk around the center to get a view from all sides. Upstairs is a tropical forest exhibit, with the world's smallest monkeys plus parrots, touch tanks, and numerous other exhibits on fossils and shark teeth. You can't miss the gift shop—you pass through it on the way out. **HOURS:** July–Aug., daily, 10–10; winter, daily, 10–5. **ADMISSION:** $$. Discounts: Seniors, children. Under 3 free. **TELEPHONE:** 732-899-1659. **WEBSITE:** www.jenkinsons.com/aquarium.

Marine Mammal Stranding Center: Located in the beach town of Brigantine just north of Atlantic City, this center was created mainly as a rescue center, so don't expect to find dolphins or whales here, because the garage-sized pool isn't large enough to hold them. You may find harbor seals or turtles, however. The Visitor Center contains a large fish tank where you can peer through a magnifying glass at some exotic species. There are also animal replicas, exhibits on conservation, and a gift shop filled with T-shirts and educational items. **LOCATION:** 3625 Brigantine Blvd. (on the circle), Brigantine (Atlantic County). **TELEPHONE:** 609-266-0538. **WEBSITE:** www.marinemammalstrandingcenter.org.

WHALE AND DOLPHIN WATCHES

Another way to visit fish and other sea creatures is to go out to meet them in their own environment. There are a number of boats at the Jersey Shore that run excursions for whale and dolphin watches or skim through the interior canals to view birds and swamp life. Here are a few. Please note that sailing times, dates, and schedules may change due to weather or other circumstances. Always check ahead.

Cape May Whale Watch and Research Center: The M/V *Whale Watcher* is a 110-foot catamaran designed for whale and dolphin watching, complete with food service. An onboard naturalist instructs passengers on spotting techniques. Whale watches last three hours, dolphin watches two. **HOURS:** Trips at 10, 1, and 6:30 in summer; May, Sept., Oct., 9:30 and 1. **FARE:** Whale watch, $$$$$; dolphin watch, $$$$. Discount: Children. Under 7 free. **LOCATION:** 1243 Wilson Dr., Cape May. Rt. 109 to 3rd Ave. to Wilson Dr. **TELEPHONE:** 609-884-5445. **WEBSITE:** www.capemaywhalewatcher.com.

Silver Bullet: This ocean-going 70-foot speedboat offers dolphin watching trips. **HOURS:** Daily at 9:30, 12, & 2:30 and an added trip at 4:30 Tue.–Thu. **FARE:** $$$$. Discount: Children. Under 2 free with adult. **LOCATION:** Docked at Wildwood Marina, Rio Grande & Susquehanna Aves., Wildwood (Cape May County). **TELEPHONE:** 609-522-6060. **WEBSITE:** www.silverbullettours.com.

Thunder Cat: This catamaran speedboat offers dolphin watching trips. **HOURS:** Daily at 10, 12, & 2 as well as 4 on Tue.–Thu. Spring and fall trips vary. **FARE:** $$$$. Discount: Children. Under 2 free. **LOCAITON:** Docked at Dolphin Cove Marina, 1001 Ocean Dr., Wildwood Crest (Cape May County). **TELEPHONE:** 609-523-2628. **WEBSITE:** www.thundercatdolphinwatch.com.

Starlight Fleet: Whale and dolphin watching cruises around the Cape May area. **HOURS:** Daily at 9:30, 1, and a 6:30 dinner cruise, May–Sept. Touch tanks onboard for 9:30 and 1 cruises. **FARE:** Whale watch, $$$$$; dolphin watch, $$$$. Discount: Children. Under 7 free with paying adult. **LOCATION:** Starlight Fleet dock at 6200 Park Blvd., Wildwood Crest (Cape May County). **TELEPHONE:** 609-729-3400. **WEBSITE:** www.jjcboats.com.

Wildlife Unlimited Tours: An enclosed 40-foot pontoon takes you on two-hour back bay and river wildlife trips. These salt-marsh safaris include birdwatching and talks on marsh life. A limited supply of binoculars is also available. N.J. Audubon sponsors some of the marsh birdwatching trips, including nesting ospreys. **SAILINGS:** Summer, three trips daily; fall, two trips. **HOURS:** Spring–fall, daily 1:30, except Sun.–Mon. at 10. On Wed. and Thu., from mid-June to Labor Day, sails from Wetlands Institute (q.v.) in Stone Harbor. **FARE:** $$$. Discount: Children. Under 6 free. **LOCATION:** Docked at Miss Chris Marina, 2nd Ave. & Wilson Dr. (across Rt. 109 from Lobster House), Cape May. **TELEPHONE:** 609-884-3100. **WEBSITE:** www.skimmer.com.

NEARBY OUT-OF-STATE AQUARIUM

New York Aquarium

It's in Brooklyn, and you can get there easily from the Verrazano Bridge since it is in the middle of Coney Island. Many people prefer visiting in the spring or fall to avoid the boardwalk amusements. For northern New Jersey, this is the only decent-sized aquarium within easy driving distance. This concrete aquarium is home to whales, sharks, seals, penguins, and a variety of tropical fish. The whales swim around lazily in the big tank—what you mostly see is their underbellies. Outside, there is a touch tank and cove where children can handle starfish, as well as a building just for sharks (mostly smaller tiger sharks).

The most dramatic exhibit is at Sea Cliffs, a 300-foot re-creation of a Pacific coastline cliff that is home to walruses, penguins, sea otters, and seals. In warm weather, a training show also takes place in an outside arena. A dolphin jumps up and takes a fish from the trainer. In any season there are always the yellow tangs, the electric eel, and other strange and beautiful denizens of the deep in various tanks. This place has a good mix of species, including seals, whales, and dolphins.

HOURS: Summer, weekdays, 10–6; weekends, 10–7; earlier closings rest of year. **ADMISSION:** Adults: $$$. Discounts: Seniors, children. Under 2 free. Parking fee. **LOCATION:** West 8th St. & Surf Ave., Brooklyn. Take Verrazano Bridge to Belt Parkway (direction of JFK Airport) until 8th St. exit. Look for signs. **TELEPHONE:** 718-265-FISH. **WEBSITE:** www.nyaquarium.com.

WILDLIFE REFUGES AND NATURE CENTERS

Great Swamp National Wildlife Refuge

The remains of a glacial pocket, the swamp serves as both a refuge for animals and as a 7,600-acre barrier to suburban development. It was saved in 1960 from being turned into an airport by local conservationists and donated to the federal government. The area is a combination of marshes, grassland, swamp, woodland, and hardwood ridges.

Wooden boardwalks at the Wildlife Observation Center on Long Hill Road let visitors traverse the wetlands and observe whatever wildlife is around. Mostly it's small—woodchucks, muskrats, frogs, geese, ducks, herons. There are deer, wild turkeys, and fox, too, though they tend to stay in the interior. There are blinds for picture taking. Swamp officials recommend visits in the early morning or late afternoon. There's also a bird-watching overlook on Pleasant Plains Road not far from the headquarters. About half the swamp is a wilderness area, and 8 miles of hiking trails cross this part of the refuge. Old sneakers or waterproof shoes are recommended. Insect repellent is especially advisable. **HOURS:** Dawn to dusk. **ADMISSION:** Free. **LOCATION:** Headquarters, 241 Pleasant Plains Rd., Basking Ridge (Somerset County). **TELEPHONE:** 973-425-1222. **WEBSITE:** www.fws.gov/ northeast/greatswamp.

While headquarters facilities in the Great Swamp are limited, there are three nature centers of interest bordering the refuge. All are free or by donation.

Somerset County Environmental Education Center: Located in Lord Stirling Park on the western edge of the Great Swamp, this modern building features classrooms, exhibits about the swamp, a book and gift shop, library, and photography and art shows. More than 8 miles of trails and wooden walkways pass ponds and cross woods and wetlands in the park's 450 acres of natural lands. Bird-watching, guided hikes, cross-country skiing, school programs, and trips are offered each year. **HOURS:** Park, daily, dawn to dusk. Center, daily, 9–5. **LOCATION:** 190 Lord Stirling Rd., Basking Ridge (Somerset County). **TELEPHONE:** 908-766-2489. **WEBSITE:** www.somersetcounty parks.org/ programs/eec/eec_main.htm.

Great Swamp Outdoor Education Center: Adjacent to the eastern edge of the Great Swamp, this 40-acre facility contains natural history exhibits on animals, a library, and classrooms. There is also an exhibit of art with a nature theme that changes monthly. Nature trails, guided walks, and wooden boardwalks lead into the swamp. Special programs such as maple sugaring are offered, plus scout and family programs. **HOURS:** Daily, 9–4:30. **LOCATION:** 247 Southern Blvd., Chatham Twp. (Morris County). **TELEPHONE:** 973-635-6629. **WEBSITE:** http://parks.morris.nj.us/aspparks/gswampmain.asp.

The Raptor Trust: This is a wildlife rehabilitation center for wounded birds, primarily birds of prey. There are several different kinds of owls, hawks, eagles, falcons, and vultures. Those that cannot be released are kept onsite in large cages for public display, for breeding purposes, and for education. Run by a nonprofit organization that also offers educational programs for school, scout, and adult groups. **HOURS:** Daily, 9 a.m.–dusk (call first). **ADMISSION:** Donation. **LOCATION:** 1390 White Bridge Rd., Millington (Morris County). **TELEPHONE:** 908-647-2353. **WEBSITE:** www.theraptortrust.org.

Edwin B. Forsythe National Wildlife Refuge

There are two divisions of this refuge, Brigantine and Barnegat. Both attract birdwatchers, photographers, and naturalists. Over 46,000 acres of grassy tidal marsh are interspersed with tidal bays and channels with some brushy upland areas that support deer, fox, and other small animals. But the main use is to protect waterfowl that use the Atlantic flyway. The snow goose, Canada goose, brant, and black duck are among the many birds that stop here. The refuge offers a seasonal calendar of wildlife events. At the Friends of Forsythe nature store you can join one-hour birding walks on Saturday mornings, March through May.

The Brigantine Division is only 11 miles from Atlantic City, and you can see the casino towers beyond the marshland vistas. But it's a world of immense quiet and peace. An 8-mile self-guided drive circles waterfowl impoundments. Spring and fall are best, but hundreds of birds are here year-round. There are four short trails through the woodlands and salt marsh as well as places where you can stop your car to take pictures. During the warm months the insect population is heavy here, so bring repellent. The Noyes Museum (q.v.) is located just before the entrance. There is a small entrance fee. The refuge headquarters is off Rt. 9 in Oceanville.

The Barnegat Division offers less access, but visitors can see wildlife from an observation platform on Bay Shore Drive as well as on the mile-long DeCamp Wildlife Trail, located at Mantoloking and Adamston Roads in Brick Township. The Holgate Unit of the Barnegat Division covers 400 acres of beach, dunes, and salt marsh at the southern tip of Long Beach Island. It is open off-season, Sept.–Mar., to pedestrians and 4WD vehicles for wildlife and nature study. Closed in summer for the piping plover nesting season.

HOURS: Headquarters, daily, 8–4; refuge, daylight except during special conditions. **ADMISSION:** Free. **LOCATION:** Brigantine Division, Great Creek Rd., Oceanville (Atlantic County). Off Rt. 9.
TELEPHONE: 609-652-1665. **WEBSITE:** www.fws.gov/northeast/forsythe.

Wetlands Institute

Set in the middle of 6,000 acres of publicly owned salt marsh, not far from the beach at Stone Harbor, this attractive cedar shake education center includes classrooms, an exhibit hall, and six research laboratories. Secrets of the Salt Marsh has more than a dozen aquarium exhibits and hands-on interactive exhibits. Terrapin Station is devoted to diamondback turtles. A book and gift shop is also on hand. There is also an observation deck that provides a view of the surrounding wetlands (and an osprey nest). The building is surrounded by native plant gardens. Periodic guided tours of the marsh, plus a number of lectures and ecology classes are available. There's also a salt-marsh trail available during visiting hours, with guided talks during the summer. A 120-foot pier at the end extends over a tidal creek and offers views of the world's largest colony of laughing gulls. Once a year, the institute hosts the "Wings 'n Water Festival," a popular wildlife art event on the third weekend in September that includes wooden duck carvings, seafood dinners, boat rides, and open houses.

> **HOURS:** May 15–Oct. 15, Mon.–Sat., 9:30–4:30; Sun., 10–4. Closed Sun. and Mon. rest of year. **ADMISSION:** $$. Discount: Children. Under 2 free. **LOCATION:** 1075 Stone Harbor Blvd. (Rt. 657), Stone Harbor (Cape May County). Off Garden State Parkway, Exit 10B. **TELEPHONE:** 609-368-1211. **WEBSITE:** www.wetlandsinstitute.org.

Meadowlands Environmental Center

The Hackensack Meadowlands Development Commission's Environmental Center is a modern circular building that sits in the center of an urban salt marsh. A wide, enclosed observation room offers panoramas of the surrounding marshland, with the Turnpike and Manhattan skyline visible in the distance. An outside deck and elevated boardwalk allow closer inspection. It is part of the larger Richard W. DeKorte Park, which includes several trails. The Marsh Discovery Trail leads across a pontoon walkway through the reeds and marshlands, where you can spot ducks, egrets, sandpipers, gulls, and ospreys. There's also a shorter trail through the adjacent Lyndhurst Nature Preserve as well as a butterfly garden next to the center.

There are some interesting displays inside. The main lobby showcases a 30-foot diorama of a salt marsh and its inhabitants. Discovery Station is an interactive center that includes computer touch screen learning, microscopes for viewing close-ups of natural specimens, and walk-through mock-ups of a cedar forest and salt marsh. The Flyway Gallery displays changing exhibits of photos, paintings, and graphics. A gift shop offers stuffed animal toys and environmentally related merchandise. The center runs regular public educational programs, guided nature walks, and pontoon boat tours.

> **HOURS:** Weekdays, 9–5; weekends, 10–3. **ADMISSION:** Free. **LOCATION:** 2 DeKorte Park Plaza, Lyndhurst (Bergen County). From Rt. 3, take Rt. 17 south, exit onto Polito Ave., then left on Valley Brook Ave., 2 miles to end. **TELEPHONE:** 201-460-8300. **WEBSITE:** www.njmeadowlands.gov/ec.

OTHER NATURE CENTERS

Flat Rock Brook Nature Center: About 150 acres of forest with trails and a brook surround a Visitor Center that offers animal and nature exhibits. It offers various weekend activities, such as tree identification and other classes for schoolchildren. A short Backyard Habitat for Wildlife Trail is among 3.2 miles of natural pathways. HOURS: Park, open daily, dawn to dusk; building, Mon.–Fri., 9–5; weekends, 1–5. ADMISSION: Free. LOCATION: 443 Van Nostrand Ave., Englewood (Bergen County). TELEPHONE: 201-567-1265. WEBSITE: www.flatrockbrook.org.

James A. McFaul Environmental Center: An 81-acre center run by Bergen County, this center includes snakes, turtles, and other small animals as well as aquariums, natural history displays, and a large room overlooking a hummingbird garden and waterfowl pond. Outside, you'll find a nature trail, picnic area, and gardens. There are also outdoor wildlife pens with deer, an eagle, and other animals. The Wildlife Exhibit Hall shows films and slide shows plus museum programs. EXHIBIT HALL HOURS: Daily, 8–4:45; weekends, 1–4:45. ADMISSION: Free. LOCATION: Crescent Ave., Wyckoff (Bergen County). Rt. 208 to Goffle Rd. north to Goodwin Ave., then one quarter mile to Crescent. TELEPHONE: 201-891-5571. WEBSITE: www.co.bergen.nj.us/parks/Parks/McFaul.htm.

Trailside Nature and Science Center: A part of Watchung Reservation, this recently expanded modern building includes an auditorium and a natural history museum. A beech tree rises through the atrium, with running water and wildlife specimens at its base. There's a fluorescent mineral room, children's discovery room, and natural history exhibits, as well as weekend programs, nature walks, and numerous children's programs. Thirteen miles of hiking trails surround the center. ADMISSION: Free. LOCATION: Coles Ave. & New Providence Rd., Mountainside (Union County). TELEPHONE: 908-789-3670. WEBSITE: www.unioncountynj.org/trailside/index.htm.

Paws Farm Nature Center: A variety of animal fun for kids. Welcome center features an education room with live animals, stuffed birds, a play area, and a gift shop. Outside, there's a dairy farm with farm animals and a barn with activities and exhibits. A historic farmhouse includes a room on small animals, a reading room, a play vet room, and a blacksmith shop. A short nature trail leads past more animals. There's also a butterfly garden and play areas. HOURS: Wed.–Sun., 10–4. ADMISSION: $. Discount: Children. Under 1 free.

LOCATION: 1105 Hainesport Rd., Mount Laurel (Burlington County). **TELEPHONE:** 856-778-8795. **WEBSITE:** www.pawsfarm.com.

Buttinger Nature Center: This popular center, located in the Stony Brook Reserve, features a Discovery Room with changing nature exhibits and numerous educational programs. There's also a Demonstration Organic Farm, a butterfly house, a birdwatching area, plus 14 miles of trails through the 830 acres surrounding the center. **BUILDING HOURS:** Tue.–Fri., 10–5, Sat., 10–4. **ADMISSION:** Free. **LOCATION:** 31 Titus Mill Rd., Pennington (Mercer County). Off Rt. 31, 2.5 miles north of Pennington Circle. **TELEPHONE:** 609-737-3735. **WEBSITE:** www.thewatershed.org.

Merrill Creek Reservoir Environmental Preserve: Hiking, wildlife observation, and photography are offered in a 290-acre preserve. The Visitor Center has hands-on wildlife exhibits, a roomful of stuffed animals and birds, and a butterfly garden. Guided field trips and other activities are offered. Numerous trails. Pick up a map at the Visitor Center. **HOURS:** Open daily; preserve, dawn to dusk; Visitor Center, Mon.–Fri., 8:30–4:30; weekends, 10–4. **ADMISSION:** Free. **LOCATION:** 34 Merrill Creek Rd., Washington Twp. (Warren County). Rt. 57 to Montana Rd., left on Richline Rd., then left on Merrill Creek Rd. **TELEPHONE:** 908-454-1213. **WEBSITE:** www.merrillcreek.com.

Poricy Park Nature Center: This 250-acre township park offers trails, a nature center, fossil bed, and a colonial farmhouse. A modern building houses nature and fossil displays, art programs, and an extensive list of school programs. Poricy Brook Fossil Beds, where you can explore for fossils, are just a short drive away. Guided tours are available for groups. The Joseph Murray Farm, built before 1780, is the site of special historical programs throughout the year and monthly tours. **HOURS:** Trails, dawn to dusk; nature center, Mon.–Fri., 9–4; Sun., 12:30–3:30; farmhouse, 1–2:30 last Sun. of month (exc. Oct., Feb., & May). **ADMISSION:** Free. **LOCATION:** Oak Hill Rd., Middletown (Monmouth County). Just west of Rt. 35. **TELEPHONE:** 732-842-5966. **WEBSITE:** www.monmouth.com/~poricypark.

Sandy Hook Visitors Center: Summer activities include canoe trips and dune walks. The center has slide shows, some terrariums, and an exhibit on the U.S. Life-Saving Service (once headquartered in the building). Year-round weekend activities include holly forest walks and school classes. Brochures for the lighthouse, Fort Hancock, and beaches are available here. **HOURS:** Daily, 10–5. **ADMISSION:** Free. **LOCATION:** Sandy Hook, Gateway National Recreation Area (Monmouth County). **TELEPHONE:** 732-872-5970. **WEBSITE:** www.nps.gov/gate/shu/shu_home.htm.

Cooper Environmental Center: The center exhibits live reptiles, turtles, and fish, plus hands-on seasonally oriented displays about the local environment, including shells, stuffed mammals and birds, and fossils. There are guided hikes on Cattus Island Park's 5 miles of trails through 500 acres of fresh and saltwater marshes and upland forest as well as bird-watching lessons, slide shows, and a junior naturalist program. **HOURS:** Park, daily, dawn to dusk; center, daily, 8–4:30. **ADMISSION:** Free. **LOCATION:** Cattus Island County Park, 1170 Cattus Island Blvd., Toms River (Ocean County). **TELEPHONE:** 732-270-6960. **WEBSITE:** www.co.ocean.nj.us/parks/cattus.html.

Tenafly Nature Center: The Nature Center Building on this 52-acre site next to 330-acre Lost Brook Preserve offers interpretive displays as well as a variety of nature and wildlife education programs. There's also an outdoor exhibition of backyard habitats for butterflies. **HOURS:** Trails, open daily, dawn to dusk; building, Tue.–Sun., 9–5. **ADMISSION:** Free. **LOCATION:** 313 Hudson Ave., Tenafly (Bergen County). Right off Engle, just north of Clinton Ave. **TELEPHONE:** 201-568-6093. **WEBSITE:** www.tenaflynaturecenter.org.

Wells Mills Nature Center: This nature center is set amid a 900-acre county park that includes a scenic lake and cedar swamp. The exhibit room features a variety of rotating displays on Pinelands environment, history, and wildlife. There's an observation deck with views of the lake and surrounding woodlands. Nature programs are offered. Canoe rentals, spring to fall. **HOURS:** Park, daily, dawn to dusk; center, daily except holidays, 10–4. **ADMISSION:** Free. **LOCATION:** Wells Mills Rd., Waretown (Ocean County). Garden State Parkway northbound, Exit 69, west on Rt. 532 (Wells Mills Rd.); or southbound, Exit 74 to Lacey Rd., east to Rt. 9 to Rt. 532 west. **TELEPHONE:** 609-971-3085. **WEBSITE:** www.ocean.nj.us/parks/wellsmills.html.

Woodford Cedar Run Wildlife Refuge: This lodge-like Education Center on a 184-acre preserve offers workshops, field trips, and hands-on exhibits about wildlife and the Pinelands. There are some live animals, especially in the snake room, plus a puppet theater and play room. The refuge also has a wildlife rehabilitation hospital that treats 2,000 animals a year and includes an outdoor live-animal compound with foxes, hawks, owls, and deer. Wonderful Wildlife Weekends (Sat., 10–4, and Sun., 1–4) focus on specific species. Outdoor Adventures include Pinelands canoe trips, off-road biking, guided hikes, tracking by compass, and outdoor skills. **HOURS:** Mon.–Sat., 10–4; Sun., 1–4. **ADMISSION:** $. Discounts: Seniors, children. Under 2 free. **LOCATION:** 6 Sawmill Rd., Medford (Burlington

County). Rt. 73 to Marlton Parkway, right on Hopewell Rd. to W. Centennial, then to Borton Rd. Make a right, then a left onto Sawmill. **TELEPHONE:** 856-983-3329. **WEBSITE:** www.cedarrun.org.

Warren E. Fox Nature Center: Displays depict area history, ecology, and environmental principles. The greenhouse has a live animal collection. Programs include bird-watching, orienteering, night excursions, reptile and amphibian walks, and other themes. Field studies combine lecture and on-site, hands-on instruction. **HOURS:** Daily, 8–4. **ADMISSION:** Free. **LOCATION:** Estell Manor County Park, Rt. 50, Mays Landing (Atlantic County). **TELEPHONE:** 609-625-1897. **WEBSITE:** www.aclink.org/parks/mainpages/nc.asp.

New Jersey Audubon Society

The society operates a number of centers, wildlife sanctuaries, and bird observatories throughout the state (908-204-8998; www.njaudubon.org). Here you might find art shows, gift shops full of books and binoculars, libraries, sample backyards with lots of birdhouses, and trail maps for the surrounding fields or forests. The centers include the following, and all are free.

Scherman-Hoffman Sanctuary: Headquarters for the society, the site is a combination of two former estates. The 260-acre sanctuary runs programs such as nighttime or morning rambles, slide programs, art shows, school programs, canoe trips, birding weekends, and more. Free nature walks Fri. and Sat., 8–9 A.M. on 3.2 miles of upland and streamside trails. There is also a nice nature center with a nature- and birding-oriented gift shop, a bird observation window, classrooms, and a bird display room. **HOURS:** Tue.–Sat., 9–5; Sun., 12–5. **LOCATION:** 11 Hardscrabble Rd., Bernardsville (Somerset County). Exit 30B from Rt. 287. Cross 202 onto Childs Rd., then bear right on Hardscrabble. **TELEPHONE:** 908-766-5787.

Lorrimer Sanctuary: This center, in a late 1700s house, has an exhibit and lecture room, interpretive and hands-on displays, gift shop, bird observation window, and nature trails on 14 surrounding acres. Activities include nature programs and workshops plus numerous programs for school kids. Lots of birdwatching. **HOURS:** Wed.–Fri., 9–5; Sat., 10–5; Sun., 1–5. **LOCATION:** 790 Ewing Ave., Franklin Lakes (Bergen County). One mile south of Rt. 208. **TELEPHONE:** 201-891-2185.

Sandy Hook Bird Observatory: This site has a Visitor Center, a nearby observation deck overlooking New York Harbor, and hiking trails. The observatory offers field trips, morning bird and butterfly walks, bird migration watch mid-Mar. to mid-May, workshops, and many school group programs. **HOURS**: Tue.–Sat., 10–5; Sun., 10–3. **LOCATION**: 20 Hartshorne Dr., Fort Hancock, Gateway National Recreation Area (Monmouth County). **TELEPHONE**: 732-872-2500.

Weis Ecology Center: Nestled on a 160-acre preserve adjacent to Norvin Green State Forest, this center offers numerous on-site programs covering wildlife, outdoor skills, and interpretive hikes. Campsites and cabins are available, as is a dormitory for school and scout groups. Special residential programs include meals. There's also a small wildlife display area and gift shop in the center. **HOURS**: Wed.–Sun., 8:30–4:30. **LOCATION**: 150 Snake Den Rd., Ringwood (Passaic County). Take Rt. 287 to Exit 55 to Rt. 511 north for 4 miles. Left on Westbrook Rd. Left again at fork, then second left onto Snake Den. Take left fork on Snake Den. **TELEPHONE**: 973-835-2160.

Plainsboro Preserve: A 631-acre preserve features an environmental education center with interactive displays, a nature bookstore, an observation deck overlooking McCormack Lake, and more than 5 miles of trails. There are natural history programs, interpretive hikes, and slide programs for groups. **HOURS**: Tue.–Sat., 9–5; Sun., 12–5. **LOCATION**: 80 Scotts Corner Rd., Plainsboro (Middlesex County). Rt. 1 to Scudders Mill Rd., then left on Dey Rd. to Scotts Corner. **TELEPHONE**: 609-897-9400.

Rancocas Nature Center: This is a favorite for bird-watchers. It covers about 120 acres on the edge of Rancocas State Park and has nature displays, a book and gift shop, and a classroom inside and nature trails beyond. **HOURS**: Tue.–Sat., 9–5; Sun., 12–5. **LOCATION**: 794 Rancocas Rd., Mt. Holly (Burlington County). **TELEPHONE**: 609-261-2495.

Nature Center of Cape May: The nature center on the harbor has exhibit aquariums, classrooms, a gift shop, and display and children's gardens. A full schedule of natural history programs runs throughout the year. Extensive program for schools and other groups. **HOURS**: Varies by season, opens around 10 A.M. **LOCATION**: 1600 Delaware Ave., Cape May (Cape May County). **TELEPHONE**: 609-898-8848.

Cape May Bird Observatory: The Northwood Center is the prime bird-watching area in the state. It is famous for its World Series of Birding weekend in early to mid-May, when millions of birds can be tracked, but there is birding activity year-round. Birding workshops and daily walks and programs. Also, local birding guides are available for hire. There's also an information center and book and gift shop. **HOURS:** Daily, 9–4:30. **LOCATION:** 701 East Lake Dr., Cape May Point (Cape May County). **TELEPHONE:** 609-884-2736.

The Center for Research and Education: This is an 8,600-square-foot building surrounded by 26 acres of marsh and upland that offers lecture rooms, a large gift shop, observation deck, wildlife art gallery, a model backyard habitat and displays, and many educational activities. **HOURS:** Daily, 9–4:30. **LOCATION:** 600 Rt. 47, Goshen (Cape May County). **TELEPHONE:** 609-861-0700.

The Great Outdoors

Trout fishing is popular from spring to fall in the many streams and rivers of the state's parks and forests. *(Photo by Patrick Sarver)*

SKI AREAS

Snowy winters come—and go. As a result, some ski areas of the past are no more. But those that are still around have largely found ways to weather the changes, with the regional skiing picture as reliable as it can be with snowmaking equipment and the addition of terrain parks for snowboarders and tubing runs. Still, not all trails or facilities listed may be available. The number of trails change all the time. The number of lifts may be upgraded from one season to the next. Typical price for an adult day ticket is $45. Please call first.

New Jersey Ski Areas

Mountain Creek: By far the largest ski area in New Jersey, covering 170 skiable acres. Ski and snowboard instruction is available at all levels. Night skiing and half-day tickets are available. Eleven lifts, including a gondola. Four peaks, forty-six trails, ski and snowboard rentals. Cafeteria and bar at base lodges. Vertical drop of 1,040 feet. For snowboarding, there are a Zaugg superpipe and five terrain parks, with more than twenty rails, including a 60-foot roller-coaster rail, S-rail, double kink rail, and many EZ-slide rails for learners. A total of sixty "hits" in all. There are also seven snowtubing runs. Construction is also underway on a new resort village. There's a new lodge and there are stores, and the rest of the village will be built over a ten-year period. **HOURS:** Weekdays, 9 a.m.–10 P.M.; Sat., 8 a.m.–10 P.M.; Sun., 8 a.m.–5 P.M. **LOCATION:** Rt. 23 to Rt. 94 north, between McAfee and Vernon (Sussex County). **TELEPHONE:** 973-827-2000. **WEBSITE:** www.mountaincreek.com.

Hidden Valley: Once partially private, now a public ski area with day, twilight, and night skiing. Twelve trails, five lifts, a variety of trails, 620-foot vertical. Ski lessons, rentals, and separate racing program. Snowboarding terrain park. Five tubing chutes. Cafeteria, bar, grill, special events. **HOURS:** Mon.–Thu., Sat., 10–4; Fri., 9 a.m.–10 P.M.; Sun., 9–5. **LOCATION:** 44 Breakneck Road, Vernon (Sussex County). Rt. 23 north to Rt. 515, 8 miles, then right on Breakneck. **TELEPHONE:** 973-764-4200. **WEBSITE:** www.hiddenvalleynj.com.

Campgaw Mountain (Bergen County): For beginners and intermediates. 100 per cent snowmaking equipment. Five beginner and intermediate trails, two double chairlifts, one tow, one conveyor lift, vertical drop of 300 feet. Lighted for night skiing; cafeteria in lodge. Lessons daily and seasonal ski and snowboarding rentals. Six runs for snowtubing with two surface lifts, half-pipe, and freestyle terrain park for snowboarding. **HOURS:** Mon.–Thu., 2–8; Fri.–Sat.; 9–10; Sun., 9–8 & holidays, 9–9. Tubing sessions are two hours. **LOCATION:** Campgaw Rd., Mahwah (Bergen County). Off Rt. 202. **TELEPHONE:** 201-327-7800. **WEBSITE:** www.skicampgaw.com.

Note: Cross-country skiing is available at most state parks and in many county parks in New Jersey.

Poconos Ski Areas

Shawnee Mountain: Just beyond the Delaware Water Gap, Shawnee offers nine lifts, twenty-three trails, snowmaking, ski school, accessory rental, cafeteria, bar, and nursery, and a 700-foot vertical.

Snowboarding, snowtubing with two tows. Family packages. **HOURS:** Day, night, and twilight skiing. **LOCATION:** Rt. 80, Exit 309, then north on Rt. 209 for 6 miles. **TELEPHONE:** 570-421-7231; snow report, 800-233-4218. **WEBSITE:** www.shawneemt.com.

Jack Frost/Big Boulder: You buy a combination ticket for these two popular mountains. Jack Frost has nine lifts, one ski carpet, and many trails that run the gamut from "Powderpuff" to "Thunderbolt." Rentals, ski school, cafeteria, nursery. There are twelve slopes at Big Boulder, twenty-three at Jack Frost. Seventeen snowtubing chutes with four tows combined. Terrain park and half-pipe at both. **HOURS:** Jack Frost: Mon.–Fri., 9–4; Sat–Sun., 8–4. Big Boulder: Mon.–Thu., 3–9; Fri., 3–10; Sat., 8 a.m.–10 P.M.; Sun., 8–8. **LOCATION:** Lake Harmony and White Haven, PA. Rt. 80, Exit 284. **TELEPHONE:** 570-443-8425. **WEBSITE:** www.jfbb.com.

Camelback: Located 15 miles west of the Delaware Water Gap and part of Big Pocono State Park, Camelback offers a variety of trails and attracts a pleasant crowd. There are thirty-three trails, thirteen lifts. This 2,100-foot mountain is the largest in the area. Three base lodges. Snowboarding, snowtubing. **HOURS:** Daily, 8 a.m.–10 P.M. **LOCATION:** Tannersville, PA. Rt. 80, Exit 299. **TELEPHONE:** 570-629-1661; snow report, 800-233-8100. **WEBSITE:** www.skicamelback.com.

New York State Ski Areas

Hunter Mountain: For groups and more advanced skiers, Hunter is very popular. A bit of a drive, but there's a 1,600-foot vertical and a large variety of trails on three peaks for all levels. Ten chairlifts, one tow, fifty-three trails; all services available. Snowboarding terrain park and half-pipe. Variety of eateries. Snowshoeing with high-tech shoes on the mountain summit. Snowtubing park with three tows (daily except Tue.). **HOURS:** Daily, 8:30–4. **LOCATION:** Garden State Parkway to N.Y. Thruway, Exit 20, to Rt. 32 to Rt. 32A to Rt. 23A, west 10 miles. **TELEPHONE:** 888-HUNTERMT. **WEBSITE:** www. huntermtn.com.

Ski Windham: Seven miles west of Hunter. Two peaks with a 1,600-foot vertical with forty-two trails and eight lifts. Includes a base lodge, restaurant, nightclub, cafeteria, ski school, nursery. Snowboard terrain park and half-pipe. Ice skating rink. **HOURS:** Sat. & holidays, 8 a.m.–10 P.M.; Thu., Fri., 9 a.m.–10 P.M.; Sun.–Wed., 8 a.m.–4 P.M. Snowtubing park with three lifts open Friday evening, weekends, and holiday Mondays. **LOCATION:** Windham, NY. Take N.Y. Thruway, Exit 21, to Rt. 23 for 25 miles. **TELEPHONE:** 518-734-4300; snow report, 800-729-4766. **WEBSITE:** www.skiwindham.com.

Mount Peter: Located just off Rt. 17A near Warwick in Orange County, NY, the oldest operating ski area in New York has three lifts and ten runs along with snowboarding. This area offers a less-expensive, lower-key skiing alternative, including free beginner ski and snowboard lessons on weekends and holidays. **HOURS:** Mon.–Thu. until 9 P.M.; Fri.–Sat. until 10 P.M.; Sun. until 5 P.M. **LOCATION:** Rt. 17A and Old Mt. Peter Rd., Warwick, NY. **TELEPHONE:** 845-986-4940; snow report: 845-986-4992. **WEBSITE:** www.mtpeter.com.

HIKING

An overwhelming majority of federal, state, and county parks offer hiking of some kind or other. In fact, according to the state, there are almost 1,200 miles of hiking trails on public land in New Jersey.

The **Appalachian Trail** traverses 75 miles of the northern tip of the state on its way from Maine to Georgia. It crosses into the state at the Delaware Water Gap and follows the Kittatinny Mountain ridge through Worthington State Forest, the Delaware Water Gap National Recreation Area, Stokes State Forest, and High Point State Park. It then turns east along the New York border to Wawayanda State Park and Abram Hewitt State Forest before heading north and out of the state at Greenwood Lake. All of these parklands offer miles of other prime hiking trails for all levels of hiker.

The **Pine Barrens** in southern New Jersey offer a completely different experience. The terrain is flat but the flora and fauna of the region are unusual. Trails and old sand roads wind through the pines and swamps. At 50 miles, the Batona Trail is the longest, extending from Carpenter Spring in Brendan Byrne State Forest to Batsto in Wharton Forest, then east to Bass River State Forest. Another, shorter trail in the Pine Barrens is the Absegami. Since trails in the Pine Barrens can be confusing and people have gotten lost, it is best to start your hike at Batsto, where you can talk with the rangers at the Visitor Center and obtain hiking guides. Check Bass River and Wharton State Forest in the state parks and forests listings.

Among the most popular county parks for hiking are the following. **North:** Watchung Reservation in Union County; South Mountain Reservation and Lenape Trail in Essex County; Mahlon Dickerson Reservation, Pyramid Mountain Natural Area and Patriot's Path in Morris County. **Central:** Lord Stirling Park and Sourland Mountain Preserve in Somerset County, Musconetcong Gorge in Hunterdon County, Hartshorne Woods in Monmouth County. **South:** Wells Mills

County Park and Cattus Island in Ocean County, and Estell Manor Park in Atlantic County. In addition, there are hundreds of miles of trails in almost all the state parks and forests. There's a list of these parks later in this chapter.

A good place to contact for hiking advice is the Sierra Club's local chapter (609-656-7612). Their hikes are led by responsible guides who are very knowledgeable about New Jersey and nearby trails. Numerous hiking and other outings are described on the N.J. chapter's Website at http://newjersey.sierraclub.org/outings.asp.

Another hiking group is the Appalachian Mountain Club, whose local New York/New Jersey chapter can be reached at 212-986-1430 (www.amc-ny.org) along with the Delaware Valley chapter (www. amcdv.org/activities). Websites list upcoming hikes.

FISHING

Saltwater Fishing

Many people think of saltwater fishing in New Jersey as offshore fishing, but there are also many opportunities for surf fishing as well as shore and small boat angling on the numerous bays along the Jersey Shore. Whether you're on the water or along the shoreline, saltwater fishing requires no license in the state.

Fishing boats are available for walk-ons at almost every coastal harbor in the state, from Raritan Bay to Cape May as well as along the Delaware Bay shore. Party boats go out seven days a week during the summer as well as quite often at other times of the year. Usually half- or full-day excursions are offered. Some boats offer overnight fishing for tuna, including trips to the offshore canyons; they come complete with tackle, bait, food and drink, although you pay for the extras, of course. These boats can often handle over a hundred people and are designed to go well out into the ocean in their quest for bluefish, weakfish, tuna, fluke, and striped bass. Charter boats are usually smaller and can be hired by groups for the day. In the busy season they must be reserved weeks in advance. Check the sports section of most newspapers (Friday editions, especially) for the names of party and charter boats. Or write or call the N.J. Division of Fish, Game and Wildlife, CN 400, Trenton, NJ 08625 (609-292-2965), for the Party and Charter Boat Directory. Or download it from www.state.nj.us/dep/fgw/prtyboat.htm#directory.

Freshwater Fishing

Fishermen have several traditional favorites in New Jersey, many of them in state parks. Anyone over 14 years of age must have a license for freshwater fishing, which you can get at any sporting goods or bait-and-tackle store. For those who like lake fishing, Round Valley Reservoir (Hunterdon County) is deemed by some to have the best fishing, with twenty-two species of fish, including rainbow and lake trout and large- and smallmouth bass. Nearby Spruce Run is another favorite for trout, bass, and muskellunge. Big and Little Swartswood Lakes in Swartswood State Park (Sussex County) are both known for their fishing quality. Greenwood Lake (Passaic County and New York State) is a huge lake, popular with anglers with boats.

Trout fishing seems to attract a lot of interest, especially in spring, when cooler waters throughout the state support an active trout-stocking program. Among the notable trout streams in the northwestern part of the state are the Pequest River, Flat Brook, and the Paulinskill and Black Rivers, not to mention the South Branch of the Raritan in the Ken Lockwood Gorge Wildlife Area. The Delaware River from Trenton north to High Point on the state's western border is also a popular fishing area, especially during the spring shad run. But there are also large- and smallmouth bass, muskellunge, and many other species. The best fishing in the Delaware is by boat, since the deeper part of this broad river is often inaccessible from shore. But there are many areas of public access along the river.

With so many bays in southern New Jersey, saltwater fishing tends to be more popular here. However, the Pine Barrens still offer some good freshwater fishing, especially for pickerel, bass, and catfish. Try the Batsto and Wading Rivers and the many lakes in parks throughout the southern part of the state, such as Parvin and Bass River State Forests.

The Division of Fish and Wildlife publishes "New Jersey Places to Fish," which lists inland waters by county that are open, along with the general quality of fishing by species (www.njfishandwildlife. com/fishplc.htm). Boating ramps are available at most state parks, but you must bring your own boat. Canoes and rowboats can also be rented in selected areas.

CAMPING

New Jersey has many state parks that offer beautiful, clean, and well-equipped campgrounds. All you have to do to enjoy them is bring your own camping equipment, a minimal entrance fee, and tote your own garbage out (state policy; they provide the bags). Call the campgrounds for details. The state park service publishes a brochure listing camping facilities and regulations at state parks (800-843-6420;

www.state.nj.us/dep/parksandforests/parks/camping.html). A listing of state parks can be found at the end of this chapter.

Bass River and Swartswood state parks are excellent for family outings. Campsites are adequately sized. Facilities include flush toilets and showers, and they are kept fairly clean. Swimming, boating, and picnic areas are close to the sites. At Bass River, the shallow lake allows for canoeing and paddle boating. Swartswood Lake is good for sailing as well. Canoes, rowboats, and paddleboats can be rented.

For good-weather weekend camping, reservations are recommended. At most state parks, half of the available sites can be reserved ahead so long as you stay a minimum of two days. The rest are given out on a first-come, first-served basis. Group sites can always be reserved in advance. Your chances are always better in midweek, especially if you just show up looking for a camping spot.

Wawayanda and Worthington parks are definitely primitive. Wawayanda is especially suitable for group camping and day trips to the beach or for fishing. No flush toilets are to be found at Worthington on the Delaware. Located a few hundred feet from the Delaware, this large open site will appeal to those who choose to fish, raft, or canoe on the river. For the truly hardy, scenic Round Valley Reservoir offers real wilderness camping. Campers must hike or boat to the sites. The key interest here is sailing, boating, and fishing. Spruce Run, with facilities for boating, fishing, and swimming, takes camping out of the woods and puts it in the sunshine, which can be hard to handle as the sites are on a hill with no shade. Again, there is a beach with the usual facilities. Swimming, boating, and fishing in state parks are also usually available daily in season for noncampers.

There are also hundreds of sites in many private campgrounds around the state. The Pine Barrens and the southern portion of New Jersey abound with these camps, which usually offer more sophisticated facilities than the state-run sites (higher rates, too). A limited number of county parks offer camping also (check park listings later in chapter). For a brochure from the N.J. Campground Owners Association listing private camping and RV sites in the state, call 609-465-8444; www.newjerseycampgrounds.com.

ADVENTUROUS OUTINGS

For those who like to add the element of adventure to their summer activities, a number of options are available. You don't have to live in California to windsurf, skydive, parachute, or raft down a river. Here are a few of the places where you can jump into action.

Soaring and Skydiving

Skydiving/Parachuting: If you want to learn how to skydive and parachute, you can learn both in one day. You get jump training on the ground, then you're taken up and out. One outfit specializing in freefall and tandem jumping is *Skydive Sussex,* affiliated with the U.S. Parachute Association. **HOURS:** Open Apr.–Nov. **LOCATION:** Sussex Airport, scene of a popular summer air show, on Rt. 639, Sussex. **TELEPHONE:** 973-702-7000. **WEBSITE:** www.skydivesussex.com.

Two skydiving schools with lessons tailored for new and experienced skydivers are offered at *Freefall Adventures/Skydive Cross Keys.* Freefall Adventures introduces beginners and novices to the sport, while Skydive Cross Keys is geared for experienced and licensed skydivers. **LOCATION:** Cross Keys Airport, Rt. 555, Williamstown (Gloucester County). Rt. 322, 5 miles east of Glassboro to left on Rt. 555. **TELEPHONE:** 856-629-7553. **WEBSITE:** www.freefalladventures.com.

Soaring: You soar in a glider (which is towed aloft by an airplane) over the Delaware Water Gap, the Kittatinny Ridge, and other scenic areas. Good picture-taking possibilities. Open year-round. Contact *Eagle Ridge Soaring,* 36 Lambert Rd., Blairstown Airport, Blairstown (Warren County) (908-362-8311).

Hot Air Ballooning

Hot air ballooning offers fancy flights (often with champagne included) at prices to match. Flights are almost always at sunrise and about two hours before sunset, because that's when wind conditions are calmest. If winds are up or if the weather's bad, then the flights are canceled. A few places fly year-round, but most operate spring to fall. The hotbed for ballooning in the state is Hunterdon and Somerset Counties, largely along the Rt. 78 corridor, with several major balloon ports along Rt. 173 near Clinton. Some scattered balloon flights can be found elsewhere in the state as well. Some of the larger companies are the following:

> *In Flight Balloon Adventures* leaves from the Coach 'n Paddock restaurant in Clinton (Hunterdon County).
> **TELEPHONE:** 888-301-2383. **WEBSITE:** www.balloonnj.com.

> *Balloons Aloft* flies out of the Sky Manor Airport in Pittstown (Hunterdon County). **TELEPHONE:** 866-800-4386.
> **WEBSITE:** www.njballoon.com.

> *Above & Beyond Ballooning* flies from the Clinton area (Hunterdon County). **TELEPHONE:** 908-208-1869.
> **WEBSITE:** www.njhotair.com.

Balloonatics & Aeronuts is north of Phillipsburg (Warren County) off Rt. 519 and flies from the Rt. 78 corridor. **TELEPHONE:** 877-438-6359. **WEBSITE:** www.aeronuts.com.

Odyssey Hot Air Balloons, located in Moorestown, flies out of the South Jersey Regional Airport in Lumberton (Burlington County). **TELEPHONE:** 856-234-5165. **WEBSITE:** www.odysseyballoons.com.

Have Balloon Will Travel is also out of Phillipsburg (Warren County), north of Rt. 78. Or they will travel to other locations. **TELEPHONE:** 800-608-6359. **WEBSITE:** www.haveballoonwilltravel.com.

Dancing on Air flies in the Flemington area (Hunterdon County). **TELEPHONE:** 877-HOTAIR4. **WEBSITE:** www.hot-air-ride.com.

Blue Sky Adventures is located in East Brunswick (Middlesex County). **TELEPHONE:** 732-940-6558. **WEBSITE:** www.njhotair.com/bluesky.

Tewksbury Balloon Adventures launches near Whitehouse Station (Somerset County). **TELEPHONE:** 908-439-3320. **WEBSITE:** www.tewksburyballoon.com.

Sky Sweeper Balloon Adventures flies from Clinton (Hunterdon County). **TELEPHONE:** 800-462-3201. **WEBSITE:** www.skysweeper.com.

If you just like to watch hot air balloons, then head to the New Jersey Festival of Ballooning, held at the Solberg Airport in Readington (Somerset County) in late July. There are usually around 125 balloons, many with special shapes, along with concerts by pop music stars. **TELEPHONE:** 800-HOTAIR9. **WEBSITE:** www.balloonfestival.com.

ADVENTUROUS WATER SPORTS

Windsurfing

Popular areas are at lakes in such state parks as Round Valley and Spruce Run. The bay side of the Jersey Shore also offers windsurfing territory for experienced practitioners. Sandy Hook is popular, and you can find windsurfing rentals on Long Beach Island and other shore resorts.

Canoeing, Kayaking, and Tubing

Kittatinny Canoes in Dingman's Ferry, PA, is one of the biggest canoe renters along the Delaware River and also offers rafting, kayaking, and tubing trips. A number of trips are available, from north of Port Jervis, NY, to the Bushkill area and range from 2.5-mile tubing trips to overnight canoe camping (800-FLOAT-KC; www.kittatinny.com). Further south is **Bucks County River Country,** which offers canoeing, leisure rafting, kayaking, and river tubing upriver to Point Pleasant, PA (Bucks County). A variety of trip lengths are offered, from two hours to overnight. Picnic facilities are available at the base. (215-297-5000; www.rivercountry.net).

The other prime area for canoeing and kayaking in New Jersey is the Pine Barrens, with outfitters scattered throughout the southern part of the state. Among the popular waterways are the Wading, Mullica, Oswego, and Batsto Rivers, which run through Wharton State Forest and other state forests of the region. The New Jersey Pinelands Commission maintains a list of outfitters in this area on its Website at www.state.nj.us/pinelands/pastimes/canoe.

OUTDOOR SKILLS

Mohican Outdoor Center: This southernmost Appalachian Mountain Club facility stands near Catfish Pond and the Appalachian Trail in the Delaware Water Gap National Recreation Area. An extensive program of outdoor-skills workshops is offered here year-round. Courses include rock climbing, backpacking, yoga and hiking, mountain biking, orienteering, wilderness first aid, bird-watching, Native American lore, photography, and astronomy. There are cabins and campsites along with a dining hall with meals available in summer. LOCATION: 50 Camp Rd., Blairstown (Warren County). Rt. 94 west of Blairstown to Mohican Rd. Left on Gaisler Rd., then right on Camp Rd. TELEPHONE: 908-362-5670. WEBSITE: www.mohicanoutdoor center.com.

STATE PARKS AND FORESTS

Following is a listing of the state parks and forests in New Jersey. Park areas with swimming charge a parking fee on summer weekends; some charge every day in summer. Other parks are free. The state offers special yearly park passes, which can be a bargain if you visit a lot of parks in summer. For more information on state parklands, visit www.njparksandforests.org.

State Parks

Allaire State Park, Rt. 524, Allaire (Monmouth County): Its 3,068 acres include restored Allaire Village, a narrow-gauge railroad, picnicking, hiking and horse trails, camping, fishing, golf course, nature center, lively calendar of events. **TELEPHONE:** 732-938-2371.

Allamuchy Mountain State Park, Allamuchy (Warren County): Mostly undeveloped forested hills with some fishing and trails. Also the site of Waterloo Village (q.v.). **TELEPHONE:** 908-852-3790.

Barnegat Lighthouse State Park, Barnegat Light (Ocean County): This is a 172-foot lighthouse with a 217-step spiral staircase. Picnicking, fishing from restored jetties, no swimming. Nearby museum. **TELEPHONE:** 609-494-2016.

Bull's Island Natural Area, Stockton (Hunterdon County). This natural area covers a portion of a small forested island surrounded by the Delaware River and the Delaware & Raritan Canal. **TELEPHONE:** 609-397-2949.

Cape May Point State Park (Cape May County): Picnicking, tours of restored lighthouse, wetlands boardwalk trails, bird-watching, swimming, nature center, surf fishing. **TELEPHONE:** 609-884-2159.

Cheesequake State Park, off Garden State Parkway, Exit 120, Matawan (Middlesex County): A 1,361-acre park consisting of wetlands and upland forest. Several miles of hiking trails lead through a variety of terrain, including a boardwalk through a cedar swamp. There's also camping, a swimming beach, fishing, picnicking, and a nature center. **TELEPHONE:** 732-566-2161.

Corson's Inlet State Park, Rt. 619 south of Ocean City (Cape May County): Beach, small boat launch, fishing. **TELEPHONE:** 609-861-2404.

Delaware & Raritan Canal State Park (Somerset County): A long, narrow strip of land between the old canal and the Millstone River, with many canal structures along the way. Canoeing, fishing, bicycling, hiking. **TELEPHONE:** 609-924-5705.

Double Trouble State Park, Double Trouble Road (Rt. 530), Berkeley Twp. (Ocean County): Includes a small historic village, hiking trails beside cranberry bogs, and canoe trips on Cedar Creek. **TELEPHONE:** 732-341-6662.

Farny State Park, off Rt. 513, Marcella (Morris County): A wilderness-type area, it offers hiking trails through the Farny Natural Area and overlooking the adjacent Splitrock Reservoir. **TELEPHONE:** 973-962-7031.

Fort Mott State Park, Fort Mott Rd., off Rt. 49, Pennsville (Salem County): A 104-acre park surrounding the remains of an 1890s fort (q.v.). Picnicking, playgrounds, and fishing. Next to Finn's Point National Cemetery. Ferry to Pea Patch Island and Fort Delaware, a Civil War prison. **TELEPHONE:** 856-935-3218.

Hacklebarney State Park, 119 Hacklebarney Rd., Long Valley (Morris County): Off Rt. 124 west of Chester. The Black River cascades through a scenic, boulder-lined gorge. Trout fishing in the river and in Trout Brook, streamside and upland hiking, picnic area, and a playground. **TELEPHONE:** 908-638-6969.

High Point State Park, Rt. 23, Sussex (Sussex County): The highest point in the state is marked by the recently restored 220-foot High Point Monument. Swimming beach at Lake Marcia. The Appalachian Trail passes through this park, part of more than 50 miles of trails at High Point. Kuser Natural Area includes a cedar swamp. Three lakes and a pond offer fishing and boating. Camping, nature tours, bicycling, and a cross-country ski center. **TELEPHONE:** 973-875-4800.

Hopatcong State Park, Landing (Morris County): Small public beach at the southern end of Lake Hopatcong, New Jersey's largest lake. Picnicking, swimming, boating, fishing, small historical museum. **TELEPHONE:** 973-398-7010.

Island Beach State Park, Central Ave. south of Seaside Park (Ocean County): Popular 9.5-mile-long beach with ocean swimming, bathhouses, surfing area, fishing, picnicking, bicycling, and two natural areas with nature trails. Year-round parking fee. **TELEPHONE:** 732-793-0506.

Kittatinny Valley State Park, Andover (Sussex/Warren County): Hike the 27-mile Paulinskill Valley Trail along the scenic Paulinskill River and 20 miles of the Sussex Branch Trail, both on former railroad rights-of-way. The Sussex Trail is still being developed (973-786-6445). For monthly hike information, call the Paulinskill Valley Trail Committee. **TELEPHONE:** 908-684-4820.

Liberty State Park, Jersey City (Hudson County), Exit 14B of N.J. Turnpike: This Hudson River–front park is known as the home of the Liberty Science Center (q.v.) and for the ferry to the Statue of Liberty and Ellis Island. There is also a 1.3-mile Liberty Walk along the Hudson, which offers great views of Lower Manhattan, Ellis Island, and the Statue of Liberty. Other points include the restored Central Railroad of New Jersey terminal, a salt-marsh natural area and interpretive center, a butterfly and sensory garden at Millennium Park, a marina, boat ramps, playground, picnicking, New York ferry,

and special events throughout the year. **TELEPHONE:** 201-915-3440.
WEBSITE: www.libertystatepark.com.

Long Pond Ironworks State Park, Rt. 511, Hewitt (Passaic County): Historic village, museum, and early American ironworks (q.v.) at Hewitt. Hiking trails lead to a small waterfall and go along Wanaque River beyond the ironworks. Fishing, boating at Monksville Reservoir. **TELEPHONE:** 973-962-7031.

Monmouth Battlefield State Park, Bus. Rt. 33, Manalapan (Monmouth County): Visitor Center, historic sites, and yearly reenactment commemorate the Battle of Monmouth of the Revolutionary War (q.v.). Picnicking and 25 miles of hiking trails. **TELEPHONE:** 732-462-9616.

Parvin State Park, Rt. 540, Pittsgrove (Salem County), 5 miles west of Vineland: This 1,309-acre wooded park surrounds Thundergust and Parvin Lakes. It offers campsites and cabins, a swimming beach, boating, fishing, picnicking, a canoe rental, 15 miles of hiking trails, and a scenic natural area and cedar swamp. **TELEPHONE:** 856-358-8616.

Princeton Battlefield State Park, 500 Mercer St., Princeton (Mercer County): Small park with historic Clarke House and Revolutionary War monument on the grounds. Open fields for walking, hiking, and picnicking. **TELEPHONE:** 609-921-0074.

Rancocas State Park, Mt. Holly (Burlington County): Nature center, hiking, and fishing highlight the activities in the heavily wooded preserve. **TELEPHONE:** 609-726-1191. Or call the Audubon Center at the park at 609-261-2495.

Ringwood State Park, Ringwood (Passaic County): Three areas of the park include Ringwood Manor, Skylands, and Shepherd Lake. Ringwood Manor (q.v.) includes the mansion of millionaire Abram Hewitt; Skylands includes a Tudor manor and the state botanical gardens (q.v.); and Shepherd Lake is a recreation area offering a swimming beach, boat rentals, and fishing. Several hiking trails cross the park, and there are nice picnicking grounds in many areas. **TELEPHONE:** 973-962-7031.

Round Valley Recreation Area, Rt. 629, Lebanon Twp. (Hunterdon County): Wilderness camping, boating, fishing, hiking, swimming beach, and picnicking at the second largest lake in the state. **TELEPHONE:** 908-236-6355.

Spruce Run Recreation Area, Clinton (Hunterdon County): A large, scenic lake that offers fishing, boat rentals, sailing, a swimming beach, and picnicking. **TELEPHONE:** 908-638-8572.

Stephens State Park, now combined with Allamuchy Mountain State Park, Hackettstown (Warren County): Camping, fishing, picnicking, and a playground in woods lining the Musconetcong River. TELE-PHONE: 908-852-3790.

Swartswood State Park, Rt. 619, Swartswood (Sussex County): Excellent fishing, boating, hiking, boat rentals, picnicking, camping, and a swimming beach on two scenic lakes. TELEPHONE: 973-383-5230.

Voorhees State Park, Rt. 513, High Bridge (Hunterdon County): Hiking, picnicking, camping, nature study, and an astronomical observatory in a wooded hillside preserve. TELEPHONE: 908-638-6969.

Washington Crossing State Park, Rt. 29, Titusville (Mercer County): Rolling hills along the Delaware River offer a nature center, outdoor theater, picnicking, playing fields, hiking, camping, and historical museums (q.v.). TELEPHONE: 609-737-0623.

Washington Rock State Park, 16 Rock Rd., Green Brook (Somerset County): Picnicking and views from atop a bluff (q.v.) overlooking the Plainfields and beyond. TELEPHONE: 201-915-3401.

Wawayanda State Park, 885 Warwick Tpk., Hewitt (Passaic/Sussex Counties): There are two main areas of the park. One, near Highland Lakes, offers camping, fishing, boat rentals, a swimming beach, hiking, and horseback riding in the forest surrounding Wawayanda Lake. The second, off Bearfort Rd., offers fishing and wilderness-style hiking. TELEPHONE: 973-853-4462.

State Forests

Abram S. Hewitt State Forest, West Milford (Passaic County): This rugged forest offers hiking and cross-country skiing but is still largely undeveloped. TELEPHONE: 973-853-4462.

Bass River State Forest, New Gretna (Burlington/Ocean Counties): Garden State Parkway, Exit 52, follow signs. This sandy Pinelands park of 26,000 acres surrounds scenic Lake Absegami. Swimming beach, picnicking, hiking, nature study, fishing, boat rentals, canoeing. Lakeside cabins and campsites. TELEPHONE: 609-296-1114.

Belleplain State Forest, Rt. 550, Woodbine (Cape May/Cumberland Counties): Lake Nummy, surrounded by a pine, oak, and cedar forest, offers beach swimming, picnicking, hiking, nature trail, interpretive center, boat rentals, camping, and fishing. The forest also includes East Creek Pond on Rt. 347. TELEPHONE: 609-861-2404.

Brendan Byrne State Forest, Rt. 72, New Lisbon (Burlington County): Pakim Pond offers swimming, picnicking, hiking, and camping amid

Pinelands forests and cedar swamps. Whitesbog Village (q.v.) offers a look at historic town and cranberry bogs. **TELEPHONE:** 609-726-1191.

Jenny Jump State Forest, Hope (Warren County): Mountaintop trails lead to rocky overlooks of the Delaware Water Gap and Great Meadows. A separate section about 2 miles south near Mountain Lake includes hilly woodland hiking trails. There's picnicking, camping, hiking, nature study, and an astronomical observatory. **TELEPHONE:** 908-459-4366.

Norvin Green State Forest, Ringwood (Passaic County): Hiking trails begin from a nearby Audubon nature center and lead to a panoramic view atop Wyanokie High Point that includes Manhattan in the distance. **TELEPHONE:** 973-962-7031.

Penn State Forest, off Rt. 563, Jenkins (Burlington County): Lake Oswego offers swimming, picnicking, hiking, fishing, camping. A few paved roads beyond the lake have wide potholes but most are just sand. **TELEPHONE:** 609-296-1114.

Ramapo Mountain State Forest, Skyline Dr., Oakland (Bergen/Passaic Counties): A streamside trail climbs from lower parking area off I-287 to scenic Ramapo Lake, which is circled by a level path. A semi-paved, private road from an upper parking area is much more level and great for biking. A lot of people also seem to bring their dogs here. A side trail leads to Castle Point and the ruins of a 1910 stone mansion. A nice place for hiking, bicycling, fishing, and picnicking. **TELEPHONE:** 973-962-7031.

Stokes State Forest, Rt. 206, north of Branchville (Sussex County): The forest includes Tillman Ravine, a 10,000-year-old hemlock-lined gorge, great views from atop Sunrise Mountain, a swimming beach at Stony Lake, beaver meadows along Big Flat Brook, and more than 17 miles of marked trails. Plenty of swimming, picnicking, hiking, camping, and fishing throughout the forest. **TELEPHONE:** 973-948-3820.

Wharton State Forest, Rt. 542, Hammonton (Burlington, Atlantic, and Camden Counties): At 115,000 acres, this largest parkland in the state lies deep in the heart of the Pinelands. At Batsto (q.v.), there is a historic village and a scenic lake and stream. Atsion Recreation Area on Rt. 206 offers a swimming beach, bathhouse, and nearby camping and cabins. There's a boat ramp on the Mullica River at Crowley's Landing east of Batsto on Rt. 542. There are canoe launch areas off Rt. 542 near Batsto, at Atsion, and on the Wading River south of Jenkins and at Speedwell on Rt. 563. Plenty of camping, canoeing, hiking, and picnicking throughout the forest, including the Batona Trail. **TELEPHONE:** 609-561-0024.

Worthington State Forest, Rt. 80, Exit 1 (Warren County): Because of its location, a lot of people think it's part of the Delaware Water Gap National Recreation Area, but it's actually state land. Among the attractions are the Dunnfield Creek hiking area, where the Appalachian Trail leads to Sunfish Pond atop the Kittatinny Ridge and other trails lead to the top of Mount Tammany, overlooking the Water Gap from 1,500 feet. Along the Delaware north of the Water Gap you'll find the historic Copper Mine Inn and campgrounds. Alternate trails lead from this area to Sunfish Pond. Plenty of fishing, hiking, picnicking, backpacking, and camping in this area. **TELE-PHONE:** 908-841-9575.

County Parks

The extent of county parks varies considerably throughout the state, with some counties, like Morris, having a well-developed system of nature-oriented parks while other counties have fewer or focus more on urban amenities. However, you'll find some nicely developed county parks throughout the state. Unlike state parks, they rarely charge entrance or parking fees. There may be a fee for programs, however. Here is a selection of the more notable ones. Call for directions, since many large parks have several entrances. Also check the "Garden Variety" chapter for gardens run by county parks. Nature centers and zoos in county parks are described in more detail in the "Animals" chapter.

Atlantic County Park, in Estell Manor: This park consists of 1,742 acres and includes a nature center, biking, cross-country ski and hiking trails, fishing, and picnic areas. Historic sites. Rt. 50 south of Mays Landing. **TELEPHONE:** 609-625-1897, 645-5960.

Berlin Park, Park Drive, Berlin (Camden County): Almost 150 acres, with fishing, hiking, picnic area, and playground. Site of Camden County Environmental Studies Center. **TELEPHONE:** 856-795-7275.

Campgaw Mountain Reservation, Mahwah (Bergen County): Winter ski area, plus hiking trails, and camping. **TELEPHONE:** 201-327-7800.

Cattus Island County Park, 1170 Cattus Is. Blvd., Toms River (Ocean County): Nature center and hiking trails on a peninsula in Barnegat Bay. **TELEPHONE:** 732-270-6960.

Colonial Park, Mettlers Rd., Franklin Twp. (Somerset County): Rose garden and fragrance gardens, arboretum, tennis courts, boating, fishing, hiking, and picnic areas. **TELEPHONE:** 908-722-1200.

Cooper River Park, Haddonfield (Camden County): The paved Cooper River Trail follows the stream for 9 miles through the Camden County suburbs.

Davidsons Mill Pond Park, Deans (Middlesex County): Fishing and picnicking at old mill pond. Rt. 130, east on River Rd, then right after second bridge. TELEPHONE: 732-745-3995.

Duke Island Park, Old York Road, Bridgewater (Somerset County): Fishing, picnicking, concerts, hiking along Raritan River. TELEPHONE: 908-722-1200.

Eagle Rock Reservation, Eagle Rock Ave., West Orange (Essex County): Overlook atop Watchung Mountain offers great views of New York skyline, a 9/11 memorial, and hiking in the woods. Private restaurant in park (Highlawn Pavilion).

Garret Mountain Reservation, Valley Road, Paterson (Passaic County): Hilltop park includes Lambert Castle (q.v.), scenic overlook of Paterson and Manhattan skyline, hiking, fishing, stables, and riding trails. TELEPHONE: 973-881-4832.

Hartshorne Woods Park, Middletown (Monmouth County): The Rocky Point section offers woodland trails with overlooks of the Navesink River. TELEPHONE: 732-842-4000.

Holmdel Park, Longstreet Rd., Holmdel (Monmouth County): Historical farm, large arboretum, picnic pavilion, fishing lake, and hiking. TELEPHONE: 732-946-9562.

Hunterdon County Arboretum, 1020 Rt. 31 N., Lebanon Township: This 73-acre park includes a 20,000-square-foot display garden, picnicking, wetlands study area, and hiking trails. TELEPHONE: 908-782-1158.

Johnson Park, River Rd., Piscataway (Middlesex County): Large picnic areas, small horse track, small animal zoo, ball fields, hiking trails, and restored village on the banks of the Raritan River. TELEPHONE: 732-745-3900.

Lewis Morris Park, Rt. 124, Morris Twp. (Morris County): Woods and grassy fields adjoin Jockey Hollow. Lake offers swimming beach and fishing. Hiking, picnic areas, and ice skating. TELEPHONE: 973-326-7600.

Lord Stirling Park, Basking Ridge (Somerset County): Home of the Environmental Center adjacent to the Great Swamp (q.v.), this 900-acre park has 8.5 miles of trails and boardwalks that cross forests and wetlands, as well as a public riding stable. **TELEPHONE:** 908-722-1200.

Mahlon Dickerson Reservation: Weldon Rd., Jefferson Township (Morris County): Large park offers hiking, mountain biking, equestrian trails, fishing, canoe rentals, and group picnic area. Small camping area for trailers and some tents. **TELEPHONE:** 973-326-7600.

Manasquan Reservoir: Windler Rd., Howell Township (Monmouth County): More than 1,200 acres and a lake for rowboats, fishing, and hiking. **TELEPHONE:** 732-842-4000.

Mercer County Park, Rt. 535, West Windsor Township (Mercer County): Includes a large lake with a marina, fishing, ice skating, picnic facilities, and hiking trials. **TELEPHONE:** 609-989-6530.

Musconetcong Gorge Section, off Rt. 519, Holland Township (Hunterdon County): Scenic hikes in undeveloped woodland hills above the Musconetcong River. **TELEPHONE:** 908-782-1158.

Ocean County Park, Rt. 88, Lakewood (Ocean County): Once a vacation site for John D. Rockefeller, today it includes a swimming lake, fishing lake, playgrounds, and tennis courts. Cross-country skiing in winter. **TELEPHONE:** 732-506-9090.

Pyramid Mountain Natural Historical Area, Boonton Ave. (Rt. 511), Montville Township (Morris County): Its 1,000 acres of rocky hills offer hiking and overlooks. Main feature is Tripod Rock, a huge boulder balanced on three smaller rocks since the last ice age. **TELEPHONE:** 973-326-7600.

Roosevelt Park, Oakwood Ave., Edison (Middlesex County): A compact park known for its summer theater series in an outdoor amphitheater. Lake fishing, trails. **TELEPHONE:** 732-745-3900.

Schooleys Mountain Park, Camp Washington Rd., Long Valley (Morris County): Swimming beach and lake, boating, hiking, bridle trails, summer environmental center. **TELEPHONE:** 973-326-7600.

Scotland Run Park, Clayton-Williamson Rd., Clayton (Gloucester County): Nature center, boating, swimming, fishing, picnicking, and hiking on almost 1,000 acres. **TELEPHONE:** 856-881-0845.

South Mountain Reservation, Northfield Rd., West Orange (Essex County): Includes ice skating rink, Turtle Back Zoo, fishing, hiking, scenic views, cross-country skiing, and picnicking. **TELEPHONE:** 973-268-3500.

Thompson Park, Newman Springs Rd. (Rt. 520), Lincroft (Monmouth County): Grounds include a display rose garden, fitness trails, picnic area. Many activities with summer theater in barn. TELEPHONE: 732-842-4000.

Turkey Swamp Park, Georgia Rd., Freehold (Monmouth County): One of the few county facilities to include camping (with a restroom and showers). There are sixty-four campsites plus a lake for boating and fishing. Trails, playgrounds, ball fields. TELEPHONE: 908-462-7286.

Van Saun Park, Forest Ave. off Rt. 4, Paramus (Bergen County): Includes Bergen County Zoo (q.v.), lake, fishing, ice skating, large picnic area, playground, and walking paths. TELEPHONE: 201-262-2627.

Warinanco Park, St. Georges Ave., Roselle (Union County): Lake for rowing, fishing, ice skating in winter. Picnic area. TELEPHONE: 908-298-7850.

Watchung Reservation, Mountainside (Union County): Part of the Watchung Mountains, includes trails, picnic areas, nature center, horseback riding stables, and fishing. TELEPHONE: 908-789-3670.

Wells Mills County Park and Nature Center, 905 Wells Mills Rd., Waretown (Ocean County), 5 miles west on Rt. 532. Inside the Pinelands, this 810-acre park includes a nature center, hiking trails, cedar swamp, lake fishing, and canoe rentals in season. TELEPHONE: 609-971-3085.

FEDERAL AND INTERSTATE AREAS

Sandy Hook

This division of the Gateway National Recreation Area encompasses the Visitor Center with nature displays, pamphlets, and maps; several guarded beaches with bathhouses, changing rooms, and concession stands. Picnicking allowed. Although most people come for the beach, there is also Fort Hancock (q.v.), which has a small museum, restored officers' quarters, and remnants of 1890s concrete gun emplacements; the Sandy Hook lighthouse (q.v.); and hiking and bird-watching in the natural areas. Fishing is allowed at several points. Windsurfing and snorkeling on the bay side.

LOCATION: Across bridge from Highlands (Monmouth County).
Rt. 36 east from Garden State Parkway, Exit 117.
TELEPHONE: 732-872-5970.
WEBSITE: www.nps.gov/gate/shu/shu_home.htm.

Delaware Water Gap National Recreation Area

This scenic parkland encompasses forests, Appalachian ridges, historic villages, and 40 miles of the Delaware River along the northwestern edge of the state. The **Appalachian Trail** cuts 25 miles through the New Jersey side of this park on its way from Maine to Georgia. There are lots of other hiking trails as well as picnicking,

Canoeists enjoy a fun day on the Delaware River at the Delaware Water Gap National Recreation Area. *(Photo by Patrick Sarver)*

canoeing, swimming, fishing, bicycling, and historic sites. You'll find some real back roads here, where you can travel miles without seeing a house. You might, however, see a bear or two if you're lucky.

The 1,500-foot-high Kittatinny Ridge is dramatically cut by the Delaware River, giving the area its name. From a parking lot alongside Rt. 80 is the Dunnfield Creek hiking area, with trails that lead to Sunfish Pond and to the Water Gap overlook. The Mohican Outdoor Center (q.v.), accessible from Blairstown on the eastern side of the park, is set in a scenic nature area on Catfish Pond. It is also an overnight stop along the Appalachian Trail that is run by the Appalachian Mountain Club.

A number of scenic spots lie north of the Water Gap along the scenic Old Mine Rd. Nine miles north of the Visitor Center is the Depew Recreation Site, a popular summer beach and picnic ground along the river. Just beyond that lies Van Campens Glen, where a trail leads alongside a stream in a scenic gorge to upper and lower Van Campens falls. A mile or so north on the road (or by trail) is the Watergate Recreation Site, a popular picnicking and fishing spot with ponds set amid a large, open, grassy area (parking fee). Millbrook Village (q.v.) is a restored town from the 1800s farther along the park road. Blue Mountain and Crater Lakes, on a turnoff north of Millbrook, offer swimming, picnicking, fishing, canoeing, and hiking amid deep forests. The gravel road leading to Crater Lake also offers turnouts with sweeping views of the Paulinskill Valley from atop Kittatinny Ridge.

Continuing north, you'll find the Walpack Valley Environmental Education Center in Walpack Center, a small town along the Flat Brook, which is known for its trout fishing. Turn right into the town and continue across the brook. Just past the cemetery, turn right and travel a mile or so down a pot-holed gravel road to Buttermilk Falls, where a stream tumbles 75 feet down a steep, forested hillside. A wooden stairway climbs to two overlooks beside the falls, which is more dramatic in spring when water flows are greater.

If you turn left off the main park road a couple of miles before reaching Walpack and travel down a long gravel road, you'll pass the restored Van Campen Inn. This historic 1740s stone structure was an important stop on the Old Mine Road in colonial times. Tours are held one Sunday a month. Call the park for dates and times. Nearby is the Military Trail, where a French and Indian War encampment is held in mid-October. The Peters Valley Craft Center (q.v.), north of Walpack, offers crafts displays and demonstrations on weekends. A store and gallery in the village are open year-round.

There are also more sites of interest across the Delaware in the Pennsylvania side of the park, including Smithfield Beach, the Pocono Environmental Education Center, and Dingmans Falls. The Dingmans area, where a boardwalk trail leads to two high waterfalls, lies across the Delaware on an old private toll bridge (a tolltaker on foot asks for tolls) not far from Peters Valley.

LOCATION: Rt. 80, Exit 1. Also accessible on Millbrook Rd. from Blairstown and via Rts. 206 and 560 near Layton. **TELEPHONE:** 570-588-2435. **WEBSITE:** www.nps.gov/dewa.

Palisades Interstate Park

This scenic park stretches along the Hudson River from Fort Lee to the New York border and beyond. Hiking trails run atop the cliffs and down to the river below. Fishing is allowed in the Hudson. The undercliff park road is often closed to traffic, which adds to its popularity as a bicycling area. There are also riverside picnic areas and boat basins in Alpine, Englewood, and Fort Lee. You'll also find a historic area at Fort Lee (q.v.) plus scenic cliff-top overlooks of the river at Fort Lee, State Line Lookout, and elsewhere.

ADMISSION: Parking fees are charged at riverfront areas in the summer. **TELEPHONE:** 201-768-1360. **WEBSITE:** www.njpalisades.org.

NEARBY OUT-OF-STATE AREA

Bushkill Falls

This scenic attraction offers a day in the country set in the foothills of the Poconos. The area is cool in the summer and colorful in the fall. You enter through a "nature" museum to a pathway through the forest. Although you can get a good view of the cascading water from above, it is more impressive to see it from below by way of a "natural" log and stone stairway. The Main Falls drop over the edge of a 100-foot cliff to a deep pool below. From that point the water drops another 70 feet through a large gorge strewn with gigantic boulders.

There are three routes to the falls. The short route, with a green trail marker, takes only 15 minutes to walk. It is the "chicken" trail to a lookout where you can take a picture, then sit down. The second or "popular" route takes 45 minutes and is for those who want their money's worth. This takes you down and around the bottom of the main falls and back on a rustic wooden boardwalk through a scenic gorge. The third route takes 1½ hours. Here you travel down below the falls, then cross the stream on a long loop trail. Along the way, you pass a series of mist-laden falls and climb to a lookout where you can enjoy a panoramic view of the Delaware Valley before circling back to the gorge.

HOURS: Apr.–Oct., Mon.–Fri., 9–6; weekends and daily in mid-summer, 9–7; Nov., daily, 9–4, weather permitting.
ADMISSION: Adults: $$. Discounts: Seniors, children. Under 4 free.
LOCATION: Bushkill, PA. Rt. 80 to Exit 309, then take Rt. 209 north 11 miles to Bushkill Falls Rd. Follow signs. **TELEPHONE:** 570-588-6682 or 888-628-7454. **WEBSITE:** www.visitbushkillfalls.com.

The Garden Variety

The dramatic Indo-Persian Garden is one of numerous greenhouse rooms that make the Gardens at Duke Farms the premier garden attraction in New Jersey. *(Photo © Duke Farms Foundation)*

Gardens at Duke Farms

One of New Jersey's foremost attractions, Duke Farms offers a number of garden-oriented tours on the grounds of the Duke Estate south of Somerville. This is clearly a millionaire's legacy. The main garden exhibit is the Conservatory, which is a series of interconnecting hothouses with an amazing variety of plants. Each hothouse contains a shortened version of an international garden. The layout of the flowers and the walkways are all planned to reflect the atmosphere of that particular garden. The first one you enter is the Italian Romantic Garden. Here you find statuary amid lush plant life, birds-of-paradise, and the type of Mediterranean setting that sent nineteenth-century poets into ecstasy. Each garden is controlled for climate and humidity. In the Edwardian Conservatory, it's warm. This is a hothouse filled with tropical plants like sego palms and elephant ears and enough big, fat orchids for a senior prom.

The long English Garden, on the other hand, is temperate. A brick walkway takes you through sedate rows of hollyhocks, primroses, and manicured boxwoods. A small herb garden is here as well. The French garden is formal, with flowers set out in greenery shaped in a fleur-de-lis pattern. Latticework covers all, and a statue of a noblewoman reminds you that this is a small version of what you might find at Versailles.

The Chinese garden, with its overhanging willows, stone walkway, and arched bridge over a goldfish pond is for serene meditation. The scent of the fragrant tea olive permeates the air. Among the other gardens you will find an Arizona desert with succulents and tall cacti; a Japanese rustic-style meditation garden; and a geometric Persian garden with decorated tiles and fountains. Many gardeners tend to all these plantings, so the display flowers change seasonally, but the overall scheme remains intact. The hothouse gardens are closed in the summer. **HOURS:** Sept.–May, Wed.–Sun., tours start at 11–2:30. **ADMISSION:** $$. Discounts: Seniors, children. Under 6 free.

There are four other tours to choose from. The Park & Nature Tour is via a tour bus that takes you on an hour-long journey through the 700-acre "park" that forms the core of the Duke estate. You'll learn about natural aspects of the park, such as wildlife habitats and endangered species, as well as see historic buildings and landscaping elements like fountains, sculptures, waterfalls, and trees. **HOURS:** Mid-Apr.–Nov. at 11, 12:30, and 2. **ADMISSION:** $$.

The Country Manor tour takes you inside the estate's 67,000-square-foot mansion, with an emphasis on how flowers and plants are used to bring the outdoors inside. The Duke family's interest in horticulture is reflected in how plants are integrated into interior design, as showcased by the designs of Duke Farms' gardening staff. The rooms covered on this hour-long tour include the first floor of the main house, Doris Duke's Hollywood wing, and indoor tennis court. This tour will be held for the remainder of 2007 but may be discontinued or changed after that. **HOURS:** Tours depart Wed.–Sun., from 11 to 2:45. **ADMISSION:** $$$.

An hour-long guided tour of the Outdoor Japanese Stroll Garden wanders through the peaceful garden started by Doris Duke in the 1930s. You'll learn about the history and symbolism of various elements in the garden, including Asian statuary and carefully created landscapes. **HOURS:** Mid-Apr.–Nov., Wed.–Sun. at 10:30 and 3. **ADMISSION:** $$.

Walk on the Wild Side is a 1.25-mile self-guided nature and landscaping trail through the woodlands and fields at Duke Farms. Starting at the Visitor Center near the Conservatory, you'll see examples of wildlife and learn about Duke Farms' role as a laboratory for ongoing natural landscape restoration. A gift shop and an outdoor eatery on the grounds are both open during tour hours. **HOURS:** Wed.–Sun., 9–2:30. **ADMISSION:** $.

All tours except the Wild Side are by reservation.

LOCATION: 80 Rt. 206 south, Hillsborough (Somerset County). Turn at Duke Parkway south of Somerville. **TELEPHONE:** 908-722-3700. **WEBSITE:** www.dukefarms.org.

Leaming's Run Gardens

Leaming's Run Gardens was created as a bulwark of quiet woods and colorful plantings against the encroachment of motels and gasoline exhaust fumes near the southern shore. It can transport you back to your childhood. Everyone has probably explored a forest at least once, felt the crackling of pine needles underfoot, and heard the whippoorwill above. That's the kind of woods that covers 30 acres of sandy soil here, all interspersed with colorful gardens.

There are gardens at each bend of the road—more than twenty of them, with many assemblages of color. The yellow garden mixes gourds, gladiolas, banana peppers, and taller plants. Another garden is a medley of oranges. The English garden and reflecting pool are typical of a cottage landscape in Britain. Each garden is planted to provide color and texture during the entire season from late spring to early fall. The most recent is a sweetheart garden in the shape of a heart that attracts romantic picture takers.

Three acres are set aside for a replica colonial farm. Here you will find a traditional early-American log cabin with a fenced-in kitchen and herb garden. The interior of the cabin is authentic, and outside you'll find goats and chickens. Beyond the farm are nooks and crannies in the trail—with snapdragons, pinks, and a cinnamon walk. There are benches where you can enjoy the view. (During August there are plenty of hummingbirds around, too.)

At the end of the one-mile walk, you come to the Cooperage, a shop where you can buy a variety of dried flower arrangements and other gifts. There are a few rules for the gardens, by the way: no smoking, no pets, no drinks, and no radios.

HOURS: Mid-May–mid-Oct., 9:30–5. **ADMISSION:** $$. Discount: Children. Under 7 free. **LOCATION:** 1845 Rt. 9 North, Swainton

(Cape May County). Garden State Parkway, Exit 17, to Rt. 9, then south.
TELEPHONE: 609-465-5871. **WEBSITE:** www.leamingsrungardens.com.

Branch Brook Park

When it's cherry blossom time in Newark's Branch Brook, hundreds
of visitors descend upon New Jersey's oldest county park. Not only
do the cherry trees outnumber the ones in Washington, D.C., but
Branch Brook itself is an outstanding example of the informal urban
parks that nineteenth-century planners thought of as a respite from
city congestion. The park was designed by America's foremost landscape architect, Frederick Law Olmstead, and his son, and it includes meandering walkways, little lakes, recreational fields for
baseball and tennis, and small copses of trees and bushes.

There are now over 2,700 cherry trees, with the most luxuriant
double-blossom variety clustered at the Belleville end of the park.
The original trees were donated by Caroline Bamberger Fuld back in
1927, but they have almost doubled in number since then. The
Japanese flowering cherry does not bear fruit and comes in several
varieties, including the weeping cherry and the single and double
blossom, all in white or pink. The trees are planted along the road-
way, and people are allowed to park their cars by the road so they
can get out and take pictures. The season usually starts during the
second week of April, depending on the weather. There are also a
number of special events held in the park during the official two-
week festival.

> **LOCATION:** Rt. 280 to Newark (Essex County); make a left on First St.,
> a right on Park Ave., and then take the first right.
> **TELEPHONE:** 973-268-3500.
> **WEBSITE:** http://branchbrookpark.org/event.htm.

Colonial Park Gardens

Several attractive gardens can be found in this county park. The
original rose garden, once part of the Mettler Estate, was developed
and expanded by a horticulturist so that it now covers an acre. The
Rudolf van der Goot Rose Garden displays over 325 varieties, with
more than 3,000 bushes in a formal display garden that exhibits the
A.A.R.S. Award Winning Roses each year. Included are the original
York and Lancaster roses, tea roses, hybrids, floribundas, minia-
tures, and more. They are all labeled to show type and date of intro-
duction into the horticultural world. A flagstone walk makes for
easy ambling.

Behind the rose garden is the Fragrance and Sensory Garden,
which provides Braille plaques for the blind and a handrail for the

handicapped. There's also a perennial garden, with 5 acres of perennials, trees, shrubs, and ornamental grasses. And set inside Colonial Park is a 144-acre arboretum complete with meandering stream. Beyond that are tennis courts, paddleboats, and picnic tables for family get-togethers. A gazebo inside the 5-acre perennial garden is a popular picture-taking spot (formal pictures are by permit only).

Garden clubs, school classes, and other groups can arrange for guided tours for a fee. Otherwise the gardens are free. Major blooming at the rose garden occurs the first week of June and the first week of September.

HOURS: Daily, dawn to dusk, for park; rose garden, 8–sunset.
ADMISSION: Donation. **LOCATION:** 156 Mettlers Rd., Franklin Twp. (Somerset County). Take Rt. 206 to Rt. 514 (Amwell Rd.) east, cross Millstone River to Mettlers Rd. **TELEPHONE:** 732-873-2459.
WEBSITE: www.somersetcountyparks.org.

Reeves-Reed Arboretum

A small estate is the setting for this arboretum, hidden by tall trees on one of Summit's stately old streets. The stone and shingle manor house on a rise is surrounded by trees, shrubs, and flowering plants. But the major part of the gardens is behind the house.

You can follow the nature trails through marked oaks, maples, walnuts, and beeches. The open area of this hilly site is devoted to both flower and herb gardens. A deep depression (called a kettle hole in geological terms) is the setting for a spectacular flowering of daffodils in April, followed by summer field flowers. Azaleas, rhododendrons, a rock garden and pool, and a small rose garden are also found along the walks of this 12½-acre arboretum.

The main house offers a variety of classes and Sunday lectures. Among the brochures available there is a garden guide to help identify the plants in the arboretum. There are also a greenhouse and a small garden shop on the grounds.

HOURS: Grounds, daily, dawn to dusk; office, Mon.–Fri., 9–3.
ADMISSION: Free. **LOCATION:** 165 Hobart Ave., Summit (Union County). Take Rt. 24 to Hobart Ave. exit. **TELEPHONE:** 908-273-8787.
WEBSITE: www.reeves-reedarboretum.org.

James Rose Center

The James Rose Center for Landscape Architectural Research and Design is the former home and garden of James Rose, a founder of the modernist movement in landscape design. This site showcases Rose's ideas about interlocking indoor and outdoor spaces, combining architecture and art in a modernist residential setting. Rose designed everything here—the home, the furniture, sculpture, and garden. Three interconnected pavilions in an experimental landscape incorporate elements of Japanese design. Rose's goal was to create a radical approach to living on a small lot as an alternative to suburban tract housing. The site also shows photos of Rose's architecture and landscape designs at other locations. A self-guided brochure tour is available at the center. Some off-street and suburban street parking is available.

HOURS: Guided tours and lecture, May–Sept., 1st and 3rd Sat. of the month, 10 & 1. Self-guided tour, May 15–Sept. 1, Mon.–Fri., 10–4. **ADMISSION:** $$. **LOCATION:** 506 E. Ridgewood Ave., Ridgewood (Bergen County). Two miles west of Rt. 17. **TELEPHONE:** 201-446-6017. **WEBSITE:** www.jamesrosecenter.org.

Camden Children's Garden

What's the latest thing in interactive education for kids? Children's gardens. One of the most interesting is the Camden Children's Garden, which spruces up the outside of the Adventure Aquarium and is a pleasant spot for both kids and adults. There are lots of colorful play areas in this 4.5-acre attraction, many of which aren't just about flowers or plants. The Dinosaur Garden, for instance, offers a prehistoric environment of rock walls, waterfalls, and huge trees—not to mention a 35-foot-long Apatosaurus, created from recycled automobile parts by sculptor Jim Gary. Hand-painted benches and painted wooden violets add color to the nearby Violet Plaza, which also features an interactive water fountain. Kids can also learn and play in the Red Oak Treehouse and nearby underground maze (which is really above-ground and at eye level for children).

The Storybook Gardens have three little houses in the 3 Little Pigs Garden as well as fanciful topiaries and a chair made out of yews where children can hide and play. A giant watering can fronts the Giant's Garden, which is filled with oversize plants and foliage, and a slide sends children down a rabbit hole into Alice in Wonderland's Garden. Besides the many interactive play areas, there is now a small carousel. The Railroad Garden (fanciful plants inside small boxcars) also offers a miniature train ride.

Grownups can enjoy the statue of Walt Whitman that stands in front of the Butterfly Garden, where there's also a small Butterfly Spring ride. The statue is a fitting nod to the poet who lived his last years in this city. And the enclosed, heated butterfly house nearby allows you to experience the winged creatures and tropical plants all year-round.

The garden offers a tented picnic area for reserved groups and parties. Individuals can picnic on the benches in the small riverfront park just outside the site. A small gift shop specializes in garden-themed items. Although this is primarily an outdoor garden, it does operate year-round and has plenty of nonfoliage elements that can be enjoyed. There are also special events on Saturdays as well as a Festival of Lights, Fridays and Saturdays, late November and December.

HOURS: Daily, 10–5. **ADMISSION:** Adults, $. Discount: Children. Under 3 free. Extra fees for rides. **LOCATION:** 3 Riverside Dr., Camden. Parking garage across street. **TELEPHONE:** 856-365-8733. **WEBSITE:** www.camdenchildrensgarden.org.

Well-Sweep Herb Farm

A commercial herb-growing farm, Well-Sweep lies in a scenic rural setting about 6 miles southwest of Hackettstown. It covers 120 acres and has almost 2,000 plant varieties lining the brick and gravel walkways of its display and perennial gardens. Visitors may stroll down the paths of the formal herb garden and browse through the extensive display gardens at any time. You'll also find butterfly, medicinal, and perennial gardens here, as well as a sales area, gift shop, and farm animals (the roosters can be very noisy).

Owner Cyrus Hyde gives special lecture tours to groups by appointment. These tours offer fascinating insights into the many uses of plants. Did you know horsetail grass can be used for fine sanding? Or that tansy, planted next to the door, will keep ants away? Want the recipe for rose geranium sugar? No wonder this tour is popular with garden clubs. Special events also include guest presentations, lectures, slide shows, and craft classes, usually on Saturdays. Just make sure to reserve in advance.

Since the principal activity here is growing and selling herbs and flowering perennials, there's always a wide selection at reasonable prices. Also sold in the gift shop are pottery, books, and other garden-related items.

HOURS: Apr.–Dec., Mon.–Sat., 9–5; also open Sun., mid-Apr.–early June. Jan.–Mar., call for hours. Closed holidays. **LOCATION:** 205 Mt. Bethel Rd., Port Murray (Warren County). Off Rt. 629. **TELEPHONE:** 908-852-5390. **WEBSITE:** www.wellsweep.com.

New Jersey Botanical Gardens

The flowering preserve at Skylands Manor in Ringwood State Park is one of New Jersey's most popular garden attractions. The 96-acre site was designated the official state garden in 1984, but it is still

The New Jersey Botanical Gardens at Skylands Manor in Ringwood State Park is a showcase for flowers and plants throughout the warmer months. *(Photo by Patrick Sarver)*

known as Skylands Gardens. Because the mansion's original owner was an avid horticulturist, you'll find a large variety of flowering trees and bushes as well as flowering plants here. Most photographed is the long allee of crab-apple trees that blossom in the spring. However, the estate also has lilacs, azaleas, geraniums, and peonies among its many varieties. The formal annual garden with its stone urns and nearby perennial garden includes fall flowers and foliage.

Skylands, the forty-four-room Tudor-style mansion (q.v.), has limited visiting hours, but you may peruse the plantings that surround the house on any day. From the back of the house you can see classic terraces dotted with statues and greenery. There's quite a bit of walking to do if you want to see all the garden areas. Many of these are aligned to provide a vista; the reflecting pool especially is set up this way. A winter garden, an octagonal garden, a lily pond, formal terraces with stone balustrades, and scenic vistas make this a beautiful place year-round. Since there are only a few gardeners on hand, compared to the eighty in the days of the millionaire owner, not all sections are kept up as well. However, the volunteer group, the Skylands Association, does yeoman work here.

The association holds garden tours on Sundays at 2 P.M. from May through October. They also offer garden tours for groups and hold a Holiday Open House at the mansion the first weekend in December.

If you'd like some hands-on fun in the gardens, they offer Saturday morning volunteer garden work on various weekends in season. There are Friday evening concerts in summer on the grounds as well as other seasonal events throughout the year.

HOURS: Daily, 8–8, for park and gardens. **ADMISSION:** Parking fee, $ in season; manor fee, $. **LOCATION:** Ringwood State Park (Passaic County). Rt. 511 to Sloatsburg Rd., then Morris Rd. **TELEPHONE:** Park, 973-962-7031; Association, 973-962-9534. **WEBSITE:** www.njbg.org.

Leonard J. Buck Garden

The former estate of a wealthy Far Hills mining engineer, this 33-acre garden features native and exotic plants displayed in a naturalistic setting of woodland, rock garden, pond, and stream. A host of interesting wetland plants, perennials, flowering trees, and shrubs can be enjoyed year-round. The large fern garden features nonflowering hardy ferns intermingled with unusual shade plants. Plenty of walking here, since the terrain varies from a low-lying stream to steep hillsides, but you can pause at well-placed benches to enjoy the vista.

The rock gardens are at peak bloom in the spring, when thousands of tiny flowers peek out from designed rock formations. There are plenty of irises, azaleas, and rhododendrons and Japanese primroses in the spring, but you can find colorful autumn foliage, too. Unusual trees, a pleasant lake that is home to mallard ducks, and a small waterfall make for good picture taking. Pick up a garden map and bloom list (updated weekly) at the Visitor Center. There are many special programs and workshops at the main building, hosted by the Somerset County Park Commission, which administers the garden.

HOURS: Mon.–Fri., 10–4; Sat., 10–5; Sun., 12–5. Closed weekends & major holidays, Dec.–Mar. **ADMISSION:** $ donation. Discounts: Seniors, children. **LOCATION:** 11 Layton Rd., Far Hills (Somerset County). Off Rt. 512 about a mile south of Rt. 202. **TELEPHONE:** 908-234-2677. **WEBSITE:** www.somersetcountyparks.org.

OTHER NEW JERSEY GARDENS

Presby Iris Gardens: From mid-May to the second week in June, an outstanding display of irises can be found in this lovely suburban park in Upper Montclair. Hilly terrain and gracious homes are the setting for this local park where Frank Presby began his iris beds many years ago. Every color in the rainbow is reflected in more than thirty beds containing over 8,000 irises. There are more than 2,000 varieties of these bearded and straight-stalked flowers, planted in long linear beds that parallel the street. Some trace their lineage as far back as the 1500s. The garden has largely recovered from being vandalized in 2005, with almost all of the uprooted plants now reestablished. At the adjoining headquarters, a gift shop is open in season. **HOURS:** Daily, dawn to dusk. **ADMISSION:** Free. **LOCATION:** Mountainside Park, 474 Upper Mountain Ave., Upper Montclair (Essex County). **TELEPHONE:** 973-783-5974. **WEBSITE:** http://presbyiris. tripod.com.

Davis Johnson Park: This pleasant city park in the town of Tenafly covers 7 acres and features a rose garden, a sunken garden, and a small herb garden. Like many other local parks, it is a popular spot for photographers taking wedding pictures. **HOURS:** Daily, dawn to dusk. **ADMISSION:** Free. **LOCATION:** 137 Engle St., Tenafly (Bergen County). **TELEPHONE:** 201-569-7275.

Deep Cut Gardens: Once the property of a mafioso chief in the 1930s, these well-kept gardens still have a slight Mediterranean flavor. The 1952 ranch-style house is now a Horticultural Center where you can find a good library and some plant specimens in the enclosed porch. There are 54 acres of gardens and greenhouses that are planned as a living catalog of cultivated and native plants. Two ponds (one sporting lily pads) are home to brightly colored Koi. An azalea and rhododendron walk is a springtime favorite, while the butterfly and hummingbird garden attracts visitors in summer. Greenhouses, shade gardens, cascading pools, and a long meadow make this a pleasant place to meander. **HOURS:** Daily, 8–dusk. **ADMISSION:** Free. **LOCATION:** 352 Red Hill Rd., Middletown (Monmouth County), 1½ miles north of Garden State Parkway, Exit 114. **TELEPHONE:** 732-671-6050. **WEBSITE:** www.monmouthcountyparks.com.

Sayen Gardens: Set in the heart of a charming town, this 28-acre park displays more than 1,000 azaleas and 500 rhododendrons among its many varieties. The gardens offer walking paths, benches, a scenic bridge over a lily pond, and a host of daffodils, tulips, and snowdrops in season. Three gazebos and a 1912 bungalow-style house are part of this personal garden now made public. A popular place both for weddings and wedding pictures. The Azalea Festival held here on Mother's Day attracts thousands. **HOURS:** Daily, dawn to dusk. **ADMISSION:** Free. **LOCATION:** 155 Hughes Dr., Hamilton Square (Mercer County). Rt. 33 to north on Mercer St. to Hughes Dr. **TELEPHONE:** 609-587-7356. **WEBSITE:** www.sayengardens.org.

Cross Estate Gardens: Part of Morristown National Historic Park, the Cross Estate features a formal walled garden, wisteria-covered pergola, mountain laurel allee, shade gardens, and a native-plant area adjacent to the estate's mansion. There are also signs and a descriptive brochure covering examples of native trees important to the New Jersey Brigade, encamped here in 1780. **HOURS:** Daily, dawn to dusk. **ADMISSION:** Free. **LOCATION:** Jockey Hollow Rd., Bernardsville (Somerset County). **TELEPHONE:** 973-376-0348. **WEBSITE:** www.cross estategardens.org.

Rutgers Gardens: This 50-acre arboretum and display garden contains a wide variety of trees and flowers, including notable dogwood and holly collections as well as a rhododendron and azalea garden. There is a small formal garden, but most of this area is meant to display the variety of horticulture in the state. Among the displays are a water conservation terrace, a border of ornamental grasses, and a bamboo forest. Across the street, there is a pavilion and patio where you can picnic, and beyond that are extensive virgin woods to explore. Open House days (spring, summer, and fall) feature lectures, plant sales, and garden tours. **HOURS:** Daily, dawn to dusk. **ADMISSION:** Free. **LOCATION:** 112 Ryders Lane, New Brunswick (Middlesex County). Off Rt. 1. **TELEPHONE:** 732-932-8451. **WEBSITE:** http:// rutgersgardens.rutgers.edu.

Frelinghuysen Arboretum: Tulips, azaleas, rhododendrons, a rose garden, and a wealth of flowering trees are part of the display at this 127-acre tract that was once the home of the Frelinghuysen family. Cherry trees, crab-apple and magnolia blossoms, along with a lilac garden and a dogwood copse, bring color and contrast to the many evergreens in the collection. It serves as headquarters of the Morris County Park System, which uses the 1891 mansion for offices and library. Separate building for lectures, a nice lawn for concerts, and a gift shop specializing in garden items can all be found here. **HOURS:** Daily, 8 a.m.–dusk. Tours on weekends at 2, Apr.–Oct. **ADMISSION:** Free. **LOCATION:** 53 East Hanover Ave. (Rt. 511), Morristown (Morris County). **TELEPHONE:** 973-326-7600. **WEBSITE:** http:// parks.morris.nj.us/aspparks/Frelarbmain.asp.

Willowwood/Bamboo Brook: The Willowwood Arboretum offers extensive walking paths and a conservatory. There are flowering gardens, wildflowers, a variety of trees, and long meadows on 130 acres of rolling farmland—more than 3,500 kinds of plants in all. It adjoins the Bamboo Brook Outdoor Education Center, which includes some formal gardens and a white cedar allee surrounding the home of well-known landscape architect Martha Brookes Hutcheson. There are walking trails and small brook. **LOCATION:** Longview Rd., Chester Twp. (Morris County). **TELEPHONE:** 973-326-7627. **WEBSITE:** http://parks.morris.nj.us/aspparks/wwmain.asp.

Cora Hartshorn Arboretum and Bird Sanctuary: This 16-acre refuge includes a stone building used as a nature center. Once the estate of a millionaire's daughter, it is now a pleasant, hilly spot where you can walk on 3 miles of trails among the trees and listen to birdsongs. There are 150 species of wildflowers here as well as 45 tree species. It is known for its rhododendron dell and many rare ferns. Since there is no parking lot, you must park on the street. The nature center offers a number of nature exhibits as well as programs. **HOURS:** Grounds open daily, dawn to dusk; stone house, Mon.–Fri., 9–4:30 (9–12 in summer); Sat., 10–11:30 (closed in summer). **ADMISSION:** Free. **LOCATION:** 324 Forest Dr. South, Short Hills (Essex County). Rt. 24 to Hobart Ave., then to Forest Dr. **TELEPHONE:** 973-376-3587. **WEBSITE:** www.hartshornarboretum.com.

Sister Mary Grace Burns Arboretum: This former estate of railroad tycoon Jay Gould's son is now a college campus with four historic gardens—the Italian Garden, Sunken Garden, Formal Garden, and Japanese Garden. There is lots of statuary here as well as fountains, lagoons, and walkways plus a Japanese teahouse. **HOURS:** Daily, 8 a.m.–dusk. **ADMISSION:** Free. **LOCATION:** Georgian Court College, Lakewood (Ocean County). **TELEPHONE:** 732-987-2373. **WEBSITE:** www. georgian.edu/arboretum/index.html.

Van Vleck House and Gardens: These gardens feature rhododendrons, azaleas, and other woody plants, a wisteria-covered terrace balcony, and a small perennial and annual garden. The display greenhouse presents orchids and other tropical plants while a second greenhouse is used for various educational programs. The grounds also contain specimen trees and unusual hybrids, such as yellow rhododendrons. **HOURS:** Daily, 9–5. **ADMISSION:** Donation. **LOCATION:** 21 Van Vleck St., Montclair (Essex County). Off N. Mountain Ave., three blocks north of Bloomfield Ave. and the Montclair Art Museum. **TELEPHONE:** 973-744-4752. **WEBSITE:** www.vanvleck.org.

NEARBY OUT-OF-STATE GARDENS

Brooklyn Botanic Gardens

A trip to these gardens can be combined with one to the Brooklyn Museum, since parking in the museum lot can serve for both places.

The Brooklyn Gardens are known for the cherry blossom walk—a wide swath of lawn with Japanese double blossoms, white and pink, that come out in mid-April. Another famous display is the Japanese Hill and Pond Garden.

The gardens follow the natural cycles: daffodils in March, then lilacs and cherry blossoms, then wisteria and rhododendrons. The rose garden is spectacular but only open in certain months. The butterfly and hummingbird trail is a summer attraction. Other features are open year-round: the rock garden and brooks and the conservatories, which feature bonsai plants, cacti, and tropical plants. A Discovery Garden for children is complete with a butterfly trail in season.

HOURS: Apr.–Sept., Tue.–Fri., 8–6; weekends and holidays, 10–6. Oct.–Mar., Tue.–Fri., 8–4:30; weekends and holidays, 10–4:30.
ADMISSION: $. Discounts: Seniors, students. Under 16 free.
LOCATION: Eastern Parkway and Washington Ave., Brooklyn, NY.
TELEPHONE: 718-623-7200. **WEBSITE:** www.bbg.org.

New York Botanical Gardens

These 250 acres of grassland, trees, and formal gardens are the pride of the Bronx. The enclosed conservatories and an extensive new Children's Garden, with topiaries, indoor interactive games, and educational activities, are popular draws. A tram ride circles the park's interior; it has four major stops, takes 20 minutes, and features live narration.

The ornate main building is a Beaux-Arts structure fronted by a landmark fountain statue. Inside are orchids, an herbarium, a library, and a gift shop. The beautiful rock garden with its pond, alpine meadow, and splashing waterfalls is another stop not to miss. The Enid A. Haupt Conservatories is a 1903 "Glass Palace" with Victorian-style rotunda and structural iron framework. Inside, the tropical rain forests of the Americas are emphasized. Banana trees, native huts, and pineapple plants are in one section; tall cacti of the Arizona and Mexican desert are in another.

Outside, there are nicely stylized perennial and herb gardens with brick walkways, shaded lattices, colorful flowers, and plenty of benches. In June, the formal rose garden is lush with a variety of blooms. Tram rides, the conservatory, and children's garden are extra unless you buy a "Passport" ticket.

HOURS: Tue.–Sun. & Mon. holidays, 10–6; closes at 5, Nov.–Mar.
ADMISSION: $$. Discounts: Seniors, children. Under 2 free. Wed. free.
LOCATION: Bronx River Parkway and Fordham Rd. (Exit 7W).
TELEPHONE: 718-817-8700. **WEBSITE:** www.nybg.org.

Wave Hill

A public garden in a quiet section of the Bronx called Riverdale, Wave Hill possesses the sense of a private estate filled with beauty and serenity. There are lovely vistas of the palisades and the Hudson. Greenhouses are filled with tropical plants and cacti, and outdoor gardens are devoted to herbs and seasonal flowers. An aquatic garden, several pergolas, and many flowering trees dot the landscape.

HOURS: Mid-Apr.–mid-Oct., Tue.–Sun., 9–5:30; Wed. until 9, Jun.–July. Rest of year, 9–4:30. **ADMISSION:** $. Discounts: Seniors, students. Under 6 free. Tue. & Sat. mornings free. Also free Dec.–Feb. **LOCATION:** W. 249th St. at Independence Ave., Bronx, NY. Take George Washington Bridge to Henry Hudson Parkway to Exit 21. **TELEPHONE:** 718-549-3200. **WEBSITE:** www.wavehill.org.

Longwood Gardens

Without a doubt the most extensive formal gardens in the region, this impressive display by the DuPont family offers an amazing variety and is open year-round. Over 1,000 acres are open to the public, including some beautifully laid-out conservatories. At the main Visitor Center, you purchase your tickets and can watch a four-minute film on the highlights of the gardens. There's also a gift shop full of books and plants.

The conservatories are huge glass-enclosed rooms that surround a patio. Inside there are hanging-basket mobiles sprouting flowers, stone herons in a pond surrounded by seasonal flowers, a ballroom featuring organ concerts, and the hot and humid Palm House with its banana and breadfruit trees. There is a room for insect-eating plants, another just for orchids. The main conservatory displays change four times a year. (The Christmas display alone attracts more than 100,000 people.) Nearby is an indoor Children's Garden with mazes, stepping-stones, and hands-on activities.

Outside, directly in front of the conservatories, is the main water fountain area. The display, with many spouting water jets, is framed by trimmed boxwood. On certain nights during the summer, colored lights and music from the carillon make a spectacular show. There are even fireworks added to the fountain displays on special Saturday nights—these must be reserved in advance.

Further on are the Idea Garden, Heaths of Heather, the "Eye of God" (a low, circular water sculpture), topiary, and a rose garden. The right side of Longwood features a long walk bordered by seasonal flowers and an open-air theater with display fountains. The Peirce-DuPont House is open for an extra fee. Beyond, there are wisteria and rose gardens, forest walks and meadows, a lake with gazebo and ducks, and a complete Italian water garden.

HOURS: Open daily. Summer, 9–6; until 10 P.M. on Tue., Fri. & Sat. Hours vary rest of year. **ADMISSION:** $$$. Discount: Children. Under 6 free. **LOCATION:** Rt. 1, Kennett Square, PA. **TELEPHONE:** 610-388-1000. **WEBSITE:** www.longwoodgardens.org.

Flea Markets, Outlets, and Specialty Shopping Villages

Liberty Village in Flemington is a major outlet shopping area, with more than sixty stores in a colonial-style setting. *(Photo by Patrick Sarver)*

OUTLETS

Flemington Outlets

Flemington is a pretty Victorian town in the middle of Hunterdon County, an area that still has a fair amount of farmland. Over the years Flemington has grown from a town that offered a few discount shops to a name that has become synonymous with outlet shopping.

On Main Street you will find several shops, such as Mikasa (#95) and Flemington Glass (#156) and a number of nice lunchtime restaurants, including a tea room. Flemington Glass has sprouted annexes like crazy, so you can find not only glass there but also pewterware and dinnerware. The historic Main Street district also includes some nice Victorian Bed & Breakfasts, antiques stores, and the historic County Courthouse (see "Unique Towns" chapter).

The main stop is Liberty Village (follow signs—it has a huge parking lot behind the railroad tracks). Liberty Village started out in the 1970s as a restored colonial village but converted into an outlet center not much later. The clapboard buildings and brick walkways lend a pleasant air to the job of bargain hunting. Though the ambience is pleasant, the prices are higher these days. But Ann Klein, Liz Claiborne, Timberland, and many other outlet regulars are among the sixty stores, and Ralph Lauren has a building all to himself. Somewhere along the way, pick up the shopping booklets that contain maps and discount coupons.

Next to Liberty Village is Turntable Junction, an old-fashioned green surrounded by specialty shops and an English tea room. With some shops empty, this area has lost a little of its former luster. Across the nearby railroad tracks—where the Black River and Western Railroad (q.v.) runs during the warmer months and at Christmas—then down Stangl Road, you'll also find a Pfaltzgraff outlet in the old Stangl Pottery factory. And over at Heritage Place (Rt. 31 and Church St.) you'll find a small complex that includes Reebok and Rockport outlets. Flemington no longer has a monopoly on outlet centers, but when it comes to pleasant surroundings, this town still takes the prize. However, don't be surprised if particular stores have closed or moved elsewhere.

> **LOCATION:** Rt. 78 to Rt. 31 south, or via Rt. 202.
> From Flemington Circle follow signs for "Business District."
> **TELEPHONE:** 908-788-5729; Liberty Village, 908-782-8550.
> **WEBSITE:** www.premiumoutlets.com/libertyvillage.

Secaucus Outlets

Set in one of the busiest areas of New Jersey, across Rt. 3 from the Meadowlands Complex, the outlets here are dispersed over a huge area between warehouses, office buildings, streets, and open spaces. You definitely need a map. You can pick one up at the first outlet mall you hit (Outlets at the Cove), conveniently placed on Meadowlands Parkway. This small enclosed mall features air conditioning, clean restrooms, and a few designer outlets. At one of the stores you can pick up a Secaucus booklet that includes a map and usually offers discount coupons as well.

Farther on, at Enterprise Avenue, Hartz Way, and other streets, you will find several large outlet stores devoted to single names. Mikasa and Liz Claiborne each have their own buildings, full of merchandise at 20 to 30 percent off. Of course, if you hit a sale you can realize even more, and many people put themselves on the mailing list to take advantage of these. You will also find a number of discount chains, such as Bed Bath & Beyond. The Syms clothing store takes up a full square block.

The Harmon Cove Outlet Center (20 Enterprise Ave.) is a large enclosed mall with a variety of shops of varying value. But it also contains a food court ringed by food counters where you can rest your feet and partake of pizza, chicken, ice cream, and other types of fast food. Farther on, there's another small enclosed mall called the Designer Outlet Gallery (55 Hartz Way), which includes designers like Anne Klein. If you check your map and drive around the maze of streets, you'll find other little outlet enclaves within the area. Find a store that fits your needs or carries your brand, and the trip will be worth it. And if you wait for special warehouse sales (Mikasa has two a year), you can stock up on all your gift needs.

HOURS: Daily. Individual stores vary. **LOCATION:** Secaucus (Bergen County). Take N.J. Turnpike, Exit 16W to Rt. 3 east to Meadowlands Parkway. **TELEPHONE:** 877-OUTLET2. **WEBSITE:** www.harmonmeadow.com.

Jersey Gardens Mall

This is the ultimate Jersey experience—an indoor mall that is also an outlet. Since it's set in Elizabeth right off Exit 13A of the Turnpike, it has the advantage of being in the special 3 percent tax zone (for nonclothing items). It also has bus service from NJ Transit. Since the mall is in close proximity to the huge Toys R Us outlet, the Ikea furniture store, a megaplex movie theater, and a Rex Plex sports entertainment center, you can assume that the parking lot here will always be full.

Inside, there are plenty of tables at the food court, free strollers and wheelchairs, a huge play area for kids, and sporadic entertainment in the courtyard. The corners of the mall are anchored by mega-versions of discount chains like Marshalls, Filene's Basement, Burlington Coat Factory, and Cohoes. Between the anchors are such outfits as Off 5th-Saks 5th Avenue, Neiman Marcus Last Call, Daffy's, and Wilson's Leather Outlet. A few stores sport high-class names where you can buy a $250 Louis Vuitton tie for $125. The mall also features a bar/restaurant, a concierge desk, and lots of special events.

HOURS: Open daily. Hours vary by season. **LOCATION:** 651 Kapkowski Rd., Elizabeth (Union County). Use N.J. Turnpike, Exit 13A. **TELEPHONE:** 1-877-SAY-VALU. **WEBSITE:** www.jerseygardens.com.

Other New Jersey Outlets

The Circle Factory Outlet Center: Located just off Route 35 in Manasquan (Monmouth County) at the Jersey Shore, this center offers around thirty outlets, including Corning/Revere, Mikasa, and Geoffrey Beene. Access is not the most convenient, right off a busy traffic circle, but it services shore tourists and locals alike. **TELEPHONE:** 732-223-2300.

Jackson Premium Outlets: A popular newcomer to the outlet scene is on Rt. 537 off Rt. 195 in Jackson (Ocean County), just a few miles west of Six Flags Great Adventure. There are seventy outlets stores here, and you can find Brooks Brothers, Big Dog Sportswear (they seem to be everywhere), and Samsonite, for example. Since this outlet was built from scratch, it has a convenient design. The connected buildings sport a late-Victorian beachhouse look and form a triangle around the parking lot, which makes a shorter walk for customers. The covered walkways are another plus. **TELEPHONE:** 732-833-0503. **WEBSITE:** www.premiumoutlets.com/jackson.

Atlantic City Outlets: This seven-block retail area of upscale outlets, also called The Walk, stretches west from Bally's to the Convention Center along Michigan Ave. (Atlantic County). It features more than fifty outlet stores, including such familiar names as Ralph Lauren, Bass, Nautica, Banana Republic, Calvin Klein, and Liz Claiborne. There are a number of restaurants, spanning the range from Subway to Ruth's Chris Steakhouse. **TELEPHONE:** 609-872-7002. **WEBSITE:** www.acoutlets.com.

NEARBY OUT-OF-STATE OUTLETS

Woodbury Common

For people who live in the northeastern New Jersey, this is a popular stop. It's in New York State, so you have to pay sales tax on clothes, unlike in New Jersey and Pennsylvania. What you do get is lots of stores—220 at the moment, and 30 of them are shoe stores! Scads of clothing stores and a little of everything else (Judith Leiber, Harry & David, Godiva). Also prominent are heavy names like Armani and Versace, which undoubtedly attract people here. The place is divided into color quadrants, with a Red Apple Court, a Green, a Blue, etc. But since this is an outdoor "common," you must walk from one store to the other in all sorts of weather. Directional maps are available. A trolley tram makes the rounds in the parking lot to take you to the different sections. There's lots of territory to cover here. Special events in summer.

LOCATION: Rt. 32, Central Valley, NY. Take Garden State Parkway to Rt. 87 (N.Y. Thruway) to Harriman, Exit 16. **TELEPHONE:** 845-928-4000. **WEBSITE:** www.premiumoutlets.com.

Reading

Reading is the grandaddy of outlet towns. Someone decided to take old factory buildings and turn them into stores that would sell directly to the customer. For years people would drive from all over to get these manufacturer's goods at 50 percent off. Nowadays, with outlets everywhere, Reading has lost some of its draw. Still, the buses and cars come, and some real bargains can be found. Outlets now take charge cards, and there are several decent eating places around. On the other hand, many of the shops are actually discount stores rather than true factory outlets.

The original Reading Outlet Center can now be found in a series of buildings, some of them of the old-factory, red-brick variety, where you have to walk upstairs. Others are new and single story. Building 1, the biggest, is on Windsor Street between N. 9th and Moss. Building 2 is across the street, while Building 3 is cater-cornered to No. 1. Others are on Douglass and Oley Streets. A variety of discount shops are stuffed into these buildings. In one or the other, you will find the Kleins (Calvin and Anne), Jones New York, Liz Claiborne, and many other "names."

A highly popular destination is the VF Outlet in the neighboring town of Wyomissing (801 Hill Ave.). This "village" includes three huge buildings and several smaller ones. The big Red and Blue Buildings offer racks and racks of Vanity Fair robes and nightgowns at half price, plus lots of other goods. The complex is surrounded by gates and parking lots (with preferred parking for tour buses). There's a food court in the basement of the Blue Building.

Companies owned by VF (Lee jeans, Jansport, HealthTex) sell their goods for 50 percent off. Other sections in the complex include

Black & Decker, whose prices vary from 10 to 40 percent off. Across the street, the Designer Place sports a clean, well-lit interior. You'll find some high-fashion names here, plus a Godiva chocolate outlet.

> **HOURS:** Most stores open Mon.–Sat., 9:30–5:30 or 9:30, and Sun., 12–5 (except Jan. and Feb.). **LOCATION:** Rt. 78 to U.S. 222 to Rt. 422 west to Reading, PA. VF Outlet is on Park and Hall Rds., Wyomissing.
> **TELEPHONE:** Reading, 610-373-5495; VF, 800-772-8336.
> **WEBSITE:** VF, www.vffo.com.

Franklin Mills Mall

While many outlet centers evolved from nearby factories or the conversion of unused buildings, Franklin Mills is a superplanned, hi-tech mall designed as a magnet for shoppers from Philadelphia and New Jersey. It combines the convenience of an indoor mall with the bargain prices of discount stores and outlets. Inside the 1.8 million square foot complex, you will find hundreds of stores, food courts, plus entertainment and resting courts. Each corner of the huge complex is anchored by a large store, each section of the mall is color coded, and everything is on one level. You can also find a Levi's/Dockers outlet plus Ann Taylor Factory Store and a Saks outlet.

> **HOURS:** Mon.–Sat., 10–9:30; Sun., 11–7.
> **LOCATION:** Northeast Philadelphia, Rt. 95 to Woodhaven Rd. exit; turn right onto Franklin Mills Blvd. **TELEPHONE:** 215-632-1500.
> **WEBSITE:** www.franklin-mills-mall.com.

The Crossings

Another village created by Premium Outlets (which also did Liberty Village and Woodbury Common) and a popular favorite for those who live in northwest Jersey, the Crossings is right off Rt. 80. The left-hand turn into the complex is badly planned, but once inside, there are several streets of discount stores in this manufactured "town." People come here for Coach handbags, Carter's children's wear, or several women's plus-size places. Also, there's Timberland, Liz Claiborne, Anne Klein, and many other outlet regulars. The place is growing, and parking can be a challenge.

> **LOCATION:** 1000 Rt. 611, Tannersville, PA. Off Rt. 80, exit 299.
> **TELEPHONE:** 570-629-4658. **WEBSITE:** www.premiumoutlets.com.

Rehoboth Outlets

A trip across Delaware Bay on the Cape May–Lewes Ferry is an enjoyable outing in itself. But many people combine it with shopping at outlet malls. If you go by car (taking either the ferry or the Delaware

Memorial Bridge), you will be in a better position to bring home the big-ticket items you might pick up, for Delaware has no sales tax. Rehoboth is about 4 miles from Lewes and the ferry, but in the summertime there are shuttle buses that take passengers to the outlets. There are 130 stores strung out along Route 1 in three different outlet centers (each resembling a long strip mall), about a mile from each other. Among the stores are Pfaltzgraff, J. Crew, VF Outlet, Nike, Big Dog, Black & Decker, and Harry and David.

TELEPHONE: 866-665-8682. **WEBSITE:** www.tangeroutlet.com.

See also Penns Purchase (under Lahaska in "Unique Towns" chapter).

FLEA MARKETS

Note: Flea market hours and offerings change constantly. Always telephone first.

Englishtown Auction Sales

This is one of the world's largest flea markets, a vast dusty field set on the edge of Monmouth County's farm country. What you find is something like three hundred garage sales going on side by side with seven hundred New York street hawkers, all of them set up on tables covering a huge field. Add to that several farm stands with bins of fresh corn, tomatoes, melons, apples, and pumpkins. Then add several buildings filled with discount clothing booths, kielbasa and knish stands, a great bagel place, hamburgers and oriental food, and a complete bar and grill. Englishtown Auction Sales has everything but an auction, a term that refers to the old days when cows were sold here, too.

The flea market is open weekends only, and it opens early. You will find a mass of memorabilia, knick-knacks, new shoes, and old tires and hubcaps—practically anything in the world. A new bell for your bicycle, a collection of porcelain doorknobs, and garage sale "junque" are all mixed in with bargain basement clothing and cosmetics.

Collectors can also find something of interest, from Depression glass and comic books to paperweights and World War I German helmets and medals. More collectibles (along with food stands) are in the buildings called Red, Green, Blue, and Brown. Englishtown Auction Sales offers you a chance to buy that elusive whatnot you could never find anywhere else. But the mainstay is new merchandise sold at discount. Parking is free, with one close-by lot charging a couple of dollars.

HOURS: Sat., 7–5; Sun., 9–5. **LOCATION:** 90 Wilson Ave., Englishtown (Monmouth County). Garden State Parkway, Exit 123 to Rt. 9 south. Travel 7.5 mi., then turn right on Texas Rd. to Rt. 527. Turn left, then south 3 miles. **TELEPHONE:** 732-446-9644.

Dover Flea Market

This flea market ran for many years in Chester, then relocated to Dover and transformed itself into its own unique style. While the usual venue for such endeavors is a dusty country field or parking lot, this market takes place on the sidewalks of a small urban town. Automobile traffic is roped off for several blocks where the vendors place their stands. One advantage is that you can take the train to Dover; the flea market is only a few blocks from the station (although trains run infrequently on Sunday). Another is that cafes and restaurants are open on the main street, so you can have a regular lunch. Vendors sell a variety of new clothes, jewelry, unique items, crafts, collectibles, souvenir items, baseball cards, and such.

HOURS: Sun., 9–4, Apr.–Dec. **LOCATION:** W. Blackwell St., Dover (Morris County). Rt. 80 to Rt. 10 (Dover) exit.
TELEPHONE: 973-989-7870. **WEBSITE:** www.doverfleamarket.com.

Columbus Flea Market

This started out as a farmer's market and just grew and grew. It has rows and rows of tables filled with pocketbooks, sweatshirts,

The Dover flea market is one of many open-air flea markets that attract bargain hunters throughout the state. *(Photo by Patrick Sarver)*

sweaters, scarves, crazy items, knoc-koff perfumes, etc., as well as "garage sale" items. It's also a traditional farmer's market with fresh produce brought in from the neighboring countryside.

The indoor buildings include dozens of permanent "niche" stores plus a number of eating spots (hamburgers, bagels, etc.). In one of the buildings you can also find several Pennsylvania Dutch delicatessen counters, where you can buy Amish-style cold-cuts and breads and freshly grown produce. Don't be surprised to find furniture, window frames, and other large items in the indoor sections.

HOURS: Thu., Sat., Sun., dawn to 3 P.M. **LOCATION:** 2919 Rt. 206, just south of Columbus (Burlington County). **TELEPHONE:** 609-267-0400. **WEBSITE:** www.columbusfarmersmarket.com.

Meadowlands Flea Market

The parking lot behind the Giants Stadium had always been a venue for sporadic computer flea markets, along with a hundred other things. But for the past few years a regular flea market has been running on Wednesdays and Saturdays. It's open year-round, with more vendors on hand on Saturdays. About six hundred vendors at tables and trucks parked on the blacktop sell such clothing as sweaters, socks, and handbags, plus CDs, DVDs. There's also a large smattering of such specialties as antique telephones and African art. Of course, there are food stands, with twisted pretzels, kielbasa, Italian ices, handmade chocolates, and Amish bakeries. Many standard vendors come back year after year, so people can come back to their favorites.

HOURS: Wed., 9–3; Sat., 9–5. (Closed Wed., Jan.–Feb.) Occasionally open on other days. **ADMISSION:** Free. Also, free parking. **LOCATION:** Meadowlands Parking Lot 17, East Rutherford (Bergen County). Take N.J. Turnpike, Exit 16W, then follow signs. **TELEPHONE:** 201-935-5474. **WEBSITE:** www.meadowlandsfleamarket.com.

Other New Jersey Flea Markets

Neshanic Flea Market: This smallish (5-acre) homespun flea market is a favorite with many who come back year after year. Known for its garden equipment sales, it also has a number of household items. Various collectibles. **HOURS:** Sun., 7–2. **LOCATION:** 100 Elm St., Neshanic Station (Hunterdon County). Off Rt. 202. **TELEPHONE:** 908-369-3660.

New Egypt Flea Market Village and Auction: A collection of eighty small shops and outside tables, with antiques, collectibles, crafts, clothing, tools, used books, furniture, and other used items. Individual shops in older buildings. Outdoor tables can have everything from foundry type to garage sale items. **HOURS:** 7–2, Sun. & Wed. Auction, Sun. at I. **LOCATION:** New Egypt is 6 miles west of Six Flags in Ocean County (Rt. 537). **TELEPHONE:** 609-758-2082.

Berlin Farmer's Market and Shopping Center: A mix of traditional Jersey truck farm produce and flea market items. Indoor market houses more than eighty stores, while 300–400 vendors in outdoor spaces show new and used merchandise, including antiques, collectibles, crafts, and fresh produce. **HOURS:** Outdoor flea market open Sat. & Sun., 8–4. Inside shopping center open Thu.–Sat., 10–9; Sun., 10–6. **LOCATION:** 41 Clementon Rd., Berlin (Camden County). Just off Rts. 30, 73, and 42 between Atco and Voorhees. **TELEPHONE:** 856-767-1284. **WEBSITE:** www.berlinfarmersmarket.com.

Cowtown Flea Market: This flea and farmer's market on Saturdays and Tuesdays features around four hundred merchants. Antiques, collectibles, crafts, lots of western clothes and items. Livestock sales at noon on Tue. **HOURS:** Tue. & Sat., 8–4. **LOCATION:** Rt. 40, Woodstown. Eight miles east of Delaware Memorial Bridge. **TELEPHONE:** 856-769-3000.

NEARBY OUT-OF-STATE FLEA MARKETS

Rice's Flea Market

If it's Tuesday, it must be Rice's. That's the day this 30-acre flea market comes to life on a flat dirt field on a back road near New Hope. They're open on Saturdays, too. Officially named Rice's Country Market and Auction, it has a reputation for quality. To the neophyte it doesn't look much different than any other flea market. Its main virtue seems to be its size. Although the field is huge, getting past all the tables is not unmanageable. You can actually walk the whole market in a morning. Good thing, because by I P.M. most vendors are packing up. You can find specialty items here—one vendor sells only Guatemalan handmade goods; another specializes in ribbons and laces. There may be several booths of patterned sweaters. But the most common items tend to be college sweatshirts, tube socks, fancy scarves, and some brand-name toiletries at reduced prices. There are also a few merchandise vendors inside the small buildings.

> **HOURS:** Every Tue., Sat. (except Jan.–Feb.), and some holidays.
> **LOCATION:** New Hope, PA. Rt. 202 to Aquetong, right on Green Hill Rd., then another right. **TELEPHONE:** 215-297-5993.
> **WEBSITE:** www.ricesmarket.com.

Pocono Bazaar Flea Market

One of the largest in the area, this flea market runs year-round and has a smattering of everything. It's a mile north of Marshall's Creek, so lots of people stop by on their way to the Poconos. A central indoor market has permanent booths and scores of outdoor tables. Collectibles like porcelain dolls, old comic books, and Civil War mementos can be found at the permanent stands, while there are tables of white socks, T-shirts, sweaters, "designer" perfumes, and a hodge-podge of garage-sale items outside.

> **HOURS:** Sat., Sun., 9–5. **LOCATION:** Marshalls Creek, PA. Rt. 80, Exit 309, then Rt. 209 north for 5 miles. **TELEPHONE:** 570-223-8640. **WEBSITE:** www.poconobazaar.com.

SPECIALTY SHOPPING VILLAGES

Historic Smithville

Set around Lake Meone, and only 12 miles from Atlantic City, this "towne" started out as a colonial village that featured the authentic eighteenth-century Smithville Inn and a mix of boutique shops. It was built by Fred and Ethel Noyes, who sold the complex and donated much of their money to the nearby Noyes Museum (q.v.).

Today Smithville is devoted to shopping and eating. This is a pleasant spot, and parking is free. An old mill, a quaint bridge, and brick walkways give an old-time ambience to the village, which is dubbed Towne of Historic Smithville on one side of the lake and the Village Greene on the other. A bakery, an ice cream shop, and the Smithville Inn along with a potpourri of specialty shops, such as antiques, gift, and craft stores abound. There are about sixty establishments in all. In season there are mini-train rides, a carousel, paddleboats on the lake, puppet shows for children, and an occasional buckboard ride around town.

> **HOURS:** Mon.–Sat., 10–8; Sun., 11–6. Shorter hours off-season. **LOCATION:** Rt. 9 at Moss Mill Rd., Smithville (Atlantic County). **TELEPHONE:** 609-652-7777. **WEBSITE:** www.smithvillenj.com.

Olde Lafayette Village

In the northern part of the state, near where Rts. 15 and 94 meet just below the town of Lafayette in Sussex County, this "village" has a number of outlets mixed in with specialty shops. Colonial-style attached buildings feature such outlets as Bass, Jones New York, and Van Heusen. But specialty retailers like toy shops and bookstores are more numerous these days. There's also a farmer's market here on Sundays, June to October.

TELEPHONE: 973-383-8323. **WEBSITE:** www.lafayettevillageshops.com. Lafayette also has a nice antiques market in the center of town.

Dutch Neck Village

This small country village of quaint specialty shops is built in colonial and country style on the grounds of the original Dutch Neck Landscaping nursery. Its brick paths and landscaped grounds include a display garden with two hundred varieties of plants. Two small museums contain displays of old home furnishings memorabilia. Special sales and festivals occur throughout the year.

HOURS: Mon.–Sat., 10–5; some shops open on Sun., 12–4.
LOCATION: 97 Trench Rd., Bridgeton (Cumberland County).
Rt. 49 to Fayette St.; go one mile south, then right on Trench Rd.
TELEPHONE: 856-451-2188. **WEBSITE:** www.dutchneckvillage.com.

Other Outings

A tour through the State House in Trenton offers an inside look at the offices and chambers where the laws of New Jersey are made. *(Photo by Patrick Sarver)*

POPULAR SITES

The State House

You don't have to be on a political mission to visit Trenton. The golden-domed State House is open to the public, by guided tour only. You can see the architectural richness of this building, which predates the 1930s "institutional" style of many government structures. It is the second oldest state capitol in continuous use.

Inside, the main hall is lit by Victorian-style chandeliers, once fueled by gas. There are arches of faux marble and pilasters of dark wood. One eye-catching piece in the center of the hall is a porcelain Boehm sculpture that features the state tree (the red oak), the state bird (the goldfinch), and even the state insect (the honeybee). The rotunda features paintings of the governors. You can visit the handsome Senate Chamber with its stained glass skylight and the General Assembly Room if the legislature is not in session, which is usually Monday and Tuesday, September to June. Sometimes the Governor's Reception Room (which has even more portraits of governors) is open.

Some past governors include Civil War general George McClellan and Woodrow Wilson, the only New Jersey governor to make it to the White House. Tours run hourly, and groups of more than ten should reserve in advance. There is a cafeteria on the third floor off the parking garage. At the Visitor Center on level 2 of the parking garage atrium, there are exhibits on the path of legislation, quizzes on state history and places, as well as a gift shop.

HOURS: Mon.–Fri., 10–3, Sat., 12–3. **ADMISSION:** Free.
LOCATION: 125 W. State St., Trenton (Rt. 29 to Calhoun St. exit).
TELEPHONE: 609-633-2709.
WEBSITE: www.njleg.state.nj.us/legislativepub/visiting_guided.asp.

Battleship *New Jersey*

The most decorated battleship in the United States was also one of the most fought-over in New Jersey as three different cities wanted this refurbished ship. The Camden waterfront won out, and the *New Jersey*, with its turret guns bristling, is docked close to the Tweeter Center, not far from the Adventure Aquarium and across the river from Philadelphia (whose shipyards gave birth to it).

At 887 feet long, the *New Jersey* is one of the largest battleships ever built. Designed for a crew of 117 officers and 1,804 enlisted men in World War II, the ship had nineteen battle and campaign stars and served in World War II, Korea, Vietnam, and the Persian Gulf. Highlights of the guided tour include the ship's 16-inch gun turrets, Admiral Halsey's original cabin, the communications center, two mess areas, and crew quarters. You can watch a launch of a tomahawk missile on video and see how it's tracked in a virtual combat engagement room. There's also a multiroom museum where you can learn about life and duties onboard, see comparisons with battleships of other countries during World War II, and find out about homeland defense techniques. You also have the chance to crawl inside a gun turret, just as the crew did.

There are three types of tours: self-guided, guided, and a firepower tour. All include a lot of walking and climbing on ladders, both outdoors and inside. For those not up to steep ladder climbing, you can still walk on the main deck and enjoy a sitting room that

The big guns of the battleship *New Jersey* on the Camden waterfront are just part of the reason that the big ship is one of the most popular attractions in the state. *(Photo by Patrick Sarver)*

features two 15-minute videos about the ship and about other parts of the tour. Special tours and prices are available for school groups. There is a snack bar onboard in the crew's mess, and there are two ship stores, one onboard and a larger one on land. A 4D Flight Simulator Ride is also available for extra fee outside the gift shop/ Visitor Center.

> **HOURS:** Apr.–Sept., daily, 9–5; Oct.–Dec. & Mar., 9–3; Jan.–Feb., Fri.–Mon. only, 9–3. **ADMISSION:** $$$. Discounts: Seniors, children, vets with ID. Active duty and under 6 free. **LOCATION:** Delaware River Waterfront, Camden (Camden County). **TELEPHONE:** 866-877-6262. **WEBSITE:** www.battleshipnewjersey.org.

New Jersey Naval Museum

The New Jersey Naval Museum's USS *Ling 297* submarine is 312 feet long but only 27 feet wide, and when you consider that eighty-one men and twenty-four torpedoes were aboard during its active career in 1945, you realize that this is no place for someone with claustrophobia. Nowadays, most of the torpedoes and many of the berths have been removed to allow tour groups to move about. Indeed, the inside seems surprisingly spacious. Tickets are bought at the museum building, which also houses a number of war pictures and paraphernalia, including the periscope prism from a Japanese sub.

Tours last about 45 minutes. You begin in the torpedo room,

which still features two deactivated torpedoes. These weapons were activated only after they left the tube; they also had to be aimed correctly, since a miss would give away the sub's position. Much of the time onboard the vessel was devoted to eating and cooking. When the *Ling* first left port, space was so dear that fresh fruit and vegetables had to be stacked in one of the showerheads. Tours include the Control Room, Maneuvering Room, Main Engine Room, sleeping quarters, and more; but the conning tower and its periscope are off-limits. You are allowed to handle certain equipment, including the wheels and gauges, and the guide sounds the diving signal, which may be memorable to some from a host of old war movies.

The Naval Museum grounds also has a Vietnam-era patrol boat, a World War II Japanese Kaiten II suicide torpedo, and a German Seehund two-man coastal defense sub. An interesting place, both for older children and ex-servicemen. Birthday parties and scouting sleepovers are available.

HOURS: Weekends, 10–4; Wed. in summer, 10–3. **ADMISSION:** $$. Discount: Children. **LOCATION:** 78 River Street, Hackensack (Bergen County). **TELEPHONE:** 201-342-3268. **WEBSITE:** www.njnm.com.

Sterling Hill Mine

The last operating zinc mine in New Jersey went out of business in 1986, but the buildings are now a mining museum open for tours. (Just remember to wear a jacket and good shoes, because it's 56 degrees inside the mine, and often damp.) Besides the primary zinc deposits there are over three hundred minerals in this area, half of which are found nowhere else. Because the area around Ogdensburg and nearby Franklin has the world's largest deposits of fluorescent stones, an important stop on the tour is the Rainbow Room. This is a wall that looks like ordinary rock, but when the tour guide switches on an ultraviolet light, the red-fluorescent calcite and green-fluorescent willemite begin to glow.

There is a lot of walking on this tour not only along the tracks of the mine itself, but in the other buildings as well. The museum— where the tour usually starts—includes one huge exhibit hall that was once used by miners to change clothing. Displays include dinosaur prints, rows of zinc products, and a whole range of mining paraphernalia. There is also an impressive collection of rocks and minerals, including the local fluorescents and many others specimens from around the world.

In the mine-office building you can buy hot dogs from the grill or peruse the gift shop, which offers plenty of mineral specimens. There is also an outdoor picnic area. It can easily be combined with a visit to the Franklin Mineral Museum (q.v.), 3 miles away. You can also look for minerals yourself on the last Sunday of the month. The tour is not recommended for children under 6.

HOURS: Apr.–Nov., daily, 10–3; Mar. & Dec., appointment only. Tours at 1 and at other times. **ADMISSION:** $$. **LOCATION:** 30 Plant St., Ogdensburg (Sussex County). Rt. 517 to Brooks Flat Rd. to Plant Rd. **TELEPHONE:** 973-209-7212. **WEBSITE:** www.sterlinghill.org.

Northlandz

"Northlandz" is a combination of the Great American Railway, doll museum, La Peep Dollhouse, art gallery, and a frontier-style music hall. All are housed in a Greeklike temple of a building that's a popular destination for grandparents, families, and railroad buffs.

The huge, largely HO-scale model railroad covers 52,000 square feet and uses enough wood to build forty-two houses and plenty of plaster to create small towns and cities among the great gorges of this huge layout. There are 115 trains and 8 miles of track that cut through looming mountains, deep quarries, and unique cityscapes. They go over bridges up to 40 feet long, above rivers, and past alpine scenes. Visitors walk about a mile as they travel on ramps that rise 3½ stories to view the massive layout from different angles. You see Pennsylvania coal-mining towns, horses grazing on sloping hills, and marching bands. Some scenes are built with humor in mind. A hotel "with a view" perches precariously over a deep gorge. For drama there's a deep canyon with a complete mining town set beneath the looming railroad bridge. Some towns are peopled with miniature figures, while farms may have horses and cows set out to pasture. Anyone with any interest in model railroads will find this place interesting—even if parts of the layout could use a few repairs here and there.

The La Peep Dollhouse is not free standing but a series of ninety-four miniature rooms set into the wall, featuring home scenes including a library, indoor pool, and ballroom with doggie band. A doll museum of 150 large collectible dolls in fancy costume can be seen toward the end of the tour. The American Music Hall, in the style of a Western saloon, features a 2,000-pipe organ, which is played several times a day. Northlandz also includes a cafe and a gift shop filled with railroad memorabilia. Allow at least two hours. In good weather, there's also an outdoor mini-railroad train you can ride for an extra fee.

HOURS: Weekdays exc. Tue., 10:30–4; weekends, 10:30–5:30. **ADMISSION:** Adults, $$$. Discounts: Seniors, children. Under 2 free. **LOCATION:** 495 Rt. 202 south, Flemington (Hunterdon County).

2 miles north of Flemington Circle. **TELEPHONE:** 908-782-4022.
WEBSITE: www.northlandz.com.

New Jersey Renaissance Kingdom

Welcome to the Kingdom of Camelot, where the king and queen, knights and ladies rule at this multiweekend Renaissance festival in the South Mountain Reservation in Essex County. Follow a running storyline of love, knights, and knaves as costumed actors engage in swordplay and take on various roles. A "living chess game" is part of the entertainment, as are storytellers and puppeteers for children. Grownups can join in a Maypole dance, run around the "forest," watch weddings, and so forth. A total of twenty different shows are put on each day. Food court and vendors are on hand. The Renaissance Kingdom runs on several weekends, usually starting in late May and running through June. This group also hosts a Haunted Village at the Turtle Back Zoo in West Orange on weekends in October. Tour guides lead visitors through some scary places, filled with detailed scenery and special effects.

> **HOURS:** Kingdom, late May–June, Sat.–Sun., 11–6; Haunted Village,
> Oct. weekends, 6:30–10 P.M. **ADMISSION:** Kingdom, $$$.
> Discounts: Seniors, children. Village, $$. Discount: Children.
> **LOCATION:** South Mountain Reservation, South Orange (Essex County).
> **TELEPHONE:** 732-271-1119. **WEBSITE:** www.NJKingdom.com.

Medieval Times

Combine a horse show, a nightclub, a dinner theater, and a Renaissance festival, put it all in a circuslike arena inside a huge stucco castle, plunk it down near one of the state's busiest intersections (near the Meadowlands), and you have the New Jersey version of Medieval Times. Here you get not one but several jousts, a narrative of times gone by, and a chance to eat dinner without any utensils.

When you enter the cavernous castle to buy your tickets you are handed a paper hat with a special color. This color will determine which section you sit in and which knight you root for. These colored hats are a great gimmick, for it is in cheering for a particular champion that the audience becomes part of the show.

After a chance to look at medieval artifacts and to inspect a torture dungeon (and buy such stuff as shields and banners at the gift shop), you are ushered into the arena where chairs are set against long banquet tables. These are set in tiers so that everybody in the huge oval arena can see the show. First comes the soup (served in a porriger), then chicken, potato, and barbecued ribs, plus dessert, coffee, or punch. Since you are supposed to eat all this with your fingers, the serving wench hands you a huge napkin to be tucked into your collar Henry VIII style.

As for the show—there is a story of sorts about a king who's come back from the war and orders a tournament. The show includes some fancy prancing by the horses and a display of skills by the knights. Then it's on to the jousts. The knights not only fight on horseback but also engage in swordplay after being unhorsed. And, of course, there are several good knights and one bad apple—usually the green knight. After a few jousts and lots of clashing swords, the final victor is announced and the villain is sent to his doom. All this while the wenches are either serving supper or selling you pictures, banners, or wine.

After the show, some families stay around until their knight shows up to autograph the picture or shield their kids have bought. A popular spot for preteen parties and even dating couples. Just skip the torture museum if you have young children along.

> **HOURS:** Wed., Thu., 7:30 P.M.; Fri., 8 P.M.; Sat., 7 P.M., and Sun.,
> 4:30 P.M. **ADMISSION:** $$$$$. Discount: Children.
> **LOCATION:** 149 Polito Ave., Lyndhurst (Bergen County). Rt. 3 to
> Rt. 17 south to Lyndhurst. **TELEPHONE:** 888-WE-JOUST.
> **WEBSITE:** www.medievaltimes.com/njhomepage.htm.

The Meadowlands

Want to see how it feels to run out of the tunnel and onto the field at Giants Stadium or view the track from the press box at Meadowlands Racetrack? It's part of the guided group tour of this complex, an insider's view that includes a visit to the locker room. Meadowlands Experience tours are by appointment and require a minimum of twenty people, but they are free and last about 2 hours.

> **HOURS:** Mon.–Sat., 10 A.M. or 1 P.M. **ADMISSION:** $$. Discount:
> Students. You must furnish your own transportation throughout the
> day, but this seems like a good one for youth activity groups.
> **TELEPHONE:** NJSEA Office of Public Affairs, 201-460-4370.

Most people, of course, head to the Meadowlands for the numerous sports and entertainment events held there throughout the year. These include the following.

Meadowlands Racetrack: Both harness and flat racing have their season at this major track, which is the home of the Hambletonian, harness racing's leading event. The facility offers a glassed-in, climate-controlled grandstand. There are restaurants for those who want to combine a night at the track with dining. The fancy one is Pegasus, on the top level, with a bird's-eye view of the race, buffet stations, and high prices. Or you can opt for the tiered restaurant, which gives a better view of the track but rather ordinary food. For those watching the race from the grandstand, a large 15 by 36-foot video matrix screen allows you to see the action on the far side of the track and also flashes results almost immediately.

Giants Stadium: The stadium is named for the NFL football team that makes its home there, but the Jets and college football teams also play on the same turf. The stadium has a seating capacity of 78,000 and has a video matrix scoreboard that delights the kids and skyboxes that delight corporations. The parking lot also hosts a flea market (q.v.) plus antique shows, petting zoos, and a three-week carnival in summer. Tailgating before football games is a tradition here. The stadium also hosts special headliner concerts and other events. And starting in 2007, a new Giants-Jets stadium is being constructed.

The future of the **Continental Airlines Arena** at the Meadowlands, home of the NHL Devils and NBA Nets as well as a venue for concerts and special events, is totally unpredictable at press time. The Nets want to move to Brooklyn (although the arena there has hit road-blocks), the Devils are planning to move to a new arena in Newark, and the Meadowlands Xanadu entertainment/recreation/shopping complex being built in the arena's parking lot has been hit by law-suits and financial setbacks but is scheduled to open in 2008. Once scheduled to be torn down, the Continental Airlines Arena has recently received new money from the state to ensure its future as a concert and special events venue.

> **PARKING:** Fees vary. Come early, especially for football games.
> **LOCATION:** Off Rt. 3, East Rutherford (Bergen County). From N.J. Turnpike north, take Exit 16W for direct access; from Turnpike south, take Exit 18W. **TELEPHONE:** 201-935-8500.
> **WEBSITE:** www.meadowlands.com.

OTHER OUTINGS

Peters Valley Craft Center offers crafts displays and demonstrations. Watch students and teachers create pottery and weave, as well as practice woodworking, blacksmithing, silkscreening, and jewelry-making skills. A store and gallery in the village that focuses on fine crafts is open year-round. You can also enroll in crafts workshops designed for beginners to advanced skill levels that run for two to ten days. Peters Valley also sponsors a crafts fair, held at the Sussex County Fair Grounds in Augusta on the last weekend in September.

> **HOURS:** Self-guided tours and class demonstrations, weekends, 2–4,

from mid-May to mid-Sept. Craft auctions, Sun. at 1. Store and gallery, June–Dec., Mon., Tue., Thu., 11–6; Fri.–Sun., 11–7. Jan.–May, Thu.–Sun., 10–5. **LOCATION:** Near Layton (Sussex County). **TELEPHONE:** 973-948-5200. **WEBSITE:** www.pvcrafts.org.

Doyle's Unami Farms: Learn the history of early settlers and Indians who once hunted these fields. Visits are tailored for each season. Take part in such activities as planting or harvesting crops, get hands-on demonstrations of farm machinery, and care for farm animals. Scenic hayrides and pony rides are offered. Indian field trips tailored for all age groups include a 30-minute presentation and a hayride to an Indian campsite to visit a fire pit discovered on the farm. Owner Richard Doyle is past president of the Archaeological Society of New Jersey and has collected thousands of Indian artifacts, some of which are included on the field trip. **HOURS:** Open Apr.–Nov. Reservations required. None is needed for weekends in October (Sat., 1–8 & Sun., 1–4) when three cornfield mazes, hayrides, pony rides, and other activities are held **ADMISSION:** $$; under 3 free. **LOCATION:** 771 Mill Lane, Hillsborough (Somerset County), Rt. 206, west on Amwell Rd., right on E. Mountain Rd., then left on Mill Lane. **TELEPHONE:** 908-369-3187. **WEBSITE:** www.doyles-farm.com.

9/11 MEMORIALS

Eagle Rock: A 160-foot-long granite wall with the names of the 9/11 victims inscribed on bronze plaques and several bronze monuments to the fallen at the World Trade Center now stand at Eagle Rock Overlook. The park, which looks out on the Manhattan skyline, was a spontaneous memorial after the tragedy, with flowers and flags placed on the stone wall. **LOCATION:** Eagle Rock Reservation, Eagle Rock Ave., West Orange (Essex County).

Echo Lake Park: The Union County 9/11 Memorial is built around two steel girders from the World Trade Center. A five-sided design honors those lost at the Pentagon, and a torch of liberty honors passengers of Flight 93. The names of the 60 Union County residents lost are engraved on a stainless steel plaque. **LOCATION:** Mountainside/ Westfield.

Mount Mitchill: The Monmouth County 9/11 Memorial, in a small park atop the highest natural coastal elevation on the Atlantic and overlooking Sandy Hook and the New York Skyline, is highlighted by a large eagle clutching a beam from the Trade Center, surrounded by marble panels inscribed with the names of the 147 victims from

Monmouth County. A timeline walkway recalls the day's events. **LOCATION:** Ocean Blvd., Atlantic Highlands. Off Rt. 36.

Liberty State Park: The New Jersey state memorial to 9/11 victims is being constructed overlooking the Hudson next to the Central Jersey Railroad terminal in Liberty State Park. Plans call for twin 30 by 200-foot-long stainless-steel slabs with the names of the one hundred New Jersey victims inscribed, along with dual beams of light streaming skyward at night. **LOCATION:** Liberty State Park (Hudson County).

EXCURSION BOATS

The sightseeing cruise has been with us for a long time; the fancier excursion cruise has become more popular within the last few years. Sightseeing usually involves some narration and access to hot dogs, soda, and beer. Excursion boats more often have cocktail bars, restaurant or buffet service, and music or entertainment. The entertainment may range from a single guitarist to a five-piece band. Here are some of the larger cruises that are currently afloat. The excursion-type vessel also caters to groups for birthdays, engagement parties, proms, and business bashes.

Circle Line Tour: A standard sightseeing attraction for many years, the ferry leaves from Pier 83 at 42nd Street in New York City and travels around the island of Manhattan via the Hudson River, New York Harbor, East River, and Harlem River. There is the standard three-hour or a half-circle two-hour tour. (A one-hour tour departs from South Street Seaport for a ride around the harbor.) An announcer (or canned tape) points out the Statue of Liberty and all the monuments, skyscrapers, bridges, and churches, with appropriate anecdotes and facts. Of course, you do get to see New Jersey as well as New York when you're on the Hudson. Sailings vary by season and prices vary with the length of the tour. **TELEPHONE:** 201-915-9529. **WEBSITE:** www.circleline42.com.

The *Spirits*: *The Spirit of New Jersey* departs from Port Imperial in Weehawken for a foray along the Hudson River. This popular cruise caters to individuals as well as diverse groups, including engagement parties, junior proms, and senior citizen groups. The two-hour lunch cruise includes a buffet, a narration of top tourist spots on both sides of the river, some cabaret-style entertainment, and a DJ for dancing. The dinner cruise is more party oriented, lasts three hours, and skips the narration but has more elaborate dance sessions. **TELEPHONE:** 866-211-3805. **WEBSITE:** www.spiritcitycruises. com/ny/bridge.jsp.

The Spirit of Philadelphia departs from the pier at Penn's Landing (right across from the Adventure Aquarium in Camden) to cruise down the Delaware River and then circle back. The lunch cruise provides some historical narration for both sides of the river, and you pass the battleship *New Jersey* on one side and the historic ships on the Penn's Landing side. Cabaret entertainment, DJ, and dancing for lunch; evening parties are available, too. **TELEPHONE:** 866-211-3808. **WEBSITE:** www.spiritofphiladelphia.com.

The *Cornucopia Princess* and *Destiny:* These are 130-foot dinner cruise ships that leave from Riverview Drive in Perth Amboy for champagne brunch and dinner cruises. Both the three-deck *Princess* and the two-deck *Destiny* feature "elegant" dining. Dinner and Saturday luncheon cruises go to Manhattan, while a shorter Sunday brunch cruise explores Raritan Bay. Live band for dancing on every cruise. Advance reservations required. Call for boarding times. **TELEPHONE:** 732-697-9500. **WEBSITE:** www.cornucopiacruise.com.

A. J. Meerwald: This is New Jersey's first and only tall ship! Actually, it's a 115-foot oyster schooner that has been restored and is berthed in Bivalve on Delaware Bay. Luckily, the schooner also visits other ports (such as Liberty State Park, Philadelphia, Burlington, Camden, and Cape May) during warm weather. From spring through fall, it takes on paying passengers, who can help hoist the rigging and trim the sails. Typical trips last 2½ hours. There are also sunset sails. In spring and fall, it's booked for school groups. There's also a small museum at the home port, with displays on shipbuilding, oystering, and commercial fishing. **ADMISSION:** Morning, afternoon, or evening sails, $$$$$. Advance reservations recommended. Discount: Children. **LOCATION:** 2800 High St., Bivalve (Cumberland County). **TELEPHONE:** 856-785-2060. **WEBSITE:** www.bayshorediscovery.org.

EXCURSION RAILROADS

Black River & Western Railroad: New Jersey's best known excursion trains (both steam engine and diesel) operate from Stangl Road in Flemington, next to the outlet shops of Liberty Village, and travel to Ringoes and back three to four times a day. You can also board in Ringoes, get off in Flemington, and return on a later train. The trip meanders through the woods and farms of scenic Hunterdon County. **HOURS:** Sat.–Sun., May–Oct. Special events include the Easter Bunny Express in April, Santa Express from late November to early December, and other themed rides. **FARE:** $$. Discount: Children. Under 3 free. **TELEPHONE:** 908-782-9600 for boarding times. **WEBSITE:** www.brwrr.com.

Cape May Seashore Lines: Operates two excursion services. One is a 22-mile round trip between Cape May and Cape May Court House with a stop at Cold Spring Village in summer. The other is a Saturday excursion service between Tuckahoe and Richland in summer and fall. There are also a Santa Express, Halloween Transylvania Express and Fall Foliage tours, and a wine train from Richland and Tuckahoe. **HOURS:** Various times throughout the day. **ADMISSION:** $$. Discount: Children. **LOCATION:** Tuckahoe (Cape May County). **TELEPHONE:** 609-884-2675. **WEBSITE:** www.capemayseashorelines.org.

Delaware River Railroad: Ride along the Delaware River to Belvidere behind a steam loco in historic open-window cars from the 1940s. **HOURS:** Departs Sat.–Sun., 11, 12:30, 2 & 3. Special wine trains from Phillipsburg's Lehigh Junction (on Main St.) to Alba Vineyards, Sat. and Sun. at 12:30. Santa Claus and Easter Bunny train rides in season. **ADMISSION:** $$. Wine train: $$$$. Discount: Children. **LOCATION:** Market Square, Phillipsburg (Warren County). Off S. Main St. **TELEPHONE:** 908-454-4433. **WEBSITE:** www.877trainride.com.

Pine Creek Railroad: This popular attraction at Allaire Village (q.v.) takes riders on a 10-minute trip. The authentic narrow-gauge steam train ride, one of several park attractions, operates mostly during the summer and is on the left-hand side of the parking lot. **TELEPHONE:** 732-938-5524. **WEBSITE:** www.njmt.org.

Whippany Railway Museum: Santa Claus Special travels 10 miles round trip, with Santa onboard. **HOURS:** Weekends in Dec.; departs at 1, 2, 3 & 4. Reservations recommended. **ADMISSION:** $$. Discount: Children. **LOCATION:** Rt. 10 West at Whippany Rd., Whippany (Morris County). **TELEPHONE:** 973-887-8177. Call first. **WEBSITE:** www.whippany railwaymuseum.org.

See also New Hope & Ivyland (in the "Unique Towns" chapter under New Hope).

WINERY TOURS

Let's face it, a winery tour is just about the most popular kind of industrial tour there is. The art of wine making is so ancient and the slightly fermented air in the cellars is so heady that there is often a party air about these outings. And since wine tasting is involved, everyone seems to have a good time. Although most of the wineries have tastings, not all of them offer tours.

New Jersey is the fifth-largest wine-producing state, with wineries in ten counties. While many do not have traditional tours, all welcome visitors on weekends for tastings. And there are many festivals on tap. Even without a festival, tracking down wineries on fall weekends is a popular activity for many people. And tracking it is, because some of these places are pretty far out in the country. Luckily the New Jersey Wine Growers puts out a map, complete with directions. Most of the twenty or so New Jersey wineries combine forces for a series of wine-tasting festivals from spring to fall, where food, entertainment, seminars, and wine are on hand. Call 609-588-0085 for a map or go to www.newjerseywines.com for a list and an online map of the "wine-tasting" trail, along with festival information.

The Renault Winery

This winery near Atlantic City used to call itself the best little tourhouse in New Jersey. It certainly is the oldest winery in New Jersey (and even the whole country, according to their brochure). It is situated in the Pine Barrens about 16 miles northwest of Atlantic City, where the sandy soil lends itself well to grape production. The entrance and brick patio give it a classic Mediterranean look. With weddings and other catered affairs at an adjacent hall, and with a golf course and resort hotel, the tours aren't the only draw here.

The tour includes a sip of wine and some history of Renault. The original family brought grapes over from Europe in the 1860s, but the winery is no longer owned by the Renault clan. Of the several rooms you visit, one is full of antique wine-making equipment while another is devoted to a collection of prized historic glassware. The guide explains how the wine is poured off, and how to make champagne two different ways. You are shown early wine presses and dosage machines. After a stop in the tasting room, the tour winds up at the gift shop, where there are many accessory items for sale as well as the wine itself (it's only sold at the winery).

Renault Winery also serves lunch at a charming bistro outside the main building called the Wine Garden. A gourmet restaurant, set in an old cask room, is open by reservation for dinner and brunch. For the casual tourist, there are still some down-home attractions like a grape-stomping festival in the fall.

HOURS: Open daily; tours, Mon.–Sat., 10–4. **ADMISSION:** $.
Under 18 free. **LOCATION:** 72 North Bremen Ave., Egg Harbor City
(Atlantic County). Garden State Parkway, Exit 44 from north, right
on Moss Mill Rd., then 6 miles to Bremen Ave. From Atlantic City,

take Rt. 30 to Bremen Ave. **TELEPHONE:** 609-965-2111.
WEBSITE: www.renaultwinery.com.

Other Wineries

The newer wineries (which often look like suburban ranch houses)
are run scientifically and feature fiberglass and steel equipment, so
there isn't much to see on a tour and the information tends to be
technical. The big thing is the wine tasting. At a long bar, an atten-
dant will pour wine into little cups and explain its type and texture.
Often he or she will start with light, dry wines and proceed to
woody and fruit-flavored ones. Naturally, you are expected to buy a
few bottles after all this work.

However, most wineries will go out of their way for a group and
treat you to a full dissertation and perhaps a tour of the actual vineyards. One of these is the **Alba Vineyard.** The winemaster explains
the difference between brix and brie (pronounced the same way)
and all about reading labels and sniffing corks. Everyone gets a
series of small cups of wine—fruit-flavored ones are big in this part
of the state. Tastings take place in a special room set up with cafe
tables and chairs. The winery also has an art gallery and is a venue
for parties and jazz festivals. **LOCATION:** 269 Rt. 627, Finesville. **TELE-
PHONE:** 908-995-7800. **WEBSITE:** www.albavineyard.com.

When it comes to special events, no one seems to have as many
as the **Four Sisters Winery** in Warren County. They host a strawberry
festival, hayrides in the fall, chocolate specials on Valentines Day,
and the ever-popular grape-stomping parties. Spring, summer, and
fall, something always seems to be going on here, right next to the
Matarazzo Vegetable Market (the same family operates both). As
for the grape-stomping parties—these include food, wine, and the
right to enter an open barrel and squish grapes through your toes.
HOURS: Open daily, 9–6. **LOCATION:** 783 Rt. 519, Belvidere. **TELEPHONE:**
908-475-3671. **WEBSITE:** www.matarazzo.com/winery.

Right across the river in Pennsylvania, the **Sand Castle Winery**
offers popular tours. This building isn't quite a castle, but the view
of grape vines running in rows down the hill and the Delaware
River beyond is reminiscent of Europe. In fact, the vineyard was
developed by brothers from Czechoslovakia in the early 1990s and
offers European-style wines. They have a variety of tours: drop-ins
can take 20 minutes, and those with reservations get either the 45-
minute barrel tour or longer versions that include cheese, crackers,
or even lunch. Price varies with tour length. **HOURS:** Open daily,
except in winter. **LOCATION:** 755 River Road, Erwinna, PA. **TELEPHONE:**
800-722-9463. **WEBSITE:** www.sandcastlewinery.com.

PICK-YOUR-OWN ORCHARDS

Who would have guessed that stooping over in the hot sun and picking strawberries or blueberries would become a "bonding" experience for young families? It's also attractive to people who want to save a little money and those who want to be sure their fruit and vegetables are fresh.

Usually you buy an empty basket and fill it up, but arrangements vary. Also, weather conditions can throw off standard picking times. Most orchards are open from June until Halloween, when hayrides and contests often accompany the picking of pumpkins from the fields. Places that specialize in one fruit (such as blueberries) are open only during that season.

The best source for a list of picking farms is the Rutgers Cooperative Extension. In Burlington County, for example, there are two dozen farms that offer blueberries. The extension suggests calling first to see what is ready for picking, getting directions, and learning prices. Most farms also have already-picked fruits and veggies for those who get tired or don't want to pick. By the way, these lists also include cut-your-own Christmas trees as a crop, which could come in handy later in the season.

Some better-known farms include **Terhune's** (330 Cold Soil Road, Princeton, 609-924-2310), which also offers farm animals for petting and a busy cider mill. **Matarazzo Farms** (Rt. 519, Belvidere) runs a strawberry festival and a winery next door besides selling its own vegetables (908-475-3671). You'll find Jersey peaches and sour cherries at **Battleview Orchards** at 91 Wemrock Road, Freehold, right next door to the Monmouth Battleground State Park (732-462-0756). The **Berry Farm** (732-294-0707), which specializes in raspberries, is in Colts Neck on Route 34, very close to **Delicious Orchards**, a gorgeous indoors market with fruits, vegetables, baked goods, and candies—definitely made for the gourmet who doesn't want the thrill of picking or making his own. Even in crowded Bergen County, you can find the **Demarest Farm** at 244 Werimus Road, Hillsdale (201-666-0472), for a little touch of country. There are a lot of other places all over the state, however.

You can get a county-by-county list from Rutgers Cooperative Extension at their Website: www.ifplantscouldtalk.rutgers.edu/pyo. Also, local county extension agents and local newspapers and magazines all carry listings of farms during the picking season. The state department of agriculture also puts out a series of Jersey Fresh brochures on where to find various crops, including pick your own. **TELEPHONE:** 609-292-8853. **WEBSITE:** www.jerseyfresh.nj.gov.

THE HORSEY SET

Monmouth Park: Oceanport, Monmouth County (use Garden State Parkway, Exit 105). The oldest and, to many, the most attractive of Jersey's racetracks, is close to the seashore. There are plenty of picnic tables along the outside track, so families often come and enjoy a day's outing. Indoor and outdoor seating at grandstand. All post times 12:50 P.M. Cafeteria, food stands, plus a restaurant in the clubhouse. Thoroughbred racing from late May through September, highlighted by the Haskell Invitational in August. **TELEPHONE:** 732-222-5100. **WEBSITE:** www.monmouthpark.com.

Freehold Raceway: A beautiful track right in the heart of horse-breeding country. Standard-bred harness racing for trotters and pacers runs mid-Aug.–Feb., Tue.–Sat., and Mar.–May, Wed.–Sat. All post times 12:30 P.M. Also open days and evening year-round for simulcasting, so you can watch horse racing at other tracks around the country on TV monitors and place your bets on-site. **LOCATION:** 130 Park Avenue, Freehold (Monmouth County), junction of Rts. 9 and 33. **TELEPHONE:** 732-462-3800. **WEBSITE:** www.freeholdraceway.com.

Atlantic City Race Course: Very limited amount of thoroughbred racing. Call for schedule. Simulcasting daily. **LOCATION:** 4501 Black Horse Pike (Rt. 40/322), Mays Landing (Atlantic County). Atlantic City Expressway, Exit 12. **TELEPHONE:** 609-641-2190. **WEBSITE:** www.acracecourse.com.

Cowtown Rodeo: This is a real rodeo on the Professional Rodeo Cowboys Association circuit. It features bareback riding, calf roping, saddle bronc riding, steer wrestling, brahma bull riding, team roping, and girls' barrel racing. It's held every Saturday night from the last weekend of May to the last weekend of September at 7:30 P.M., rain or shine. The arena holds 4,000 on outdoor bleacher seats. **ADMISSION:** Adults, $$$. Discount: Children 12 and under. **LOCATION:** 780 Rt. 40, Woodstown/Pilesgrove (Salem County). Eight miles east of Delaware Memorial Bridge, off Exit 1 of the New Jersey Turnpike, or Exit 4 off Rt. 295. **TELEPHONE:** 856-769-3200. **WEBSITE:** www.cowtownrodeo.com.

U.S. Equestrian Team Headquarters: This is the home of the USET Olympic training center and headquarters. Visitors can tour the 1916 stable, one of the largest and most lavish in the United States. The trophy room displays awards won by America's leading equestrians along with a pictorial timeline on the team's development.

Guided tours by appointment. Several events are also open to the public. One, the Festival of Champions, includes show jumping, dressage, and things like four-in-hand competitions (for teams of horses). There is a charge for special events. **LOCATION**: Pottersville Rd., Gladstone (Somerset County). Just west of Rt. 206. **TELEPHONE**: 908-234-1251. **WEBSITE**: www.uset.org.

Horse Park of New Jersey: From March through November, equine events are held at this 147-acre park on most weekends and on many weekdays, including frequent multiday events. Events are frequently centered around horse shows, often on specific breeds like quarterhorses, Morgans, palominos, and Arabians. There are driving events, dressage, and even Olympic selection trials. The park has an indoor arena and five outdoor show rings. Food vendors are on site during show days. Most events are free and are usually held in daylight hours. **LOCATION**: Rt. 524, Stone Tavern (Monmouth County). Take Rt. 195, Exit 11, then east on Rt. 524. **TELEPHONE**: 609-259-0170. **WEBSITE**: www.horseparkofnewjersey.com.

ARENAS AND THEATERS

PNC Bank Arts Center: This beautiful white concrete amphitheater designed by Edward Durell Stone is the setting for nightly concerts and loads of special events throughout the summer. The "shell" is covered and offers seating for 7,000 while 10,500 more can be accommodated on the lawn. Lawn customers, however, must rent chairs from concessionaires. There are also strict rules about bringing in outside food and drink, although tailgating does take place in the parking lot. Shows range from pop and rock to jazz and country—everyone from the Beach Boys to operatic divas have appeared here. The season runs late May through September with ethnic festivals in June. **LOCATION**: Holmdel (Monmouth County). Take Exit 116 off the Garden State Parkway. **TELEPHONE**: 732-335-0400; event and ticket hotline: 732-335-8698. **WEBSITE**: www.artscenter. com.

Ocean Grove Auditorium: A cavernous 7,000-seat auditorium built in the late Victorian age is one of the attractions of this quiet campmeeting town just south of Asbury Park. The Great Auditorium, with its majestic organ, has been refurbished and restored. It is now home to many types of family-style entertainment plus a lecture series. Typical attractions are singers (including pop singers), choral groups, classical orchestral works, organ recitals, and festivals, including folk and doo-wop. Open for the summer; most performances on Saturday evenings. **LOCATION:** 21 Pilgrim Pathway, Ocean Grove (Monmouth County). **TELEPHONE:** 800-773-0097. **WEBSITE:** www.oceangrove.org/saturday_night.html.

Tweeter Center: On the Camden waterfront near the aquarium, this state-of-the-art facility presents premier artists and events year-round. It has a seating capacity of over 25,000 for rock groups and other entertainers. After the spring/summer outdoor season is over, the facility is enclosed for concerts, family entertainment, theatrical and cultural presentations, and special events. Flexible seating configurations range from 1,600 to 7,000. Secured parking is nearby. **LOCATION:** One Harbor Blvd., Camden (Camden County). **TELEPHONE:** 856-365-1300.

NJPAC: Opened in October 1997 and central to Newark's renaissance, the New Jersey Performing Arts Center is a beautiful building with a 2,750-seat auditorium worthy of the great opera houses and a small five-hundred-seat intimate theater, plus an indoor restaurant. Plenty of secured parking surrounds the center. This is a leading venue in the state for orchestras, ballet, jazz, tap, and traveling musicals. **HOURS:** One-hour guided walking tours for a small fee available by appointment. **LOCATION:** One Center St., Newark (Essex County). Take Rt. 280 to Rt. 21 (McCarter Highway), follow signs. **TELEPHONE:** 888-466-5722; tours: 973-297-5857. **WEBSITE:** www.njpac.org.

Albert Music Hall: Operated by the Pinelands Cultural Society to preserve the music of South Jersey's pines, the hall presents live shows every Sat. at 7:30 P.M., with occasional Sunday afternoon performances. This is the home of country music in New Jersey, with lots of bluegrass, country, and Pinelands tunes. The hall, built in 1997, hosts local groups with names like Cedar Crick, Piney Hollow Drifters, and the Jersey Devil & the Sugar Sand Ramblers. There's even a Pine Barrens Festival and a Legend of the Jersey Devil Show. A snack bar and gifts are available in the hall. There's also a separate Pickin' Shed, where local musicians get together to swap songs. **ADMISSION:** $. Discount: Children. **LOCATION:** 125 Wells Mills Rd. (Rt. 532), Waretown (Ocean County), one-quarter mile west of Rt. 9. **TELEPHONE:** 609-971-1593. **WEBSITE:** www.alberthall.org.

Other Arts Centers

State Theatre: Located in a cultural area next to the George Street Playhouse, this large, converted movie palace offers big-name musicals, operas, classical music, dance, variety, divas, children's shows, and occasional comedians, usually for one-night performances.

LOCATION: 15 Livingston Ave., New Brunswick (Middlesex County). **TELEPHONE:** 732-246-7469. **WEBSITE:** www.statetheatrenj.org.

Stockton Performing Arts Center: This professional theater on the Richard Stockton College campus includes the Performing Arts Center and the Experimental Theatre. Among the offerings are classic plays, from the Greeks to Shakespeare to contemporary works. Broadway classics as well as jazz, symphony, and dance troupes, and children's theater. **LOCATION:** Richard Stockton College, Pomona (Atlantic County). **TELEPHONE:** 609-652-9000. **WEBSITE:** http://intraweb.stockton.edu/pac/indexmain.asp.

Patriots Theater: Owned by the state of New Jersey, this refurbished classical venue is the place for classical, folk, and rock concerts as well as plays and operas. The building is set in a large park near the Trenton waterfront. **LOCATION:** The War Memorial, Memorial Dr., Trenton (Mercer County). **TELEPHONE:** 609-984-8400; tickets: 800-955-5566. **WEBSITE:** www.thewarmemorial.com.

Community Theatre: Housed in a former movie theater not far from the Morristown Green, this venue has undergone a major renovation, including a glass and limestone third floor, and has become one of the area's leading venues for comedy, pop, and classical performances. Afternoon shows for kids. **LOCATION:** 100 South St., Morristown (Morris County). **TELEPHONE:** 973-539-8008. **WEBSITE:** www.communitytheatrenj.com.

Count Basie Theatre: Features a wide range of shows, from musical revues and pop and rock stars to symphony, theater, comedy, and, of course, jazz and blues. There are also family-oriented matinee shows. All in a former 1926 movie theater and vaudeville house named for the legendary jazzman, who was born in Red Bank. **LOCATION:** 99 Monmouth St., Red Bank (Monmouth County). Garden State Parkway to Rt. 520 east, then left on Broad St. Follow to Monmouth St. and turn left. **TELEPHONE:** 732-842-9000. **WEBSITE:** www.countbasietheatre.org.

Theaters with Regular Seasons

McCarter Theatre: A leading regional theater, more than twenty new plays and adaptations have premiered at McCarter in the past decade. The theater season is complemented by music, dance, and special events. McCarter is the home of the Opera Festival of New Jersey and the American Repertory Ballet. **LOCATION:** 91 University Pl., Princeton (Mercer County). **TELEPHONE:** 609-258-2787. **WEBSITE:** www.mccarter.org.

Paper Mill Playhouse: New Jersey's leading venue for Broadway-style musicals and revivals, this 1,200-seat Equity theater produces notable works year-round, often with Broadway stars. Designated as the state theater of New Jersey. Art gallery upstairs and Carriage House restaurant next door. **LOCATION:** Brookside Dr., Millburn (Essex County). Take Millburn Ave. to Main St., then go right under railroad bridge to Brookside. **TELEPHONE:** 973-376-4343. **WEBSITE:** www.papermill.org.

George Street Playhouse: An intimate theater space with good viewing from all angles. The focus here is on new works for the American theater and revivals of Broadway dramas. Light refreshments in a cabaret/gallery area. Special after-show chats with performers on select Sunday performances. **LOCATION:** 9 Livingston Ave., New Brunswick (Middlesex County). **TELEPHONE:** 732-246-7717. **WEBSITE:** www.georgestplayhouse.org.

Shakespeare Theatre of New Jersey: Seasonal presentations from June to December by a repertory company that often includes Broadway names. Six to seven plays per season with at least three by Shakespeare. Some touring done during the year. **LOCATION:** F. M. Kirby Shakespeare Theatre, Drew University, 36 Madison Ave., Madison (Morris County). **TELEPHONE:** 973-408-5600. **WEBSITE:** www.shakespearenj.org.

MINOR LEAGUE BASEBALL

Everyone knows the Yankees and Mets in New York and the Phillies in Philadelphia. But remember the old-fashioned park where you and the kids ate hot dogs and cheered the locals on? That seemed to be the stuff of movies rather than real life for many years. After decades of decline, however, there's been a resurgence of minor league baseball all over the country. Especially in New Jersey, stadiums have risen in the past few years from south to north. Some teams are affiliated with major league teams at the A or AA level. Most are in independent leagues, including four that form the south division of the Atlantic League. Forget the old wooden bleachers; these are small versions of major league stadiums, with box and reserved seating, and some also offering glassed-in luxury suites. Many also offer lower-priced general admission tickets so you can sit on the grass or picnic down the lines beyond the stands. Seating capacity generally runs around 6,000. Here are the minor league teams that play in the state.

Atlantic City Surf. Atlantic League (Indep.). The Sandcastle, Rt. 40 East, Atlantic City (Atlantic County). TELEPHONE: 609-344-7873. WEBSITE: www.acsurf.com.

Newark Bears. Atlantic League (Indep.). Bears & Eagles Riverfront Stadium, Bridge St., Newark (Essex County). TELEPHONE: 866-554-BEAR. WEBSITE: www.newarkbears.com.

New Jersey Jackals. CanAm League (Indep.). Yogi Berra Stadium, One Hall Drive, Little Falls (Passaic County). On Montclair State University campus. TELEPHONE: 973-655-8025. WEBSITE: www.jackals.com.

Somerset Patriots. Atlantic League (Indep.). Commerce Bank Ballpark, East Main St., Bridgewater (Somerset County). TELEPHONE: 908-252-0700. WEBSITE: www.somersetpatriots.com

Sussex Skyhawks. CanAm League (Indep.) Skylands Park, Rt. 565, Augusta (Sussex County). Near junction of Rts. 206 and 15. TELEPHONE: 973-300-1000. WEBSITE: www.sussexskyhawks.com.

Trenton Thunder. Eastern League (AA). A Yankees affiliate. Waterfront Park, Trenton (Mercer County). TELEPHONE: 609-394-3300. WEBSITE: www.trentonthunder.com.

Lakewood Blue Claws. Southern Atlantic League (A). A Phillies affiliate. First Energy Park, Lakewood (Ocean County). Take Rt. 70 west, go right on Rt. 623. TELEPHONE: 732-901-7000. WEBSITE: www.lakewoodblueclaws.com.

Camden Riversharks. Atlantic League (Indep.). Campbell's Field, on the waterfront, Camden (Camden County). TELEPHONE: 866-742-7579. WEBSITE: www.riversharks.com.

NEARBY OUT-OF-STATE PLACES

New York Renaissance Faire

This festival, right over the New Jersey border, has become quite popular. For ten weekends from early August to mid-September, Sterling Forest in New York is taken over by knights, ladies, peddlers, jugglers, and mimes. A joust is the big attraction (usually at 2 and 6). A series of "shows" depicting outlaws, queens, and jesters are part of the festival. The mud wrestling, juggling, belly dancing, and other attractions are operated by freelancers who expect customers to come up with some coin of the realm. Rides (simple ones) and games are extra, too. Main attractions like the living Chess Game and the joust take place at particular locations at specific times. Vendors in tents also offer such unusual items as brass rubbings and flower circlets for milady's hair.

HOURS: Aug. to mid-Sept., weekends, 10–7. **ADMISSION:** $$$$.
Discount: Children. Under 5 free. **LOCATION:** Sterling Forest,
Tuxedo, NY. Rt. 17A west; look for signs. **TELEPHONE:** 845-351-5174.
WEBSITE: www.renfair.com/ny.

Crayola Factory

A popular outing for school groups, the Crayola Factory is also a place where parents can take children for a few hours of entertainment and enlightenment. It's a combination factory tour and interactive children's museum. The "Factory" takes up the second floor of a building called Two Rivers Landing, which also includes a Canal Museum on the upper floors. When you pay the admission you are handed some Crayola "coins." Upon entering the factory floor a docent explains the crayon-making process and offers a little history. Afterwards, you use your "coins" to buy a small four-crayon box. This is all for demonstration—the actual Crayola factory is 13 miles away.

The interactive sections include arts and crafts plus interesting diversions. Really young kids will enjoy the Color Garden, where giant plastic vegetables can be planted, watered, gathered, and put into bins. Other sites include a small theater where you can put on a puppet show, a "shadow play" area, and several computers featuring arty concepts. There are also huge rooms where kids sit down and work with paper or clay.

The Canal Museum upstairs is of interest to children who are not too young. You can see a mock-up of a typical flatboat from the early nineteenth century and plenty of interactive maps. The first floor of the building features local history and a small gift shop. The big gift shop, "The Crayola Store," is around the corner. Children under 16 must be accompanied by an adult.

HOURS: Summer, Mon.–Sat., 9:30–5; Sun., 11–5. Rest of year, Tue.–Sat.,
9:30–3; Sun., 12–5. **ADMISSION:** $$. Discounts: Seniors, military.
Under 3 free. **LOCATION:** 30 Centre Square, Easton, PA.
TELEPHONE: 610-515-8000.
WEBSITE: www.crayola.com/factory/index.cfm.

Culinary Institute of America

Want to run a day trip and fill up the bus? Try the Culinary Institute of America. Groups often wait months for reservations. If you go on your own, you may find it easier to reserve a table at this school where budding chefs cook, clean, and serve in the restaurants on the first floor. Many of the graduates go on to found chic, ultra-expensive restaurants, so there is a feeling of getting in on the ground floor of a good thing. But if the cooking is done by seniors, the waiters must be freshmen, because the service can vary. The food, however, is always good, if not necessarily sublime.

Set high on a hill overlooking the Hudson Valley, the red brick institute includes classrooms, student dorms, several restaurants, and a well-stocked bookstore. The Escoffier Restaurant, which specializes in the formal, multicourse European meal, includes a large window that allows patrons to watch the chefs at meal preparation. A typical formal meal might include a light hors d'oeuvre, a soup, a main course followed by salad, and then a handsome dessert. The American Bounty Restaurant offers faster service and includes such staples as roast beef and American pies. Other eating areas include the St. Andrews Café, American Pie Bakery Café, and the Italian Caterina de Medici.

A tour of the CIA is available for a fee (**ADMISSION:** $). You pass all the classrooms where students may be beheading fish or pushing pastry through a tube, and you will get the lowdown on how the institute works.

HOURS: Call first. **LOCATION:** Hyde Park, NY, 3 miles north of Poughkeepsie. **TELEPHONE:** 845-471-6608; tour reservations: 800-451-1588. **WEBSITE:** www.ciachef.edu.

Fairs and Festivals

Here is a sampling of the most popular fairs, festivals, and other special events around the Garden State.

FEBRUARY

1. Garden State Home Show, Garden State Expo Center, Somerset. Remodeling, interior decorating, and landscaping. First weekend of month. 732-469-4000.

MARCH

1. Atlantique City. Huge antiques fair inside Atlantic City's convention center. Second show in mid-October. 800-526-2724.
2. St. Patrick's Day Parade, Belmar. 732-280-2648. (Others in Kearny, Newark, Morristown, Seaside Heights, etc.) Belmar's is in early March. Others on and around March 17.

APRIL

1. Cherry Blossom Festival, Branch Brook Park, Newark (Essex County). Races, concert, tour, other events. Two weeks in mid-month. 973-268-3500.
2. Shad Festival, Lambertville. Food, crafts, sidewalk events, grilled shad. End of month. 609-397-0055.

MAY

1. American Indian Arts Festival, Rankokus Indian Reservation, Westampton (Burlington County). Artists, entertainers, food. Last weekend of month. 609-261-4747.
2. Hoboken Spring Arts and Music Festival. Crafts, artists, live music, rides on Washington St. 201-420-2207.
3. Warren County Heritage Festival, Shippen Manor, Oxford. Nineteenth-century reenactments, music, fireworks. Third weekend of month. 908-453-4381.
4. Wildwoods International Kite Festival, Wildwood (Cape May County). Memorial Day weekend. 215-736-1850.

5. Tour of Somerville, downtown Somerville (Somerset County). Memorial Day weekend. Oldest bicycle race in USA. 908-725-7223, ext. 13.

JUNE

1. Appel Farm Arts & Music Festival, Elmer (Salem County). First Saturday. Emphasis on folk, blues, and acoustic rock. Also crafts fair and children's village. 800-394-1211.
2. N.J. Fresh Seafood Festival. Gardners Basin, Atlantic City. Second weekend of month. 609-347-4386.
3. Riverfest Jazz & Blues Festival, Red Bank (Monmouth County). Three days of jazz, food, crafts, and events at Marine Park by the Navesink River. First weekend of month. 732-933-1984.
4. Battle of Monmouth reenactment. On battlefield grounds, Manalapan (Monmouth County). Weekend encampment. Costumed soldiers, overnight tenting. Last weekend of month. 732-462-9616.
5. U.S. Equestrian Team Festival of Champions. Dressage, horse-show events. Gladstone (Somerset County). Mid-month. 908-234-0848.

JULY

1. July 3 & 4. Atlantic City Fireworks. Philadelphia fireworks can be seen from Camden waterfront. Seaside Heights and Point Pleasant Beach are also popular.
2. Night in Venice, Ocean City. Decorated boats parade on inland waterway. 609-525-9300.
3. St. Ann's Feast, Hoboken. Food, vendors, entertainment. 201-659-1114.
4. QuickChek N.J. Festival of Ballooning, Solberg Airport, Readington (Somerset County). Three days of balloon ascensions, bands, clowns, vendors; usually fourth weekend of month. 800-468-2479.

AUGUST

1. Hambletonian. Meadowlands Race Track. Highest purse in trotter racing. Family events beforehand. East Rutherford (Bergen County). First Saturday of month. 201-843-2446.
2. Highlands Clam Fest (Monmouth County). Four days on first weekend featuring seafood, entertainment, rides, and games. 732-291-4713.
3. NJ State Fair and Sussex County Farm & Horse Show. Combination old-fashioned country fair and midway amusements. In Augusta. 973-948-5500.

SEPTEMBER

1. Cape May Food and Wine Festival (Cape May County). Six days in mid-month of wine tasting, gourmet marketplace, Chef's Dine-Around, harvest fair. 800-275-4278.
2. Atlantic City In-water Power Boat Show (Atlantic County). More than seven hundred power boats and yachts on display at the Farley State Marina. 609-441-8482.
3. Bloomfield Harvest Fest (Essex County). A mid-month weekend of crafts, rides, food, and special activities. 973-680-4189.
4. Wings 'n Water Festival. Wetlands Institute, Stone Harbor (Cape May County). Seafood, exhibits, decoys. 609-368-1211.
5. Fall Art & Music Festival, Hoboken (Hudson County). Crafts, artists, live music, rides on Washington St. 201-420-2207.

OCTOBER

1. Eighteenth-Century Field Day, Fort Mercer, Red Bank Battlefield, National Park (Gloucester County). Third Sunday of month. 856-853-5120.
2. Cranberry Festival, Chatsworth (Burlington County). Antiques, arts & crafts, music. Third weekend of month. 609-726-9237.
3. Chowderfest Weekend. Beach Haven (Ocean County). Everybody samples soup. 609-494-7211.
4. Victorian Week, Cape May. Ten days of house tours, band concerts, dinners, costumes. Early to mid-month. 609-884-5404.
5. Far Hills Race Meeting, Moorland Farms, Far Hills (Somerset County). Steeplechase race on open field. Tailgate spectators. Third or fourth Saturday of month. 908-685-2929.
6. New Jersey Lighthouse Challenge. Visit eleven lighthouses along the coast. Second weekend of month. 856-546-0514.

NOVEMBER

1. Annual Fall Antiques Show, indoor location near Allaire Village (Monmouth County). 732-919-3500.
2. Cape May Jazz Festival, Cape May. 609-884-7277.

DECEMBER

1. Holly Walk, Morristown. Six historical houses with Christmas decor. First weekend of month. 973-631-5151.
2. Reenactment of Washington crossing the Delaware. Christmas Day. Titusville (Mercer County). 609-737-0623.
3. Patriots Week, downtown Trenton (Mercer County). Week after Christmas. Lectures, films, tours, theater, and reenactment of the two Battles of Trenton. 877-PAT-WEEK.

Index

Index by New Jersey County

About the Author

Patrick Sarver is a former executive editor of *New Jersey Monthly* and of *Rutgers Magazine*. He has served as the editor of *Vista/USA*, the Exxon Travel Club magazine, where he was also a contributor to the Exxon Travel Guides. He is currently editorial director of the PFM Group and resides in Bernardsville, New Jersey.